Maybe having to write this is a way of exorcism.
Once you have the courage of writing down
things you know are there…
it must have a purifying effect on the spirit…

Huguette Caland

Writing in the Work of

Huguette Caland

Writing in the Work of

Huguette Caland

BRIGITTE CALAND

KAPH

TABLE OF CONTENT

Self-portrait, 1992
Mixed media on paper, 61 × 45.7 cm

Private collection, Los Angeles, California

Slightly leaning forward, fully focused, you dipped the brush delicately into ink or paint. You slowly lifted your wrist before bringing its saturated tip close to the medium you chose and placed it, motionless, on a single point.

One precise gesture and a line emerged drawn by the movement of your arm. The stroke took shape, then stopped abruptly, as if halted by an invisible force. Time itself seemed suspended. With absolute control and no room for error, one line after another, the work was created.

Regardless of the surface, whether linen or jute canvas, Canson or handmade Japanese paper, whether small enough to slip into your pocket or so vast you could stand on it, and whatever the size of the brush, it was the same ritual..

Watching you create these pieces allowed me to discover a new side of my mother. I knew you as strong, exuberant, and mischievous, yet in these moments, I found you silent, serious, and introspective, and always elegant. This series—a transition from the figurative to the abstract, from the spoken to the unspoken—which you called *Silent Letters*, moved me deeply. Its title intrigued me.

Your movements and the way you occupied space fascinated me. The intensity you poured into each piece was compelling.

The text that follows emerged from a desire to better understand this remarkable creative process, which I was fortunate enough to witness. These seemingly minimal, identical lines are full of nuances and stories; each painting, each drawing, sublimating an overflow of emotions, evoking a fragment of life.

I hope these pages will allow readers to delve into this intimate and personal body of work. I dedicate this book to you, in deepest gratitude for all that you have given me.

- Brigitte Caland

« *To silence myself, I draw lines...* it may seem like nothing, but drawing lines is a way of containing emotion, anger, anxiety. You want to scream at the world—but instead, you draw a line.»

- Huguette Caland

(*Lettres à Francine*, documentaire de F. Elkoury, Et alors production/Maison européenne de la photographie, 2000)

Slightly leaning forward, fully focused, you dipped the brush delicately into ink or paint. You slowly lifted your wrist before bringing its saturated tip close to the medium you chose and placed it, motionless, on a single point.

One precise gesture and a line emerged drawn by the movement of your arm. The stroke took shape, then stopped abruptly, as if halted by an invisible force. Time itself seemed suspended. With absolute control and no room for error, one line after another, the work was created.

Regardless of the surface, whether linen or jute canvas, Canson or handmade Japanese paper, whether small enough to slip into your pocket or so vast you could stand on it, and whatever the size of the brush, it was the same ritual..

Watching you create these pieces allowed me to discover a new side of my mother. I knew you as strong, exuberant, and mischievous, yet in these moments, I found you silent, serious, and introspective, and always elegant. This series—a transition from the figurative to the abstract, from the spoken to the unspoken—which you called *Silent Letters*, moved me deeply. Its title intrigued me.

Your movements and the way you occupied space fascinated me. The intensity you poured into each piece was compelling.

The text that follows emerged from a desire to better understand this remarkable creative process, which I was fortunate enough to witness. These seemingly minimal, identical lines are full of nuances and stories; each painting, each drawing, sublimating an overflow of emotions, evoking a fragment of life.

I hope these pages will allow readers to delve into this intimate and personal body of work. I dedicate this book to you, in deepest gratitude for all that you have given me.

- Brigitte Caland

« *To silence myself, I draw lines* ... it may seem like nothing, but drawing lines is a way of containing emotion, anger, anxiety. You want to scream at the world—but instead, you draw a line.»

- Huguette Caland

(*Lettres à Francine*, documentaire de F. Elkoury, Et alors production/Maison européenne de la photographie, 2000)

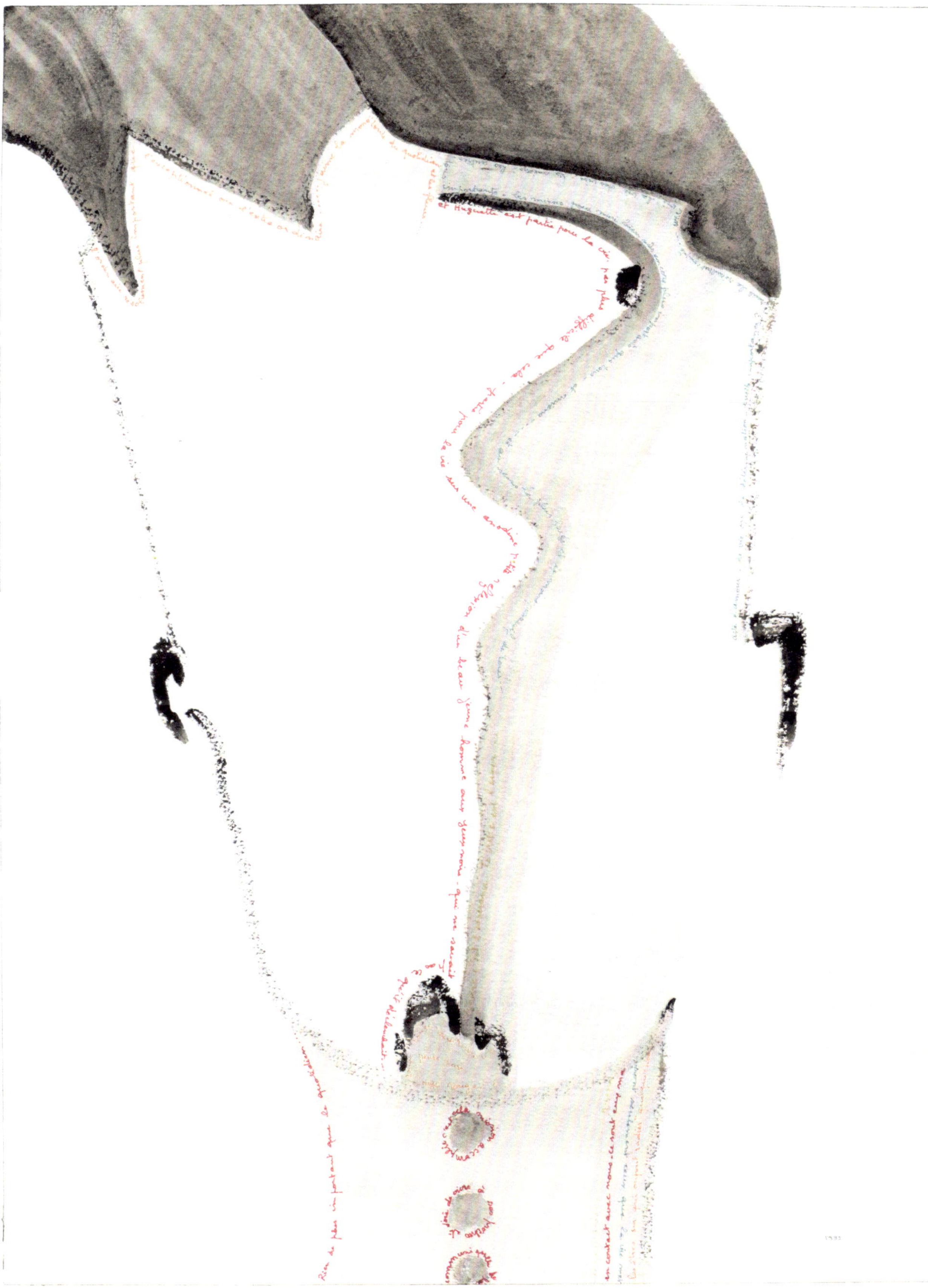
et Huguette est partie pour la vie, pas plus difficile que cela.

FOREWORD

Some things belong to the realm of the readable; others, to the visible. Brigitte Caland reminds us that making something visible is, more broadly, also an act of making it legible. In this publication, which focuses on the use of writing in the work of artist Huguette Caland, she offers a dual process of deciphering—not only what is written, but also what lies at the core of the artist's creative practice.

This perspective is particularly valuable because it is through the lens of a daughter engaging with her mother's work. In other words, no one else could have authored these pages, which trace an intimate—and perhaps even delayed—dialogue, unfolding through a dual thread of language: the words of the writer, Brigitte Caland, and those subtly woven into the paintings by the artist, Huguette Caland, unlocking interpretations.

Yet while this approach is deeply personal, it is no less scholarly. The question of writing runs throughout the history of art and warrants careful attention. Artists have long engaged with text for various reasons. The written word, when incorporated into their compositions, could serve aesthetic, narrative, or discursive purposes, and often provided a way to articulate the self. In the early twentieth century, modern art pushed this exploration of writing further: Magritte, Picasso, the Lettrists, and Paul Klee used text in ways that were at once playful and poetic. Later, in different contexts, Arab artists associated with the Hurufiyya movement made script the foundation of a visual language, reinterpreting calligraphic tradition through the lens of modernity. Other artists went so far as to mimic the act of writing itself—to perform it—creating a zone of ambiguity between what is seen and what is read.

It is likely that Huguette Caland was attuned to these various modernities and intrigued by their possibilities. Other artists of her generation, such as Etel Adnan, also worked extensively with language. Brigitte Caland's essay thus positions Huguette Caland's work at the intersection of multiple currents, as a space of hybridization—aesthetic, graphic, and linguistic. The artist wrote in three languages—Arabic, French, and English—and each of these languages becomes a declaration, affirming a multifaceted identity.

This journey through writing, which lies at the heart of Huguette Caland's intimate world, culminates in *the Silent Letters* series—letters that are, in every sense, essential. In this body of work, where the readable is literally concealed in favor of a purely visual experience, we are confronted with the paradox of showing what one cannot see and saying what one does not say. *The Silent Letters*, whose invisible words are also inaudible—because some things can only be heard within—open a space where the line becomes text, and writing becomes image.

Nayla Tamraz

Since the dawn of time, pictorial works, symbols, and alphabets have narrated the human story. Across the ages, countless artists around the world have incorporated writing into their work—whether for religious, political, poetic, or personal reasons. This study focuses on the use of writing in the art of Huguette Caland (1931–2019), who once confessed, "I could have become a writer,"[1] but chose painting instead "to be incomprehensible,"[2] to control what she reveals, what she suggests, and what she consciously—or unconsciously—keeps hidden. When asked about her creative process, Caland responded, "When I work, my hand is detached from my mind." This surrendering of control, which invites daydreaming, is what allows the unconscious to speak. Her artworks, like dreams, become expressions of fulfilled desires. This interplay of light and shadow sparks curiosity. From the very beginning of her artistic career in the 1960s, Caland began weaving written elements into her visual work. By the 1980s—and more prominently in the 1990s—her art increasingly featured texts in Arabic, English, and French. Throughout her life, Caland found joy not only in playing with colors in paintings and drawings, but also with words. Humor, metaphor, wordplay, and nostalgia appear in her titles; in poetic works like *The Women of My Country*; in recollections of a childhood steeped in political and familial events, such as *The Independence of Lebanon Told to L'Or Iman* and *The Bride/Kantari, April 1952*; and even on her smocks—loose work dresses spattered with paint, scribbled notes, and sketches.

From the 1990s onward, legible writing in her paintings, drawings, notebooks, and garments often vanishes beneath layers of color, abstract signs, or brushstrokes of ink and paint—creating a playful, enigmatic exchange with the viewer (as seen in *Sketchbook #2*). At the same time, Caland invents her own visual language, a system of recurring symbols and motifs that dances between the spoken and the unspoken. She pushes this language further into abstraction in her *Silent Letters* series, where words are replaced by regular, rhythmic lines.

In these works—often vibrant, sometimes soft, and rarely dark—repetitive motifs and signs carve out imagined landscapes, shaping their contours and borders. Scattered across the canvas, text emerges in varying degrees of visibility and legibility, inviting viewers to decipher the emotions of a moment, the memory of a day or an encounter, a fragment of childhood, or a spontaneous homage. Among these, one name recurs: Paul. Sometimes clearly written, other times hidden in plain sight, Paul becomes a lingering presence—an obsession to be exorcised. Caland writes to him, recalls him, and embeds his name across her work. Paul: her great love, her husband,

1 Huguette Caland, in *Warae elwoujouh*, an interview with Ricardo Karam, 2006, accessed on YouTube on December 14, 2021.

2 Dominique Eddé, "*The Elephant and the Poppy*," in exhibition catalog *Huguette Caland*, Solidere, Beirut, 2013, 16.

the man she ultimately chose to leave behind when the call to become an artist became irresistible.[3]

Given the large number of paintings, drawings, collages, and smocks on which Caland combines two modes of expression—visual creation and writing—this book explores the function of writing in her work through a body of pieces produced between 1968 and 2012 across France, the United States (California), and Lebanon. Structured around three central themes—The Spoken and the Game of Concealment; From Concealment to the Unspoken; and Paul, or the Narcissistic Wound—this essay seeks to better understand the conscious and unconscious motivations that led Caland to employ both visual and written languages. It investigates her impulse to conceal text, to play with the viewer, to shift between languages, to invent her own symbolic language, and to ultimately carry this process into abstraction.

3 S. Freud, Pulsion et destins des pulsions [*Drives and the Fate of Drives*], (Petite Bibliothèque Payot, Paris, 2012) On page 15; "Drive," as it happens, is a term from physics. It dates back to 1625 and means "the act of pushing," preferably in a liquid. In German, it is translated as *trieb*; in English, it is *drive*: always and again, "that which pushes." The concept had been troubling Freud for some time. In 1905, in *Three Essays on the Theory of Sexuality*, he provided this rather complicated definition: drive is the "psychic representative of a source of endosomatic excitation producing a continuous flow, as opposed to the stimulus, which is produced by an isolated excitation coming from the outside. The drive thus represents one of the concepts that mark the distinction between the psychic and the somatic." On page 24: "What is the aim of a drive? Clearly, the satisfaction or relief of the tension caused by the push."

THE SPOKEN AND THE GAME OF CONCEALMENT

This chapter focuses on the visible and legible writing embedded in various media—paintings, drawings, and smocks (work dresses)—as well as the emergence and evolution of Caland's playful strategy of concealment. She often partially obscures certain written passages, offering only fragments to the viewer and inviting a game of interpretation.

Signatures and Titles

In the 1960s, perhaps driven by a desire to assert her identity and independence, Caland typically signed her works in Arabic, placing the signature on the reverse side of the canvas. This practice preserved the integrity of the visual surface while signaling authorship—sometimes through her initials, the initial of her first name and her surname, or her full name. Later, she adopted Latin letters for her signature, following a similar pattern. Her drawings from the 1970s often bear a discreet signature at the bottom, accompanied by a date. Following her departure from Lebanon in June 1970 to settle in Paris and fully embrace her identity as an artist, a shift occurred—not only in her life, but in her work. No longer in the immediate sphere of her husband, family, or the society she left behind, she seems to have shed the need for artifice. From that point on, she primarily signed using Latin letters (French), her first language, aligning herself more closely with her new cultural environment.

While many of her earlier works in Lebanon bear titles referencing places—*Kaslik, Maameltein, City II, TV City, La Ville*—the titles begin to change after she moves to Paris. Though many works across her career remain Untitled, a new imaginative freedom emerges. At thirty-nine, alone for the first time, Caland experiences what she describes as a "midlife crisis" and an "overnight de-routinization.[4]" This personal rupture unleashes a liberated, experimental creativity, driven by a masculine libido in form and feeling—fluid and bold. Having lived much of her life under scrutiny, Caland seeks to explore the vastness of a world newly within reach.

4 P. L. Assoun, *Le Démon de midi*, (L'Olivier, Paris, 2008) On pages 21 and 110: "The 'midlife demon' in women takes on its meaning from what it exploits in the gap between the 'maternal' and the 'feminine.' Behind this dizzying interplay, a principle may be at work that could well contain its secret, like a mirror of the mythical narrative encountered earlier: the reference to the figure of the Mother. When the epiphany we know arises, this promise of happiness tied to the brand-new object comes as a relay to a faltering marital bond."

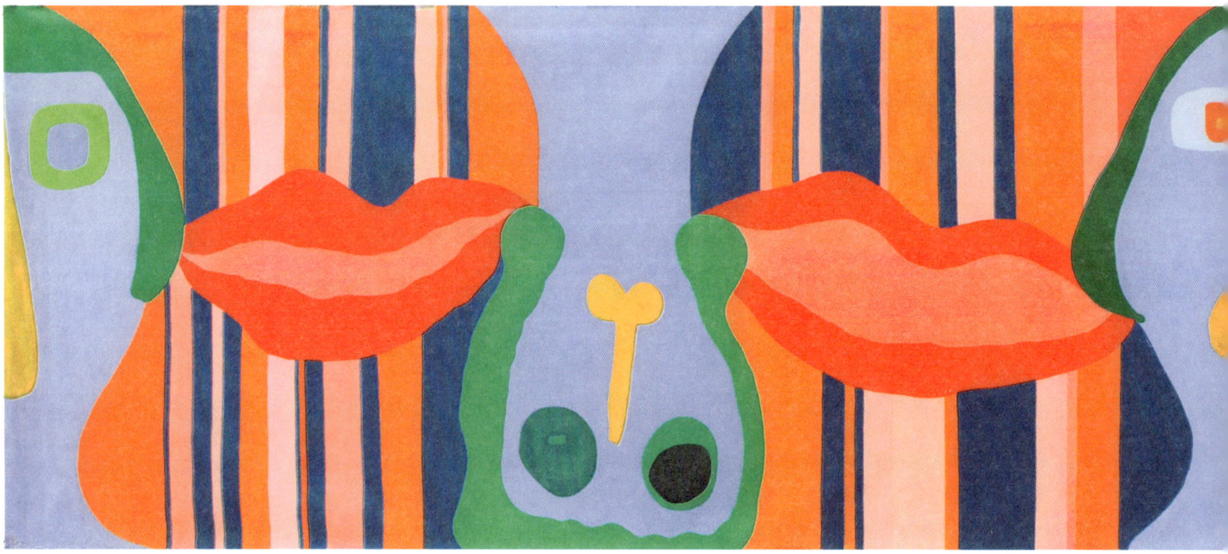

Visages sans bouche, bouches sans visage, 1970
Oil on canvas, 203 × 998 cm

Collection Ministry of Culture, Saudi Arabia

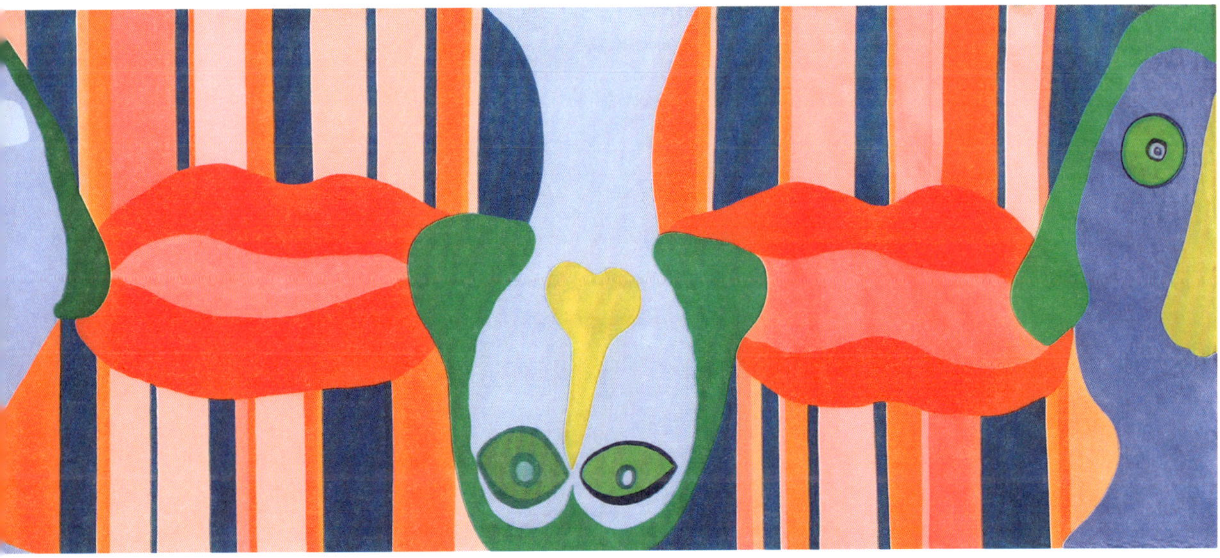

Rather than destabilizing her, this newfound freedom becomes the raw material of her artistic practice: colors are either translucent or vividly expressive; lines are refined and electrically charged, converging and nearly touching; drawings and paintings often possess an erotic quality. The titles she gives her works—concise, humorous, and evocative—infuse them with symbolic depth, challenging the viewer to decode layered meanings.[5] One striking example is *Visages sans bouche, bouches sans visage* (1970), a monumental painting measuring 203 × 1000 centimeters. Here, the disintegration of faces reflects a dual fragmentation—of figure and ground—perhaps echoing the one that Caland felt as she entered this new phase of life.

This rupture, however, also marks the beginning of her artistic emancipation. As the art critic-author Michel Butor observed, there are titles that proclaim themselves like poems—declamatory or distilled in the manner of the surrealists—and others that whisper, modest and unassuming, seeking not attention but discretion: "Don't look at me, don't pay attention to me, I am barely a word."[6] *Hi!*—a simple greeting—becomes multifaceted: a welcoming gesture, a homophone for "high" (suggesting elevation, intoxication), and a bold, condensation,[7] provocation. In just one syllable, Caland distills complex meaning: "It is in this small thing that the spirit resides."[8] She plays with language—*Witz* (wit) in German[9]—choosing not the language of her childhood, nor the dominant idiom of her upbringing, but one born of both geographical and linguistic liberation. In this playful tension, a voluptuous female figure (the artist herself) appears to take flight—legs spread, arms stretched upward or suspended—a body liberated through art and language alike.

5 M. Butor, *Les Mots dans la peinture*, (Flammarion, Paris, 2019), 16-18.

6 Ibid., 21-22.

7 S. Freud, *The Joke and Its Relation to the Unconscious*, (Gallimard, Paris, 1988), 98-99.

8 Ibid., 101-102.

9 Ibid., 33-34. In a foreword signed by J.-B. Pontalis. A German polysemic word "...which designates a faculty, wit, and its product... The *Witz* is thus linked to the fragment, the find, the surprise (including for its author: a good *Witz* also surprises the one who utters it)."

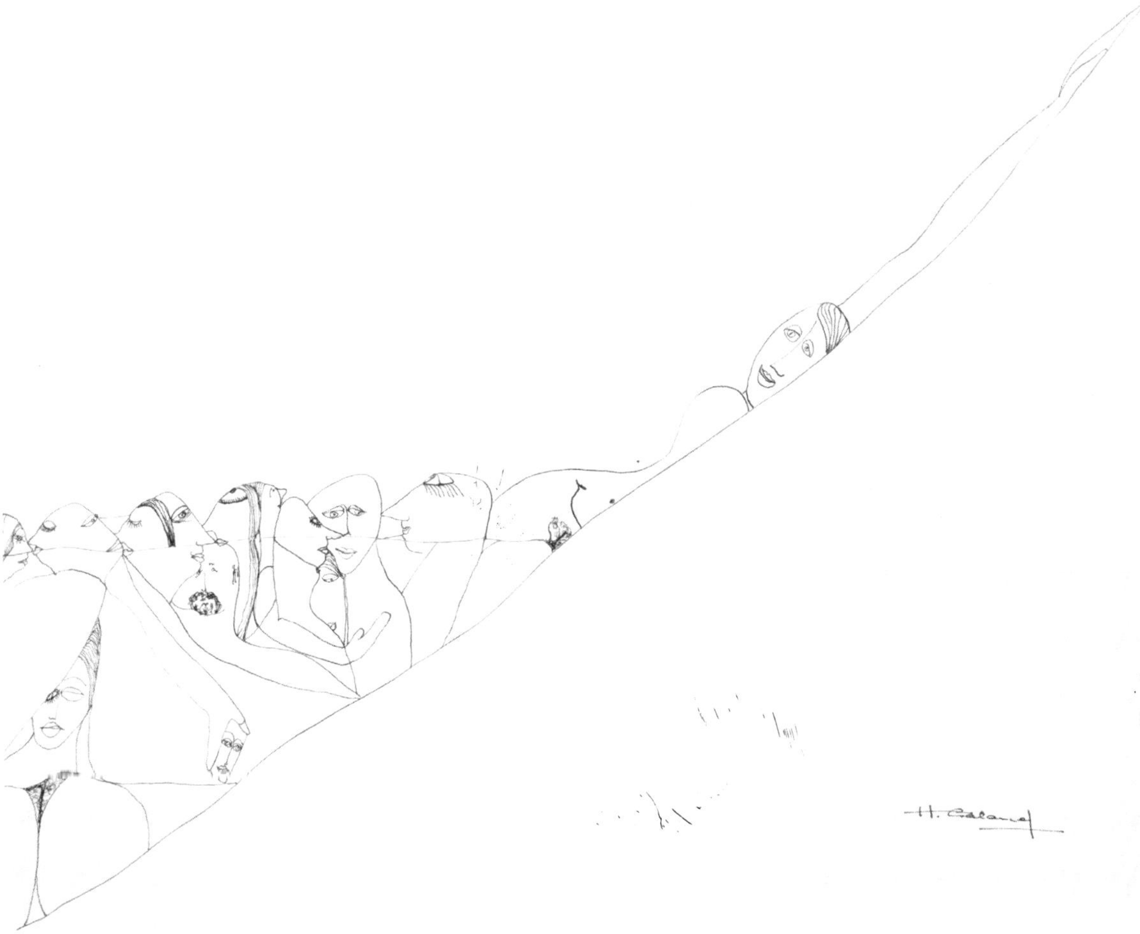

Couchée sur la colline, 1971
Ink on paper, 26.6 × 34,3 cm

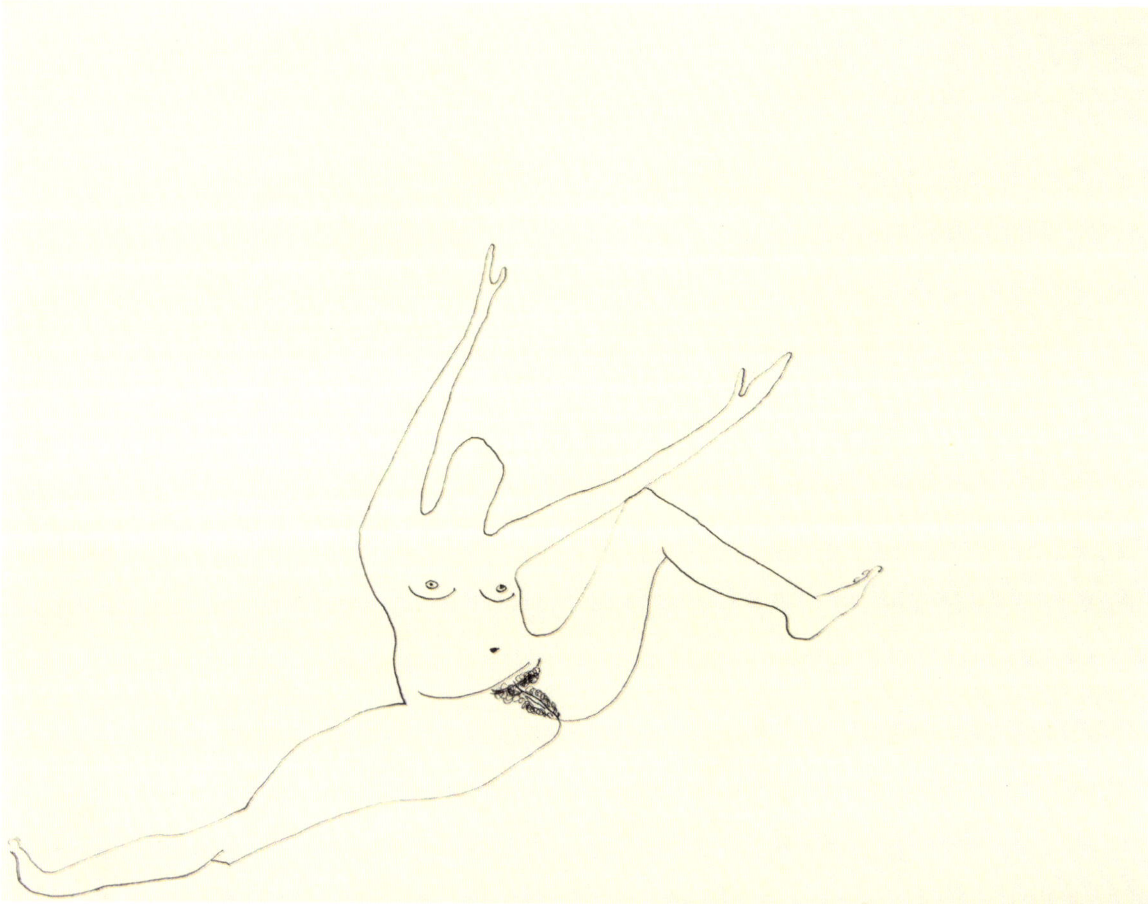

Hi!, 1973
Ink on paper, 24.1 × 31.8 cm

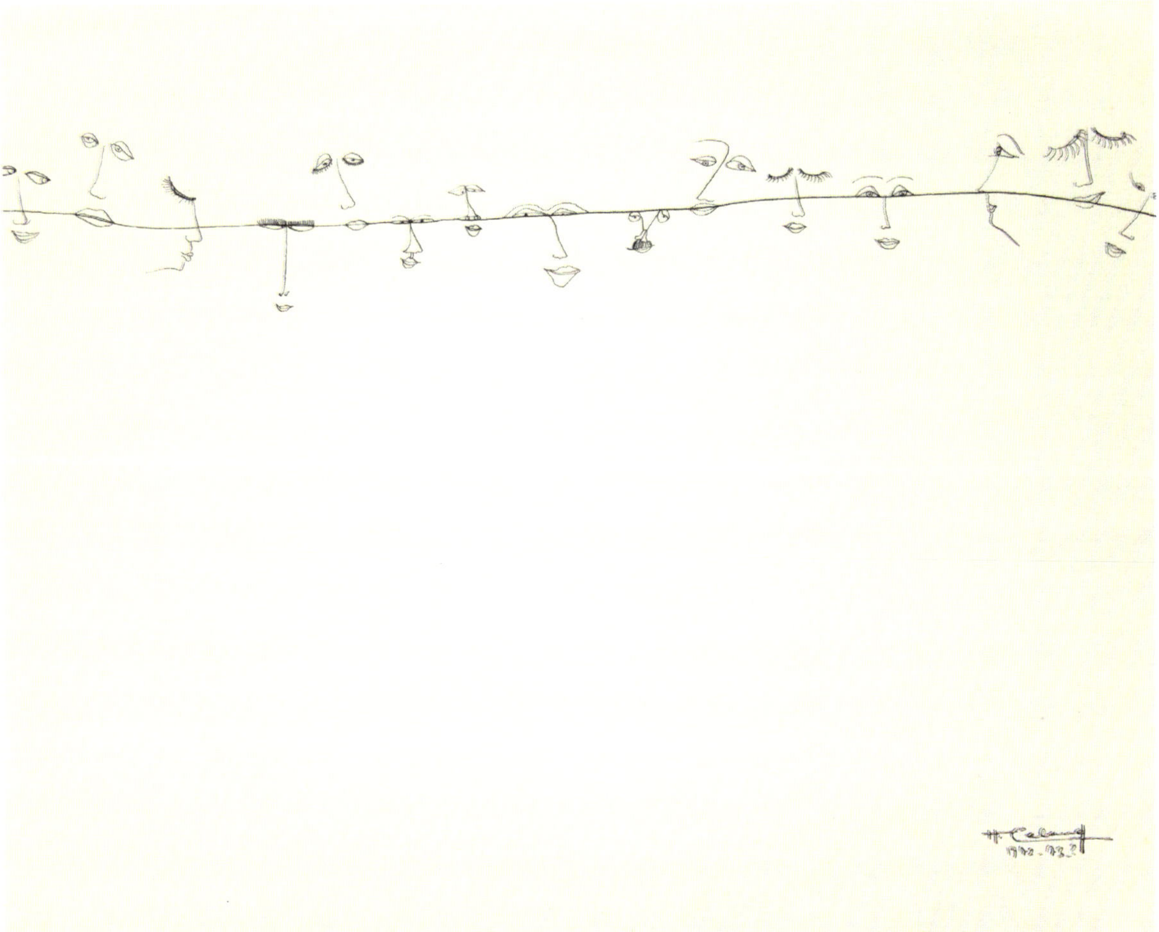

Musique, 1972-1973
Ink on paper, 26.7 × 3.9 cm

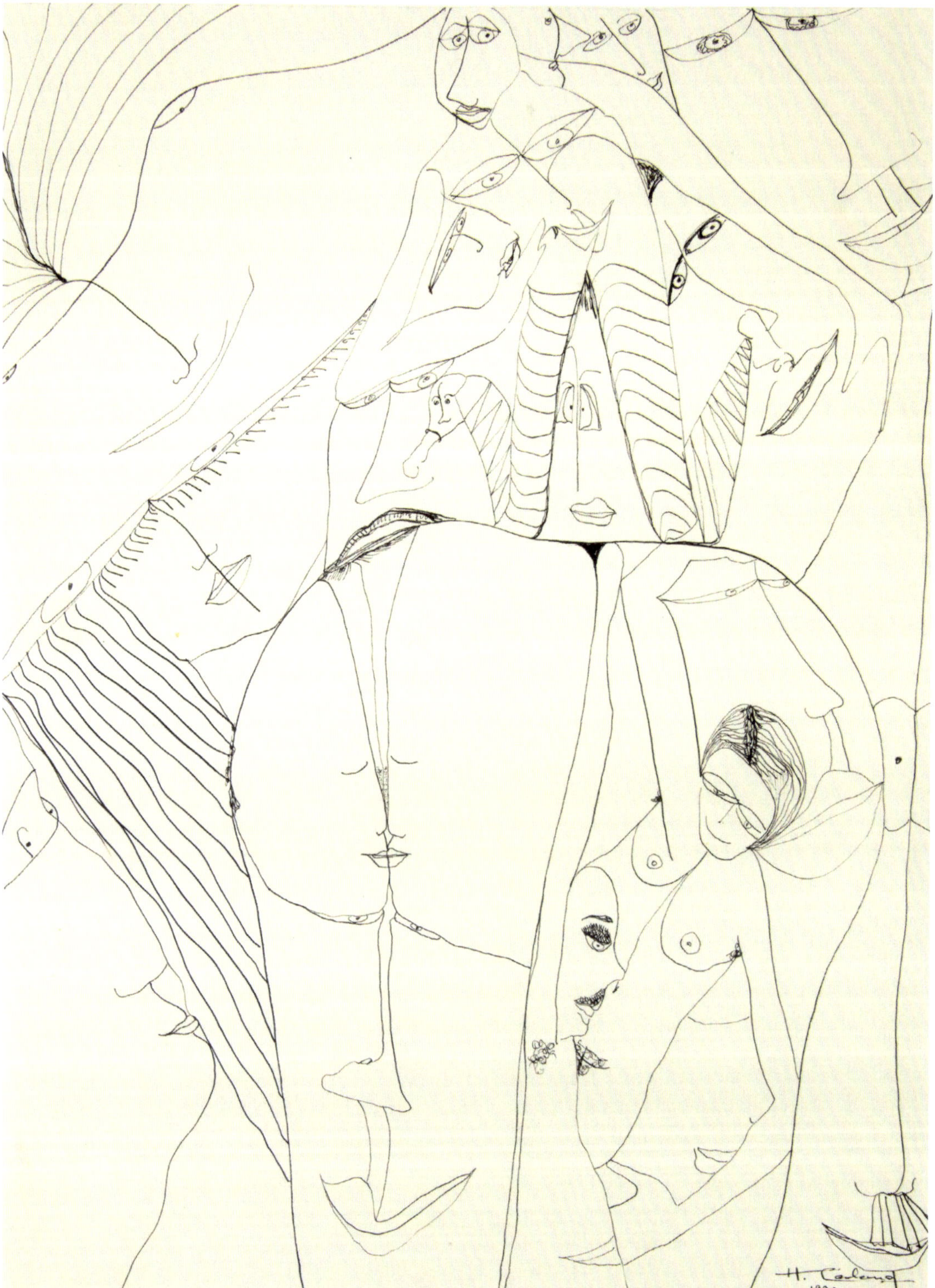

Cirque, 1972
Ink on paper, 35 × 27 cm

Partie à trois, 1971
Ink on paper, 32 × 24 cm

Gala gala, 1972
Ink on paper, 46 × 38 cm

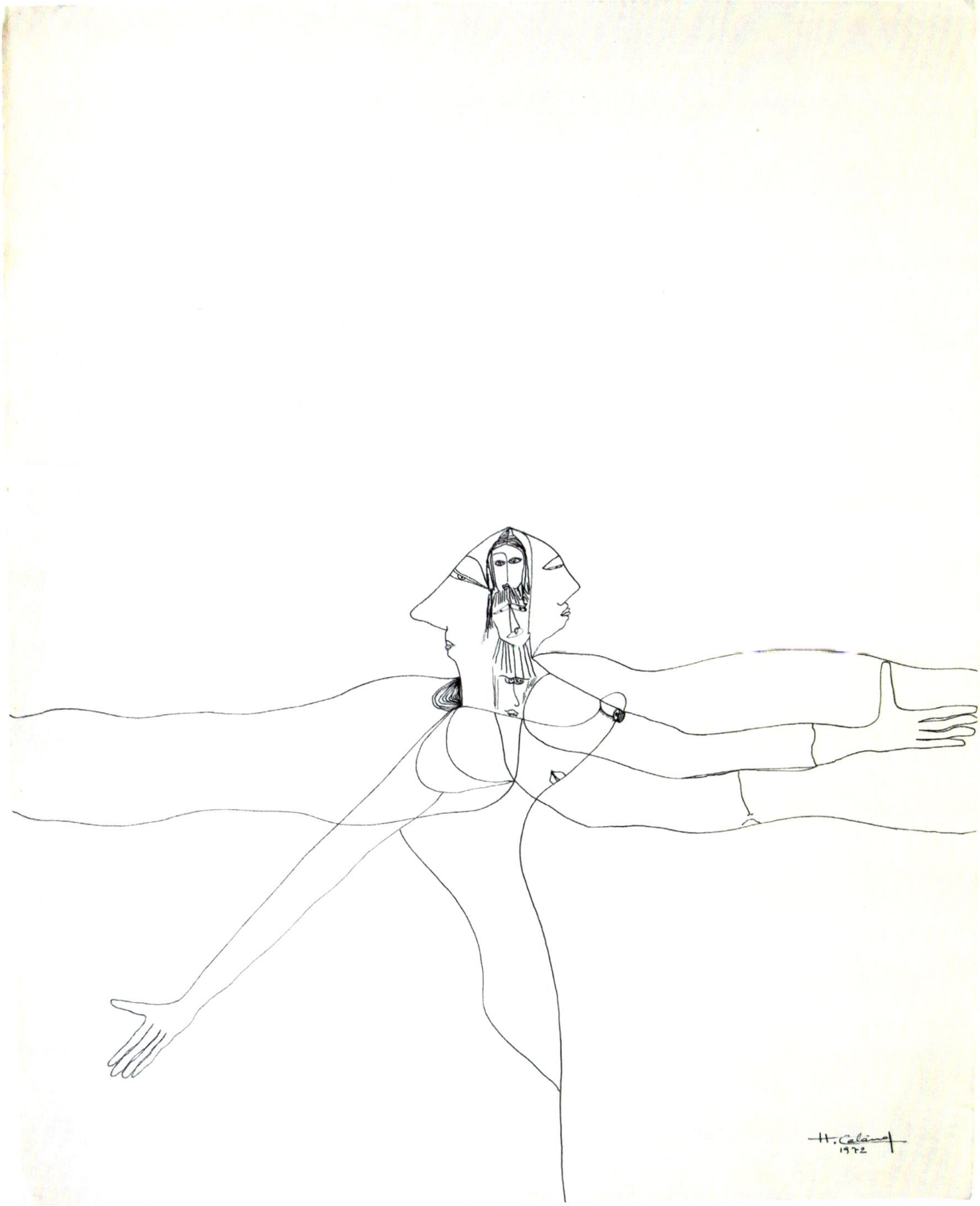
H. Calina
1972

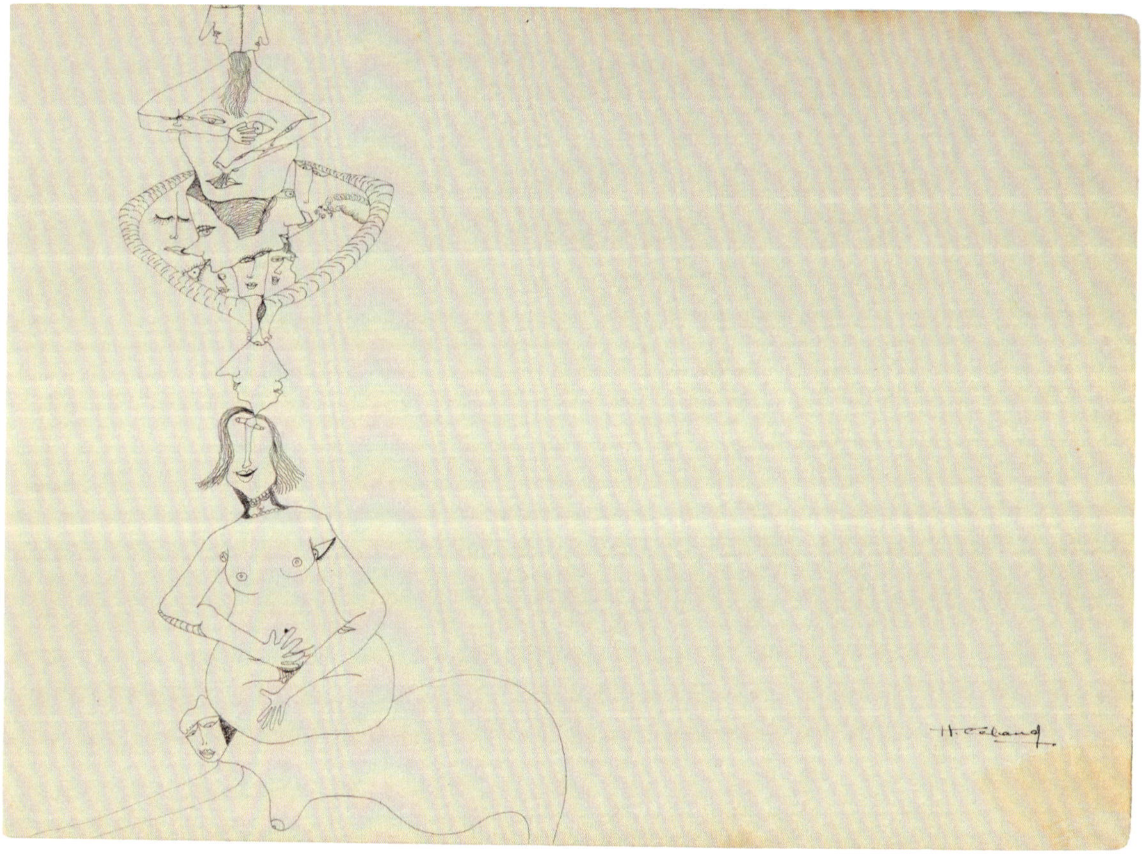

Who's the Boss, 1972
Ink on paper, 25.2 × 35 cm

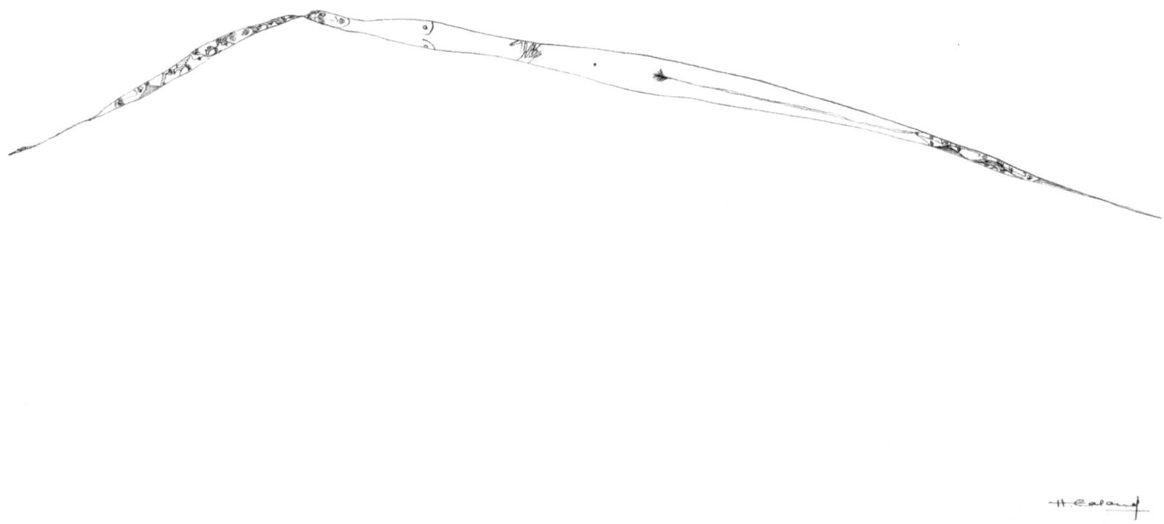

Compression, 1971
Ink on paper, 24 × 33 cm

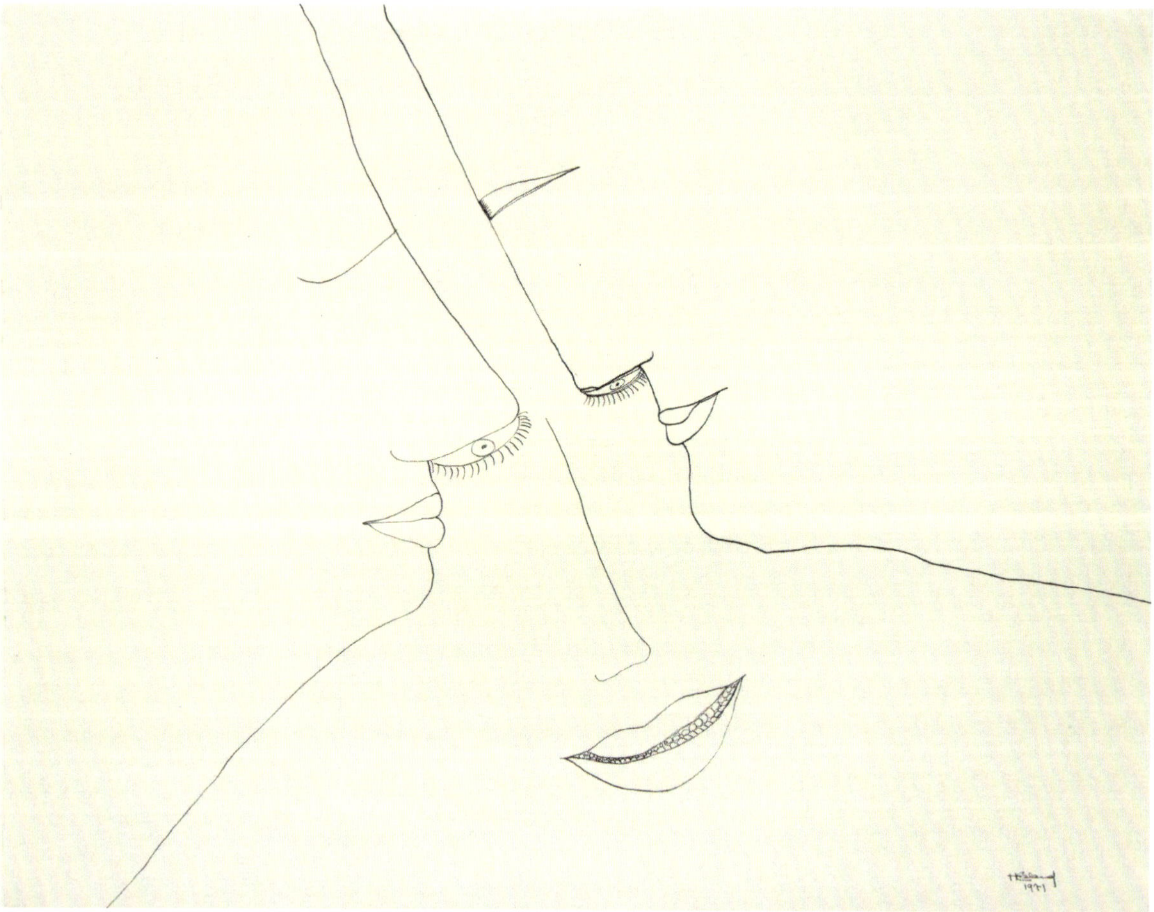

Partie carrée, 1971
Ink on paper, 27 × 35 cm

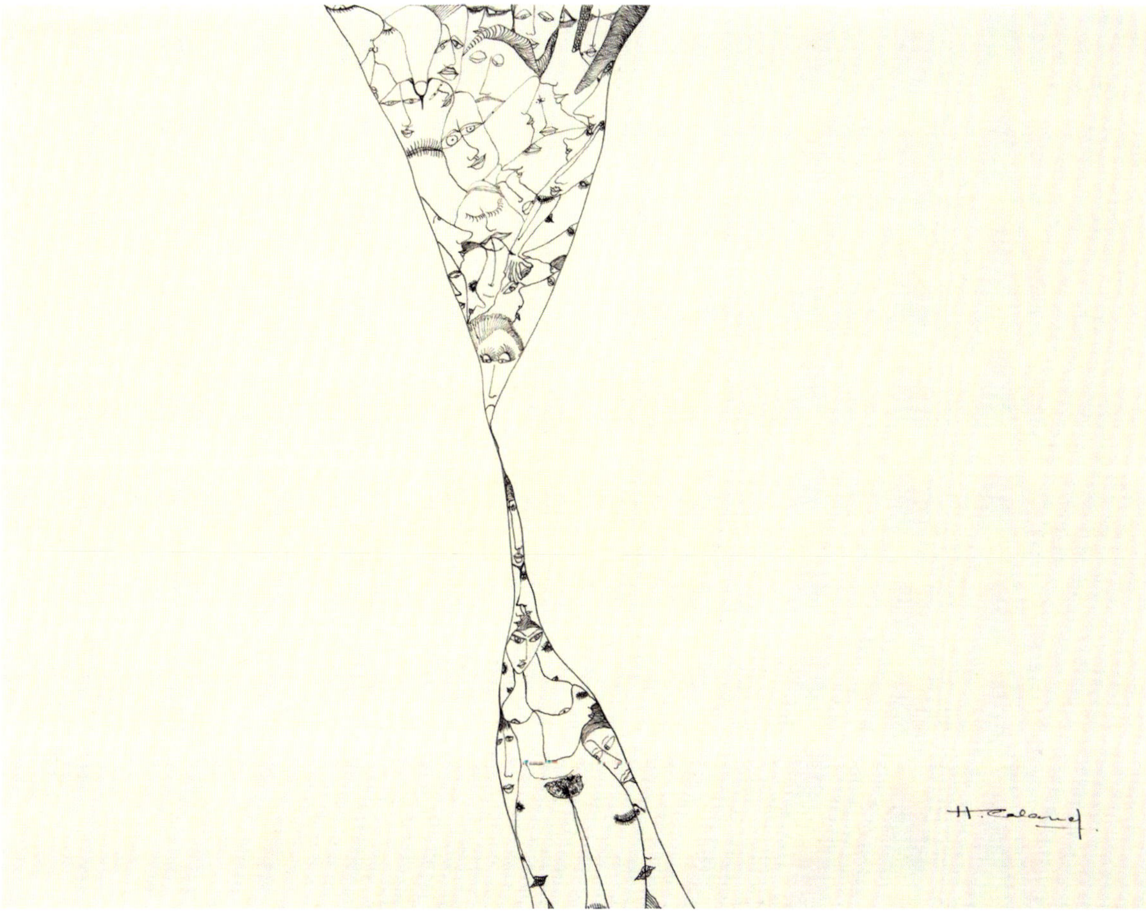

Parenthèse II, 1971
Ink on paper, 24.1 × 33 cm

Private collections, Los Angeles, California and Beirut, Lebanon

Other evocative titles from this period include *Gala gala,*[10] *Who's the Boss, Compression, Partie carrée,* and *Parenthèse* (see photos on p. 19-29). Among them, one stands out for its political resonance: *Guerre incivile* (1981), the only painting in Caland's oeuvre that directly references the Lebanese Civil War. The title—translating as "uncivil war"—functions almost like a successful Freudian slip,[11] "bringing to light something latent yet already known."[12] As the term "*incivile*" (uncivilized) underscores, incivility is a prerequisite for any war. By subverting the conventional term "civil war," Caland exposes its inherent ambiguity and absurdity. Visually, the painting emphasizes contrast. There is no overt depiction of bloodshed, but instead a central, clearly visible, amputated figure—an image of dismemberment treated with a certain distance, even abstraction. The work doesn't shy away from erotic references, and the tension between life and death instincts is palpable. Surreal figures rendered in soft hues and delicate outlines appear with vacant eyes and faces that resemble either flaccid or erect phalluses—challenging conventional representations of masculinity. Some faces are split in two, perhaps alluding to the schizophrenia of "ordinary" citizens, suddenly propelled into violence.

The *Limousin* and *Granite* series (see photos on p. 33-39) are closely tied to places—villages and quarries—visited during her time with sculptor George Apostu. By 1992, Caland was living in California when the Clarence Thomas hearings rocked the United States. Anita Hill's testimony, centered on a single pubic hair, ignited a national scandal. In response, Caland created a series of small, delicately painted works on paper mounted to wood, which she titled *Homage to Pubic Hair* (see photos on p. 40-51)—a bold, humorous, and subversive tribute to bodily autonomy and feminine presence.

10 The verb *galah* comes from the Semitic root g-l-h (from which the words "discover," "exile" in Aramaic and Hebrew, and the expression "wash the dishes" in Arabic derive). It is also the words said by magicians in Lebanon when they reveal something unexpected.

11 Freud, *The Joke and Its Relation to the Unconscious*, op. cit., in a preliminary note by J.-B. Pontalis, 34.

12 Ibid., 51.

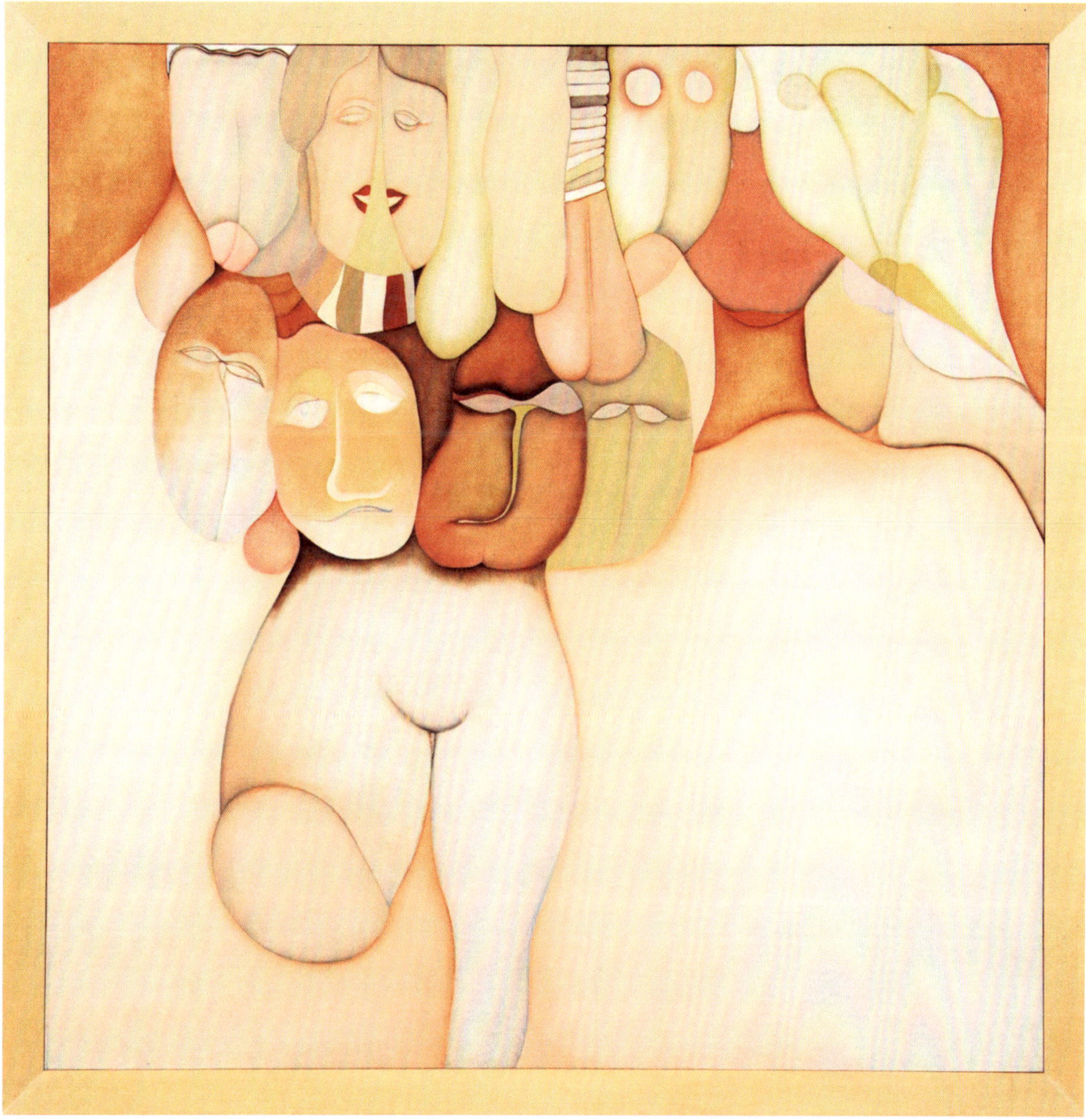

Guerre incivile, 1981
Oil on canvas, 155 × 155 cm

Private collection, Los Angeles, California

Sketchbook #5 (extracts pages 8, 12, 13, 14, 17, 19), 1986
Ink and watercolor on paper, 15.8 × 22.8 cm

Private collection, Los Angeles, California

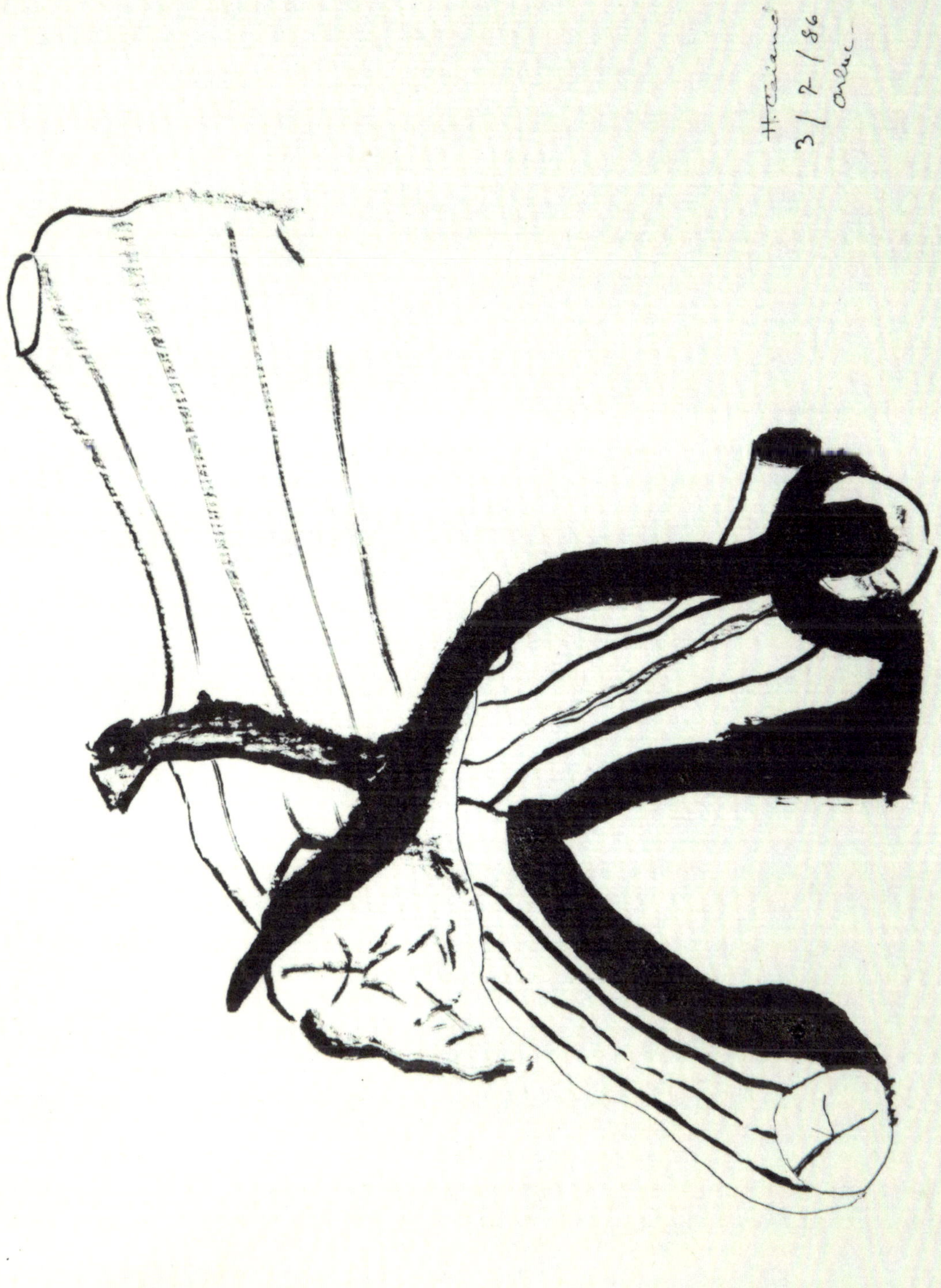

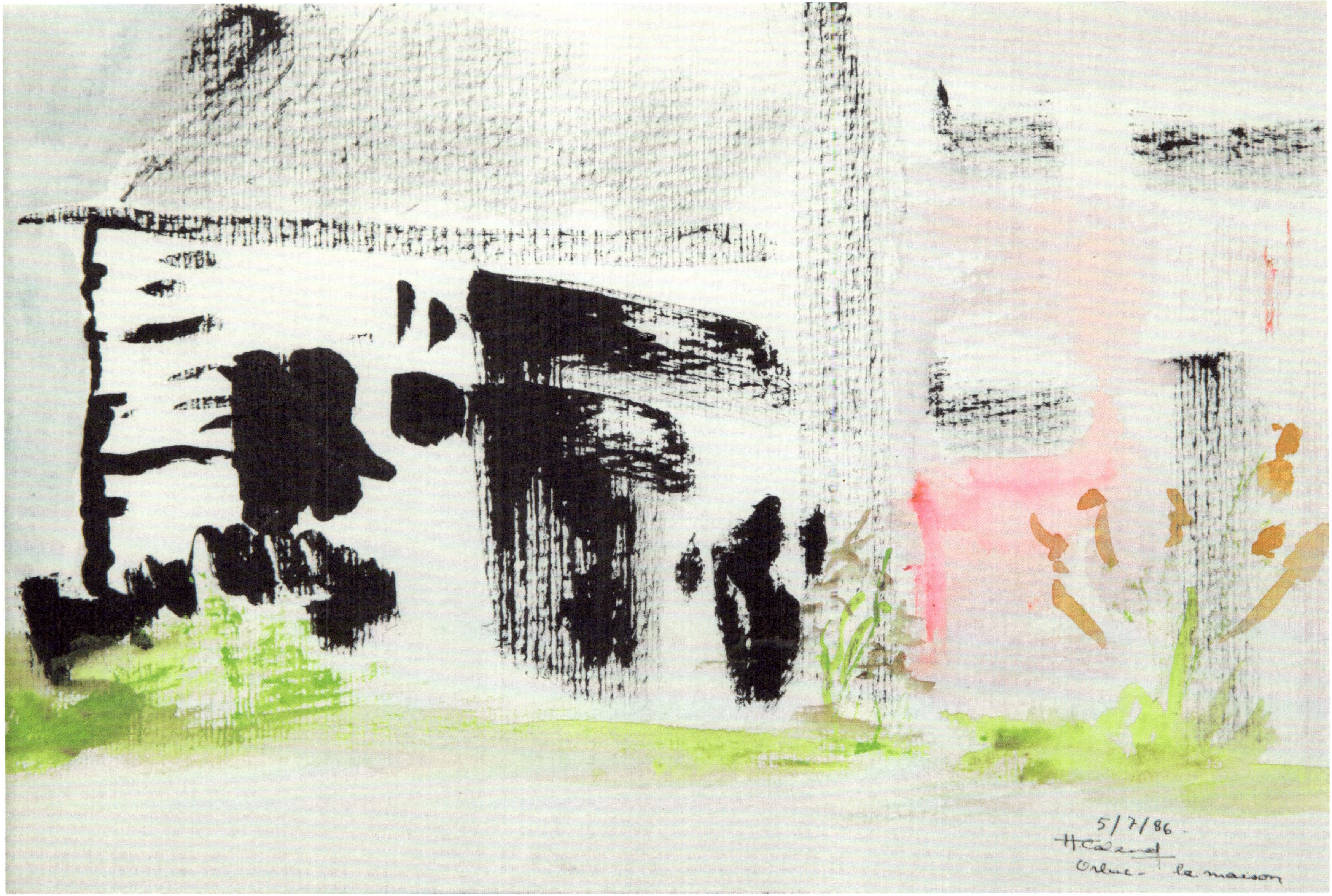
5/7/86.
la maison

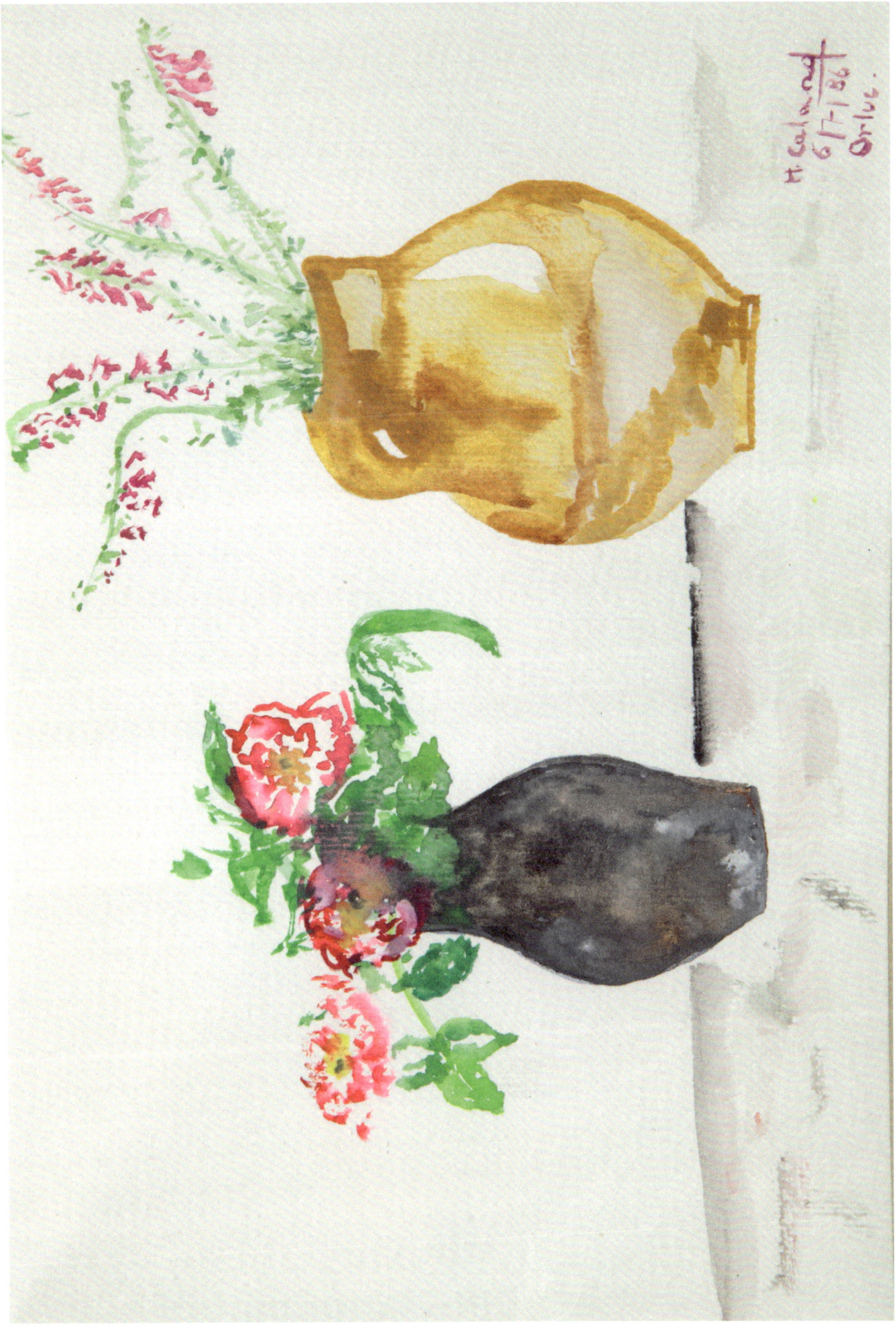

Paris - le 19/12/86 -

Apostu est mort le 13 Octobre -
Pour moi - dans la nuit du 6 Juillet au 7 -
En fait le 6 - vers 11 heures du soir -
Il a eu une hémorragie - elle devait arriver - je l'attendais presque -
En faisant comme si de rien n'était - en vivant - dormant -
aimant - ayant peur -
Ce carnet s'est arrêté le 6 juillet 1986 -
La nuit de Samedi à Dimanche a été parfaite -
Il constatait souvent : " Dormir contre ton cœur - c'est le paradis(?)"
J'aimais mon cœur qui lui procurait un peu de paix -
Il m'avait dit aussi : "Tu ne comprends pas - je ne peux resister à ta p..."
J'aimais ma "p"... parce qu'il disait qu'il ne pouvait pas y résister.
"Le sommeil avec toi est plus pervers(e) (sic) que le footing..(sic)....
Le sommeil n'était pas pervers - il a été le plus pur et le plus merveilleux des sommeils -
J'ai découvert la chorégraphie du sommeil - le rituel du sommeil -
l'improvisation du sommeil - la créativité du sommeil -
Nous attendions avec émotion et une patience controlée le sommeil en question -

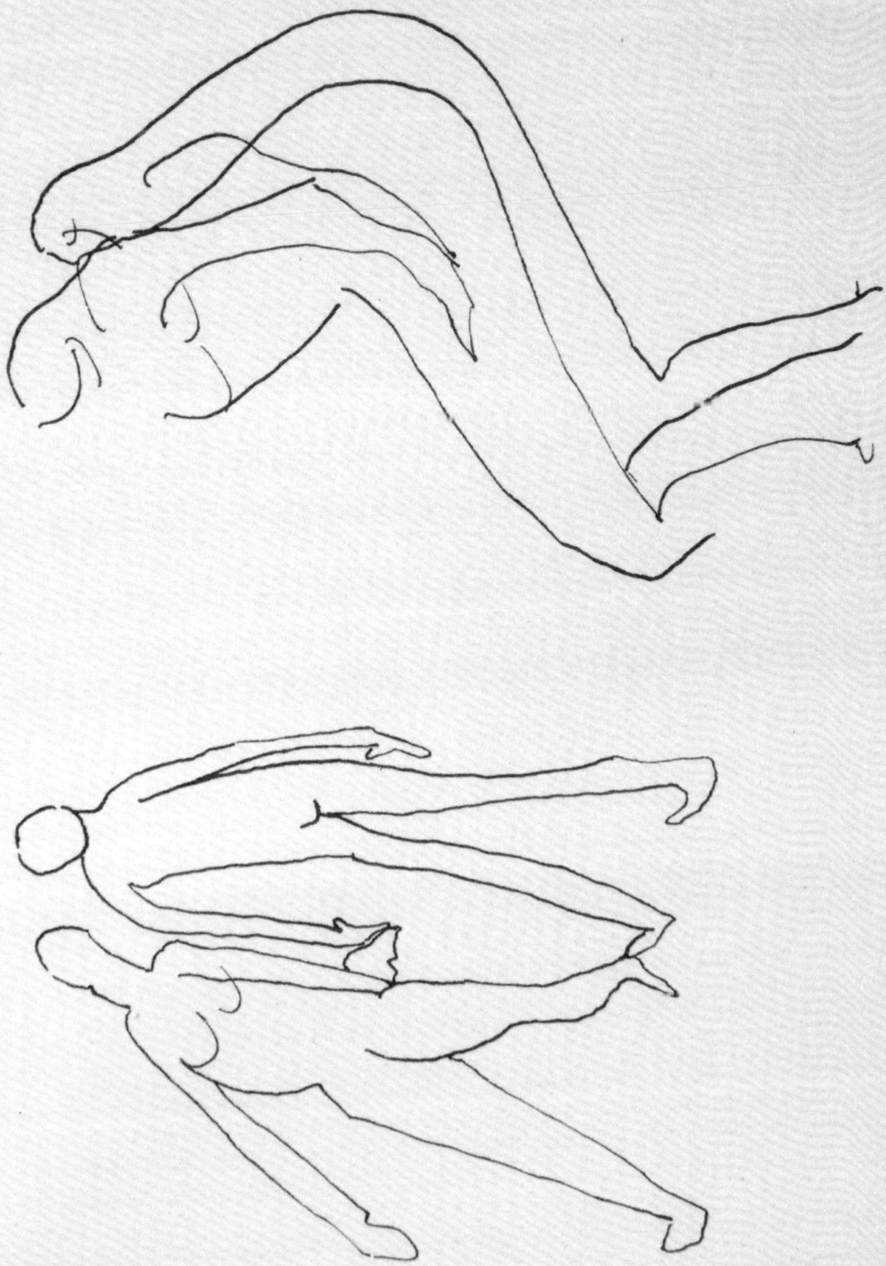

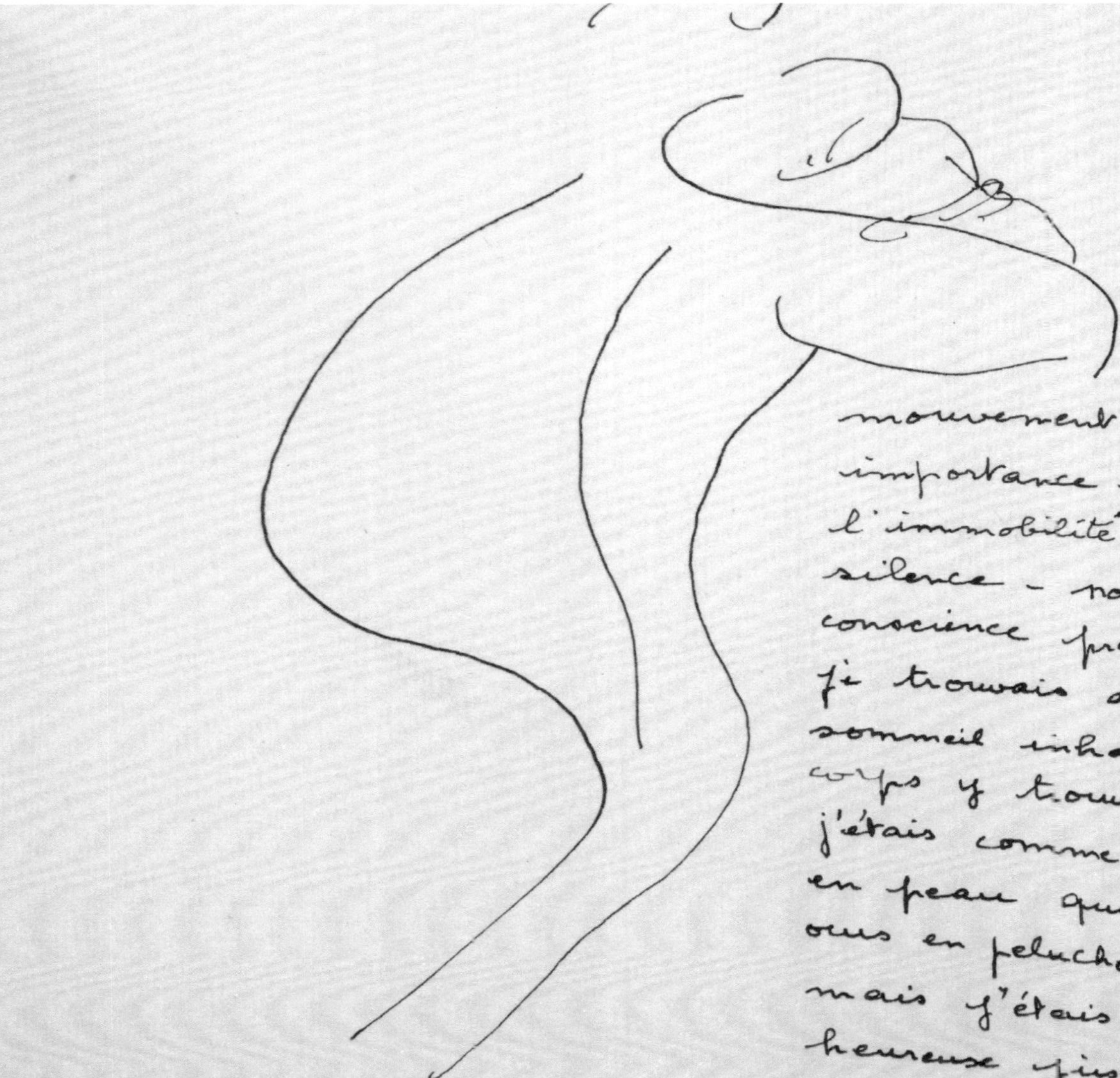

nous inventions
le sommeil –

il en était né une
chorégraphie pratiquée
rituellement – le moindr.
mouvement prenait une immense
importance –
l'immobilité totale était un autre
silence – nous avions une presque
conscience presque permanente –
je trouvais d'instinct des positions de
sommeil inhabituelles pour que son
corps y trouve un confort momentané –
j'étais comme un immense jouet
en peau qui lui servait comme un
ours en peluche aux petits enfants –
mais j'étais un jouet aux aguets.
heureuse jusqu'à l'épuisement de
remplir son rôle de jouet

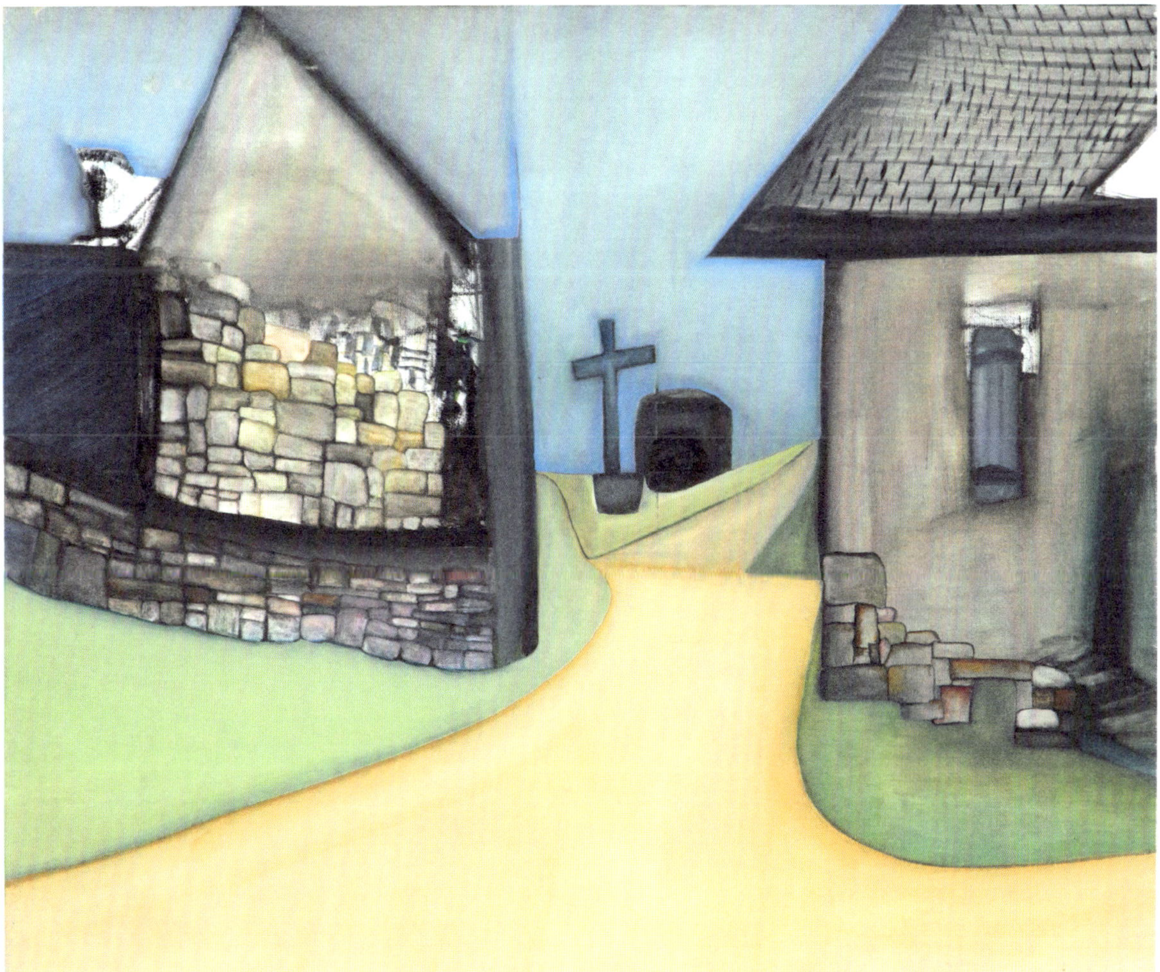

Limousin, 1985
Oil on canvas, 54.6 × 81.3 cm

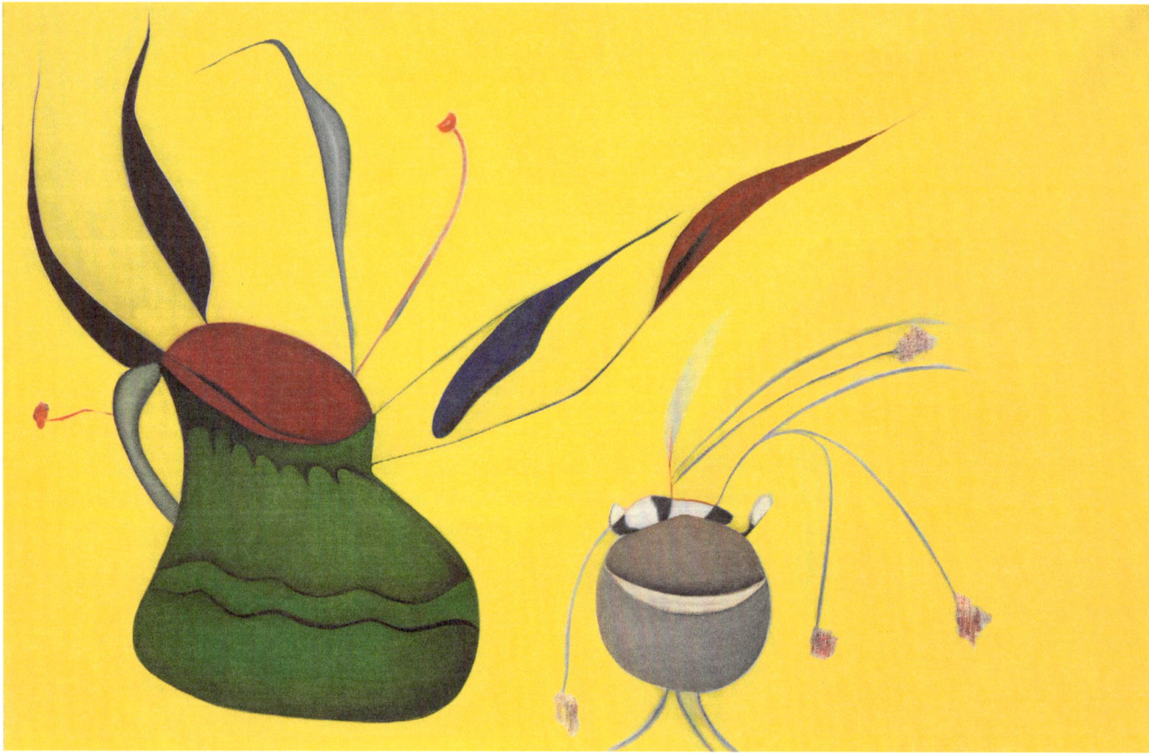

Limousin, 1985
Oil on canvas, 45.7 × 26.6 cm

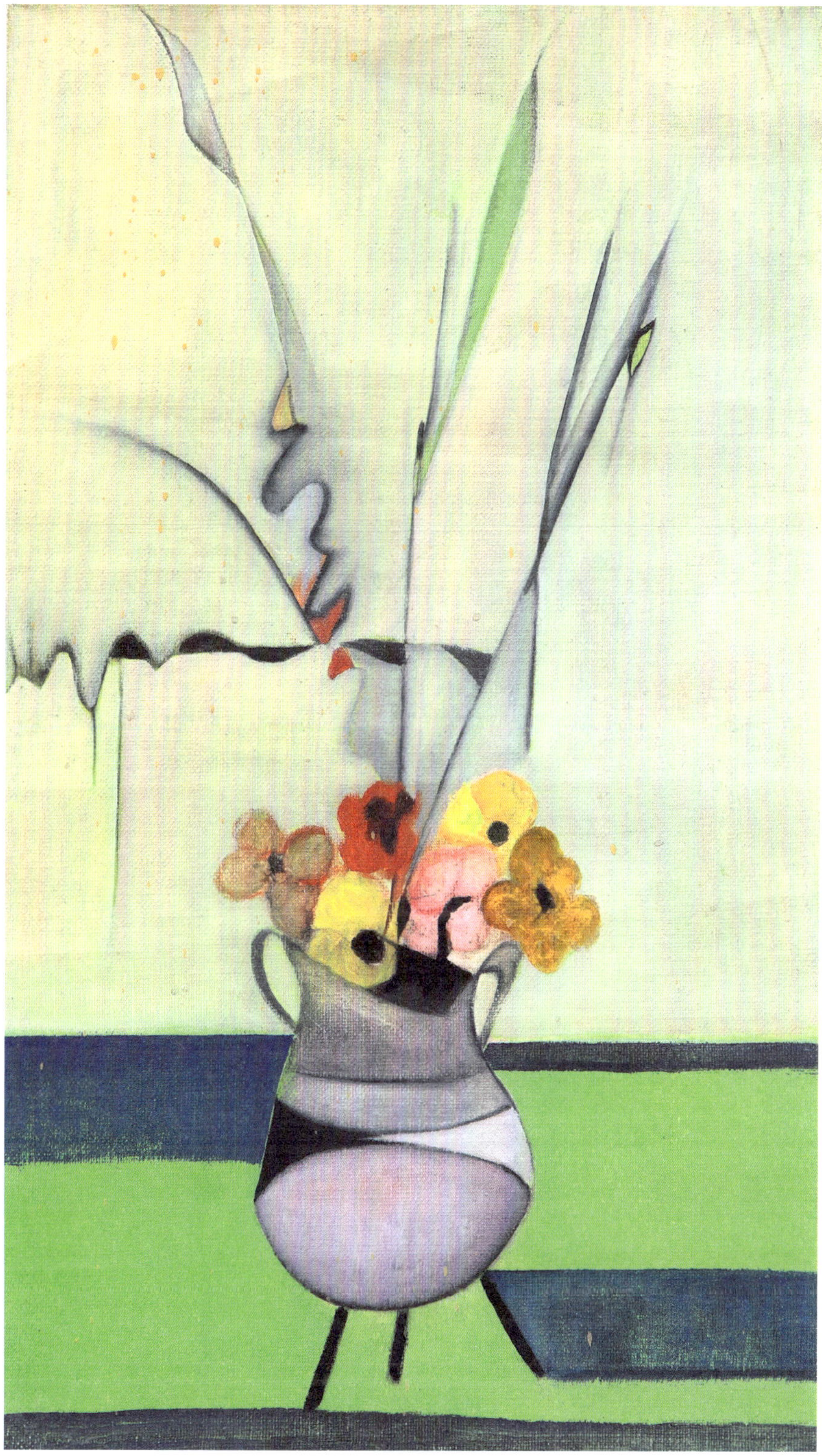

Limousin, 1985
Oil on canvas, 59.7 × 72.4 cm

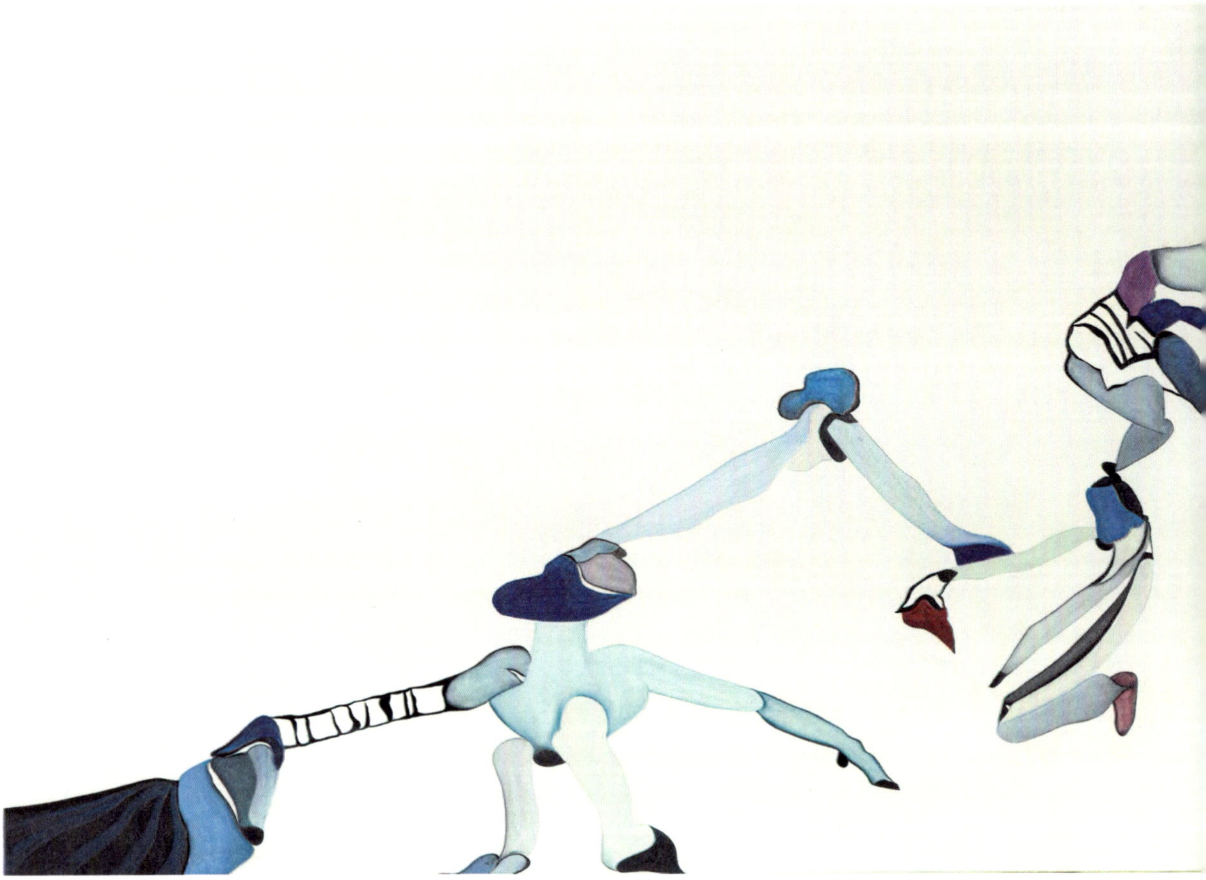

Granite I, 1985
Oil on canvas, 49.5 × 148.6 cm

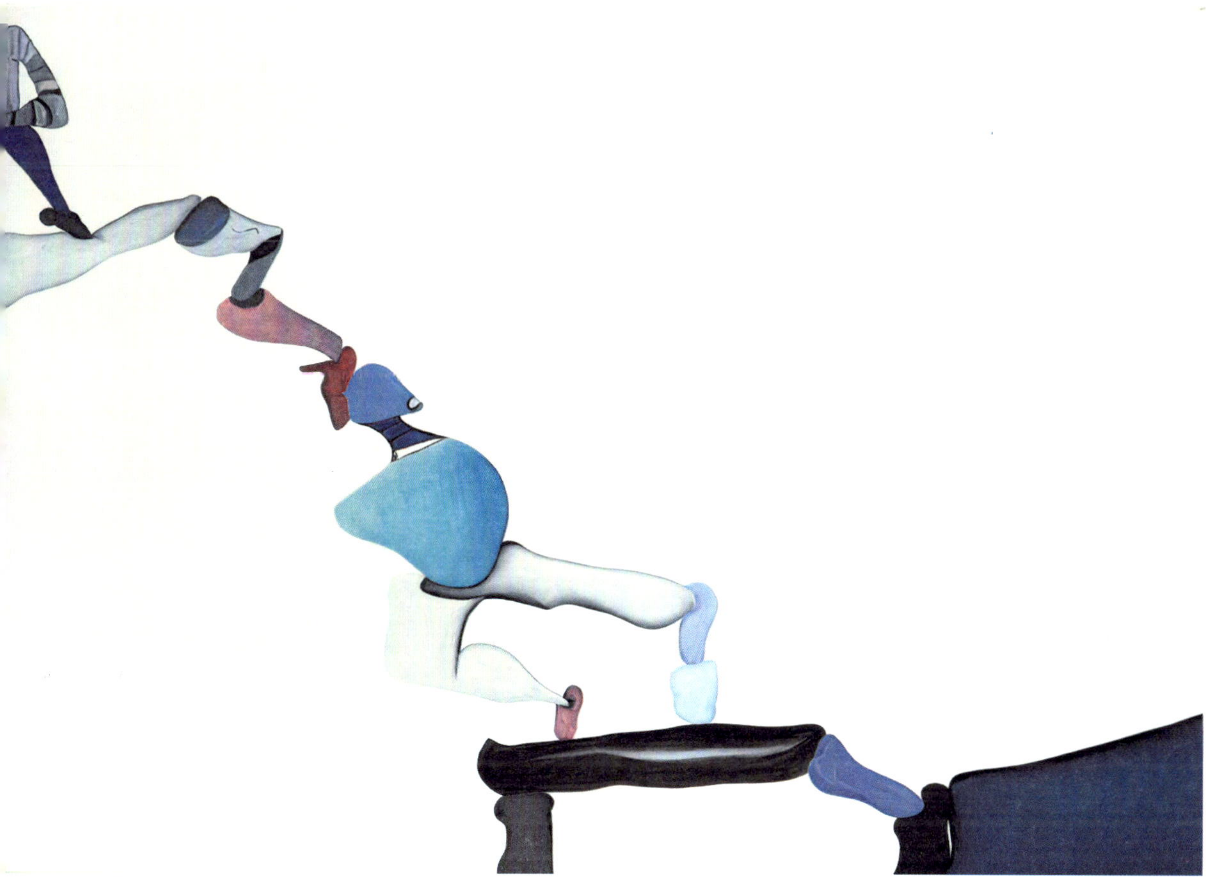

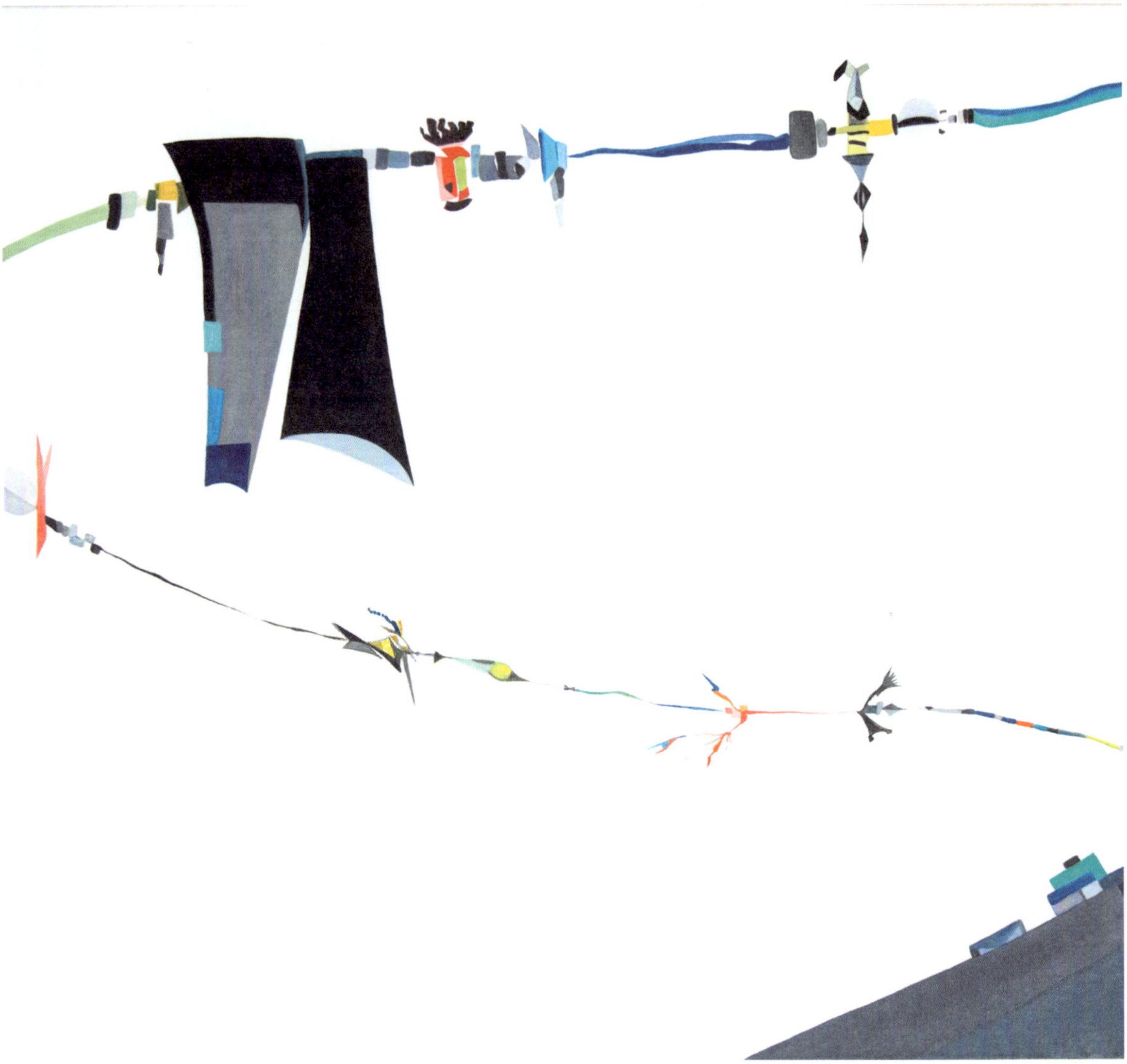

Untitled
Oil on canvas, 54 × 65.4 cm

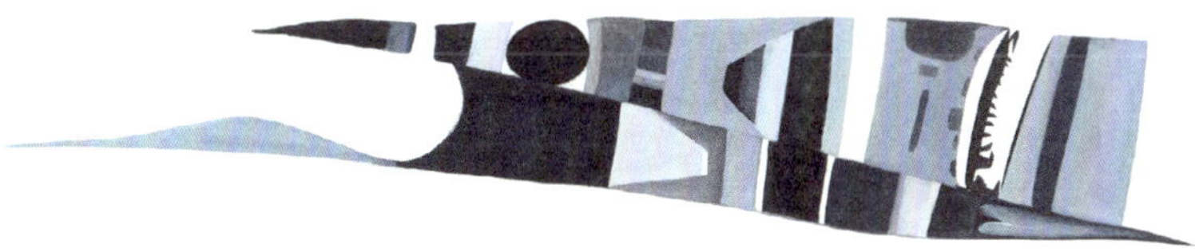

Untitled, 1986
Oil on canvas, 100.3 × 100.3 cm

Private collections, Los Angeles, California

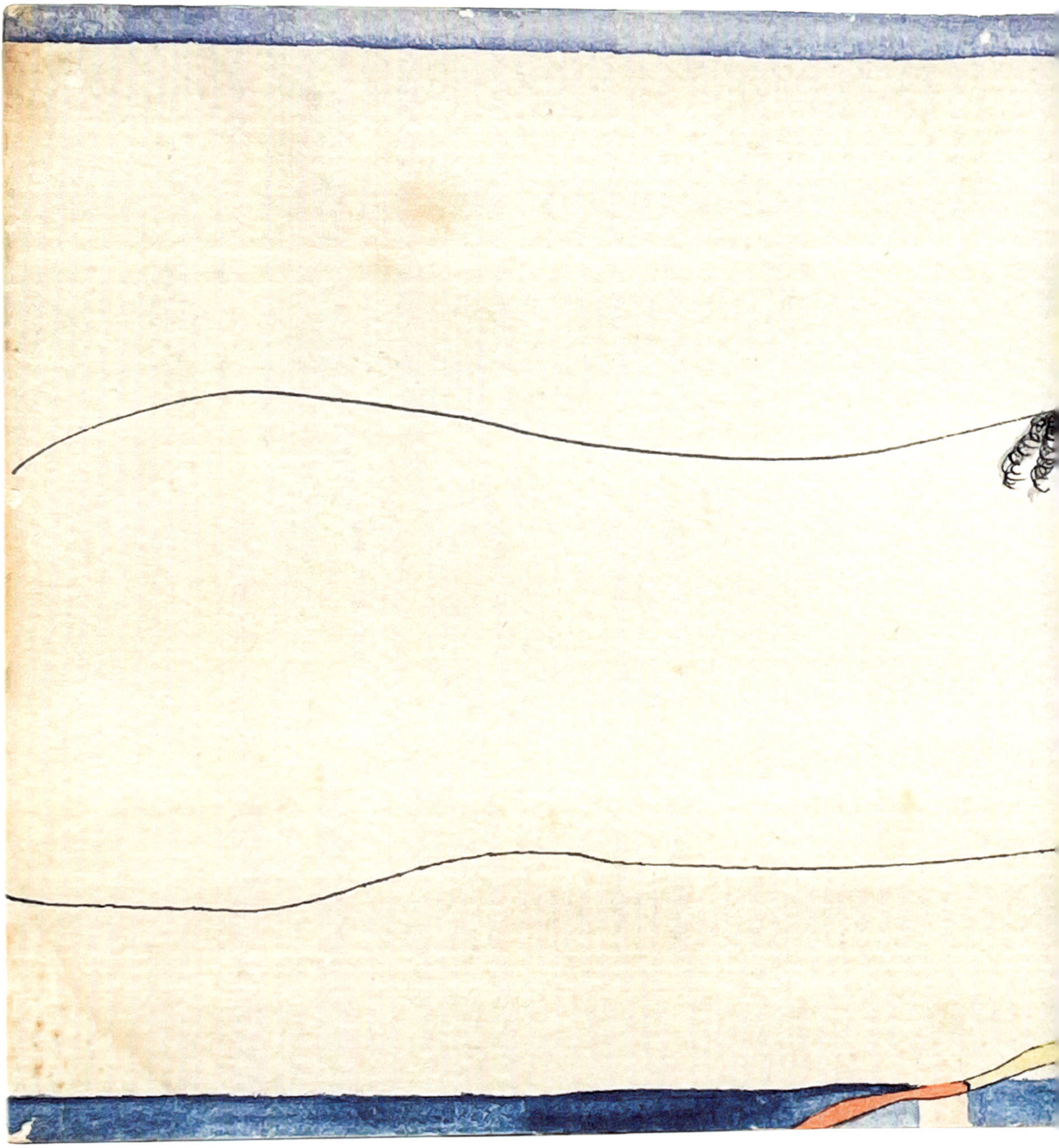

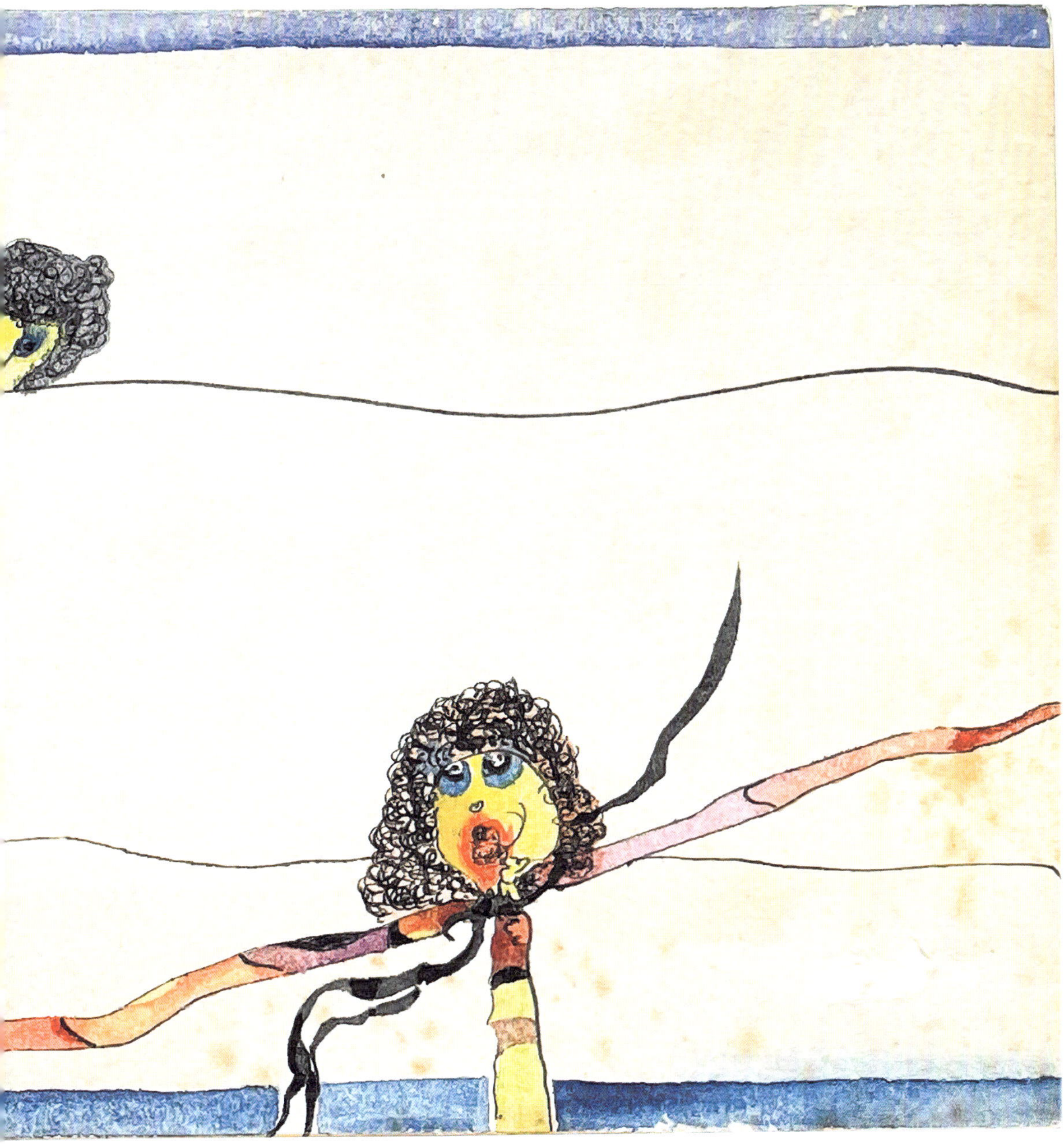

Homage to Pubic Hair, 1992
Mixed media on paper mounted on wood, 12.7 × 25.4 cm

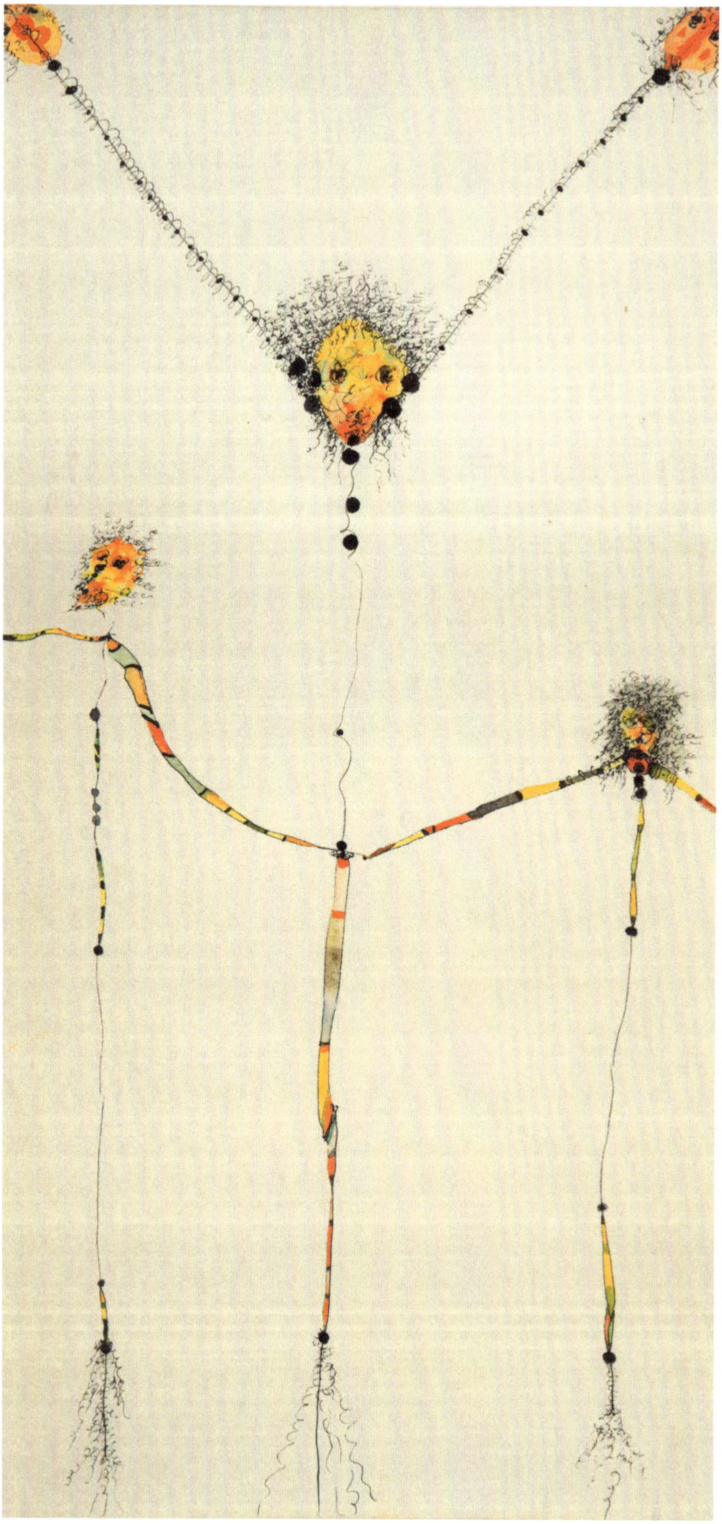

Homage to Pubic Hair, 1992
Mixed media on paper mounted on wood, 50.8 × 25.4 cm

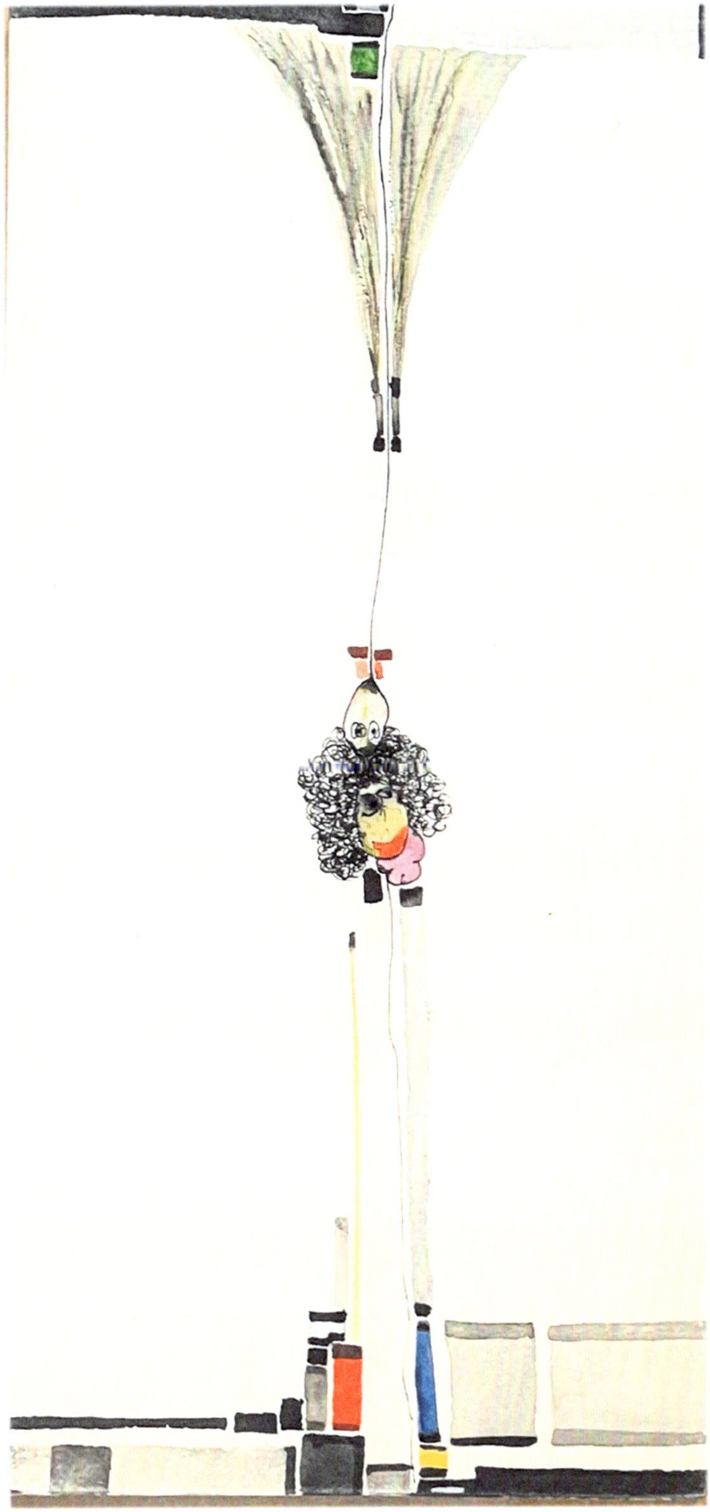

Homage to Pubic Hair, 1992
Mixed media on paper mounted on wood, 25.4 × 12.7 cm

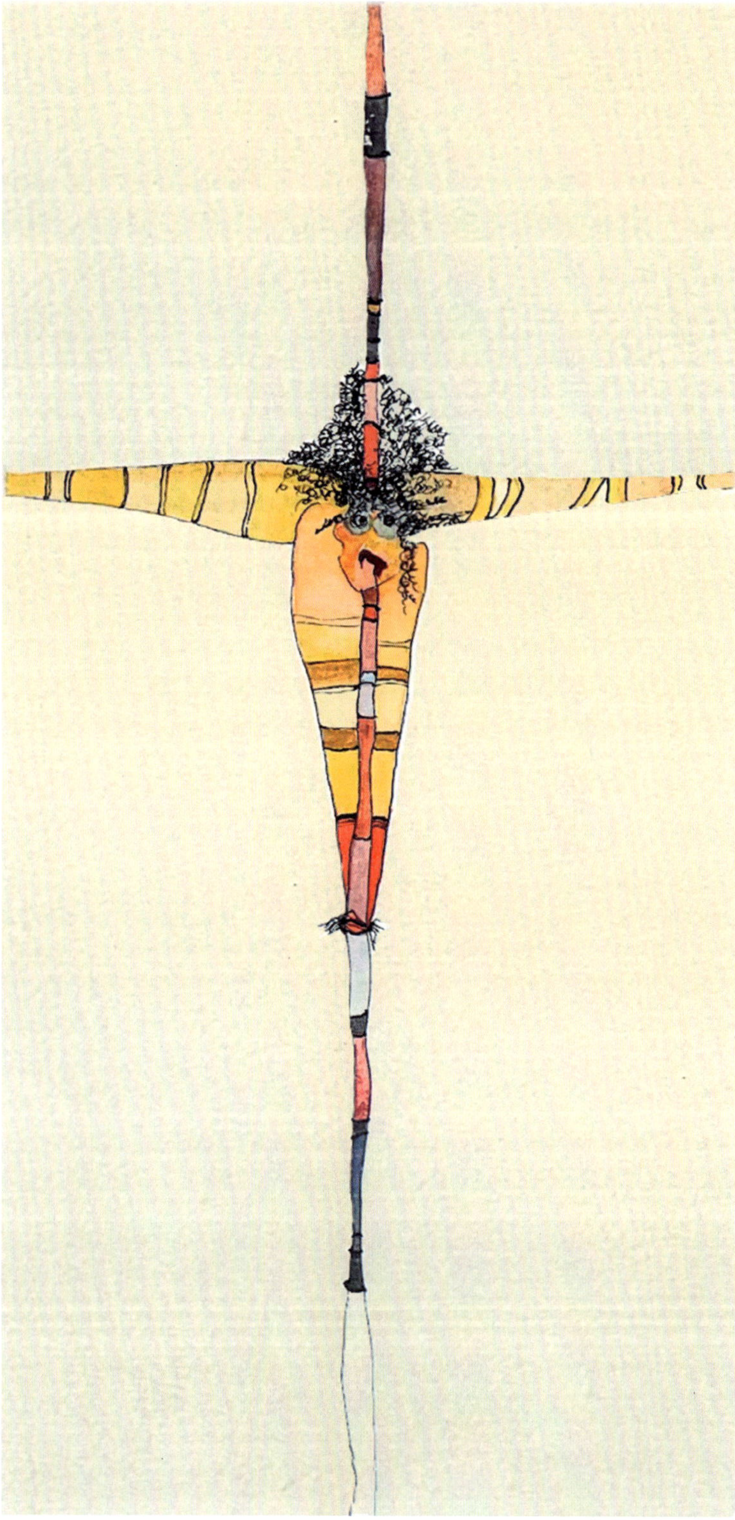

Homage to Pubic Hair, 1992
Mixed media on paper mounted on wood, 25.4 × 12.7 cm

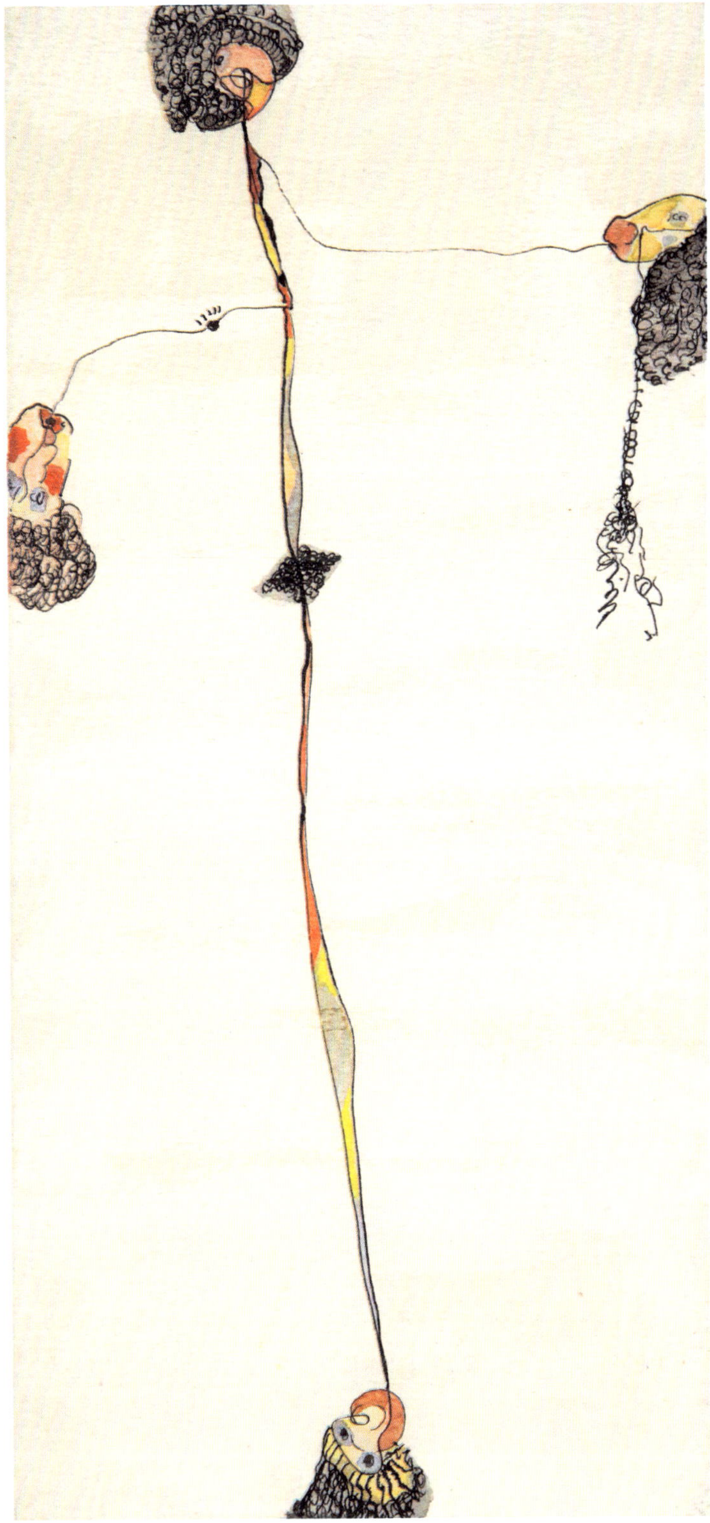

Homage to Pubic Hair, 1992
Mixed media on paper mounted on wood, 26.7 × 12.7 cm

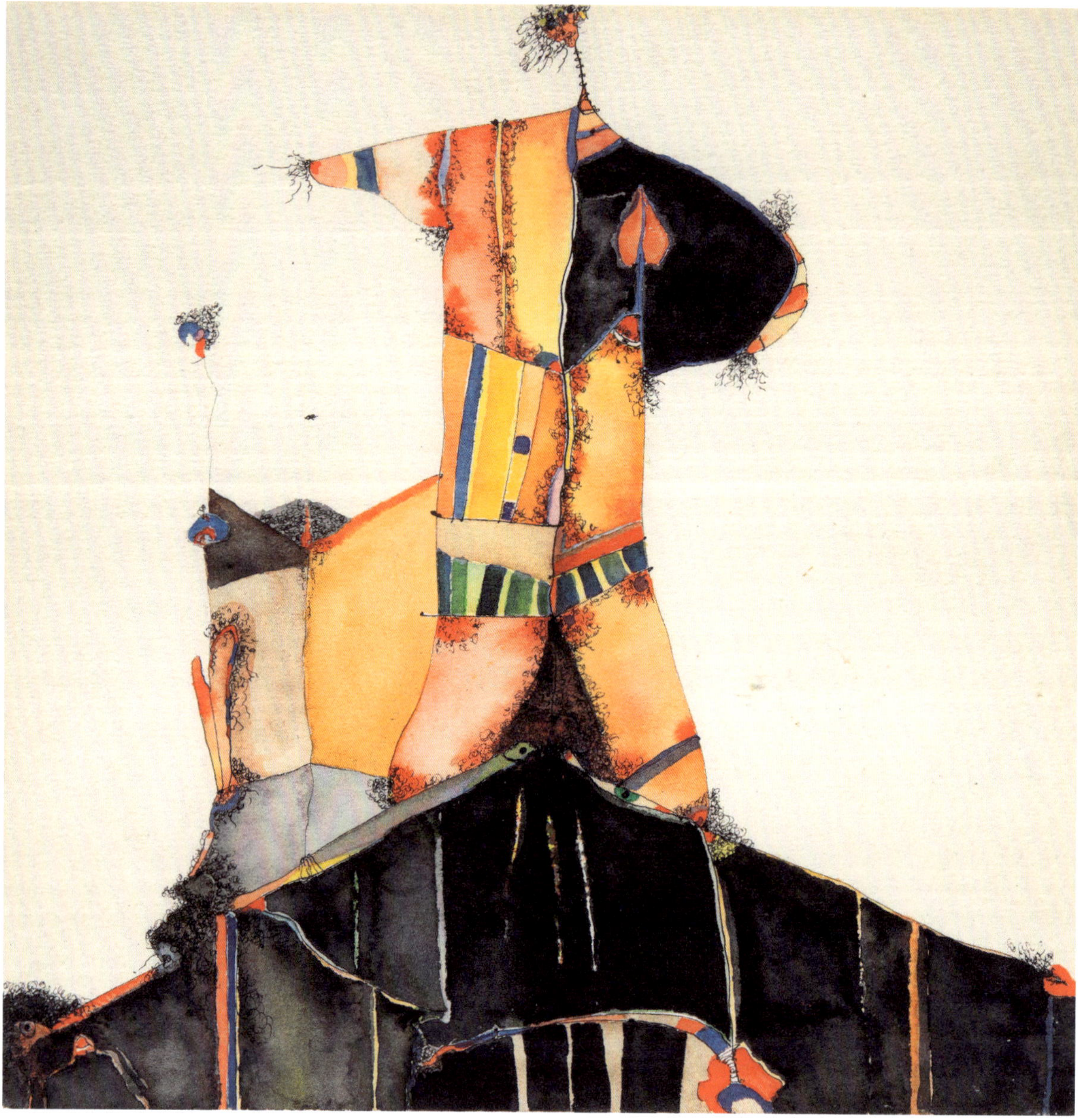

Homage to Pubic Hair-Sarcasm, 1992
Mixed media on paper mounted on wood, 2.4 × 25.4 cm

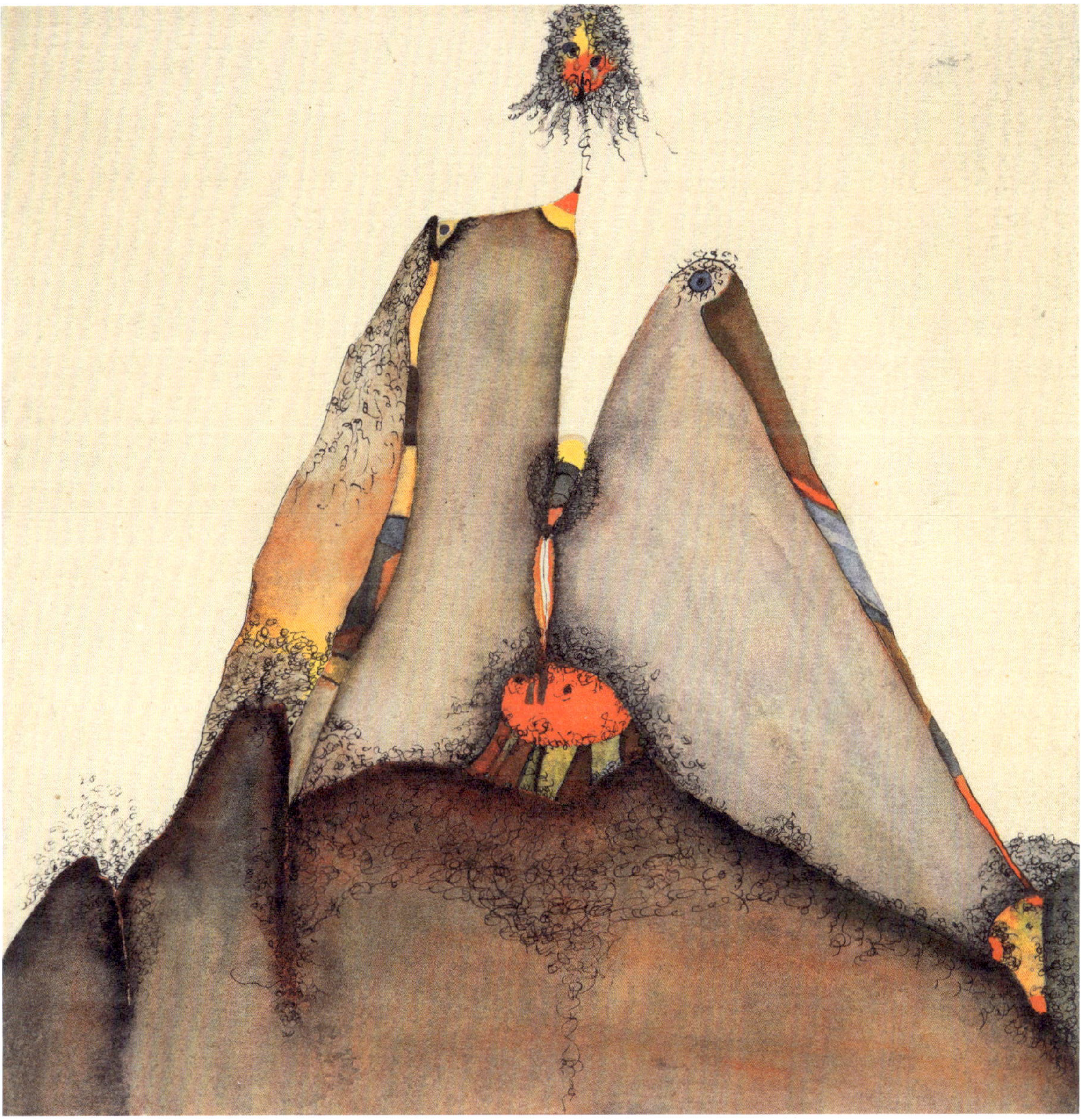

Homage to Pubic Hair, 1992
Mixed media on paper mounted on wood, 25.4 × 25.4 cm

Homage to Pubic Hair-Sarcasm, 1992
Mixed media on paper mounted on wood, 25.4 × 25.4 cm

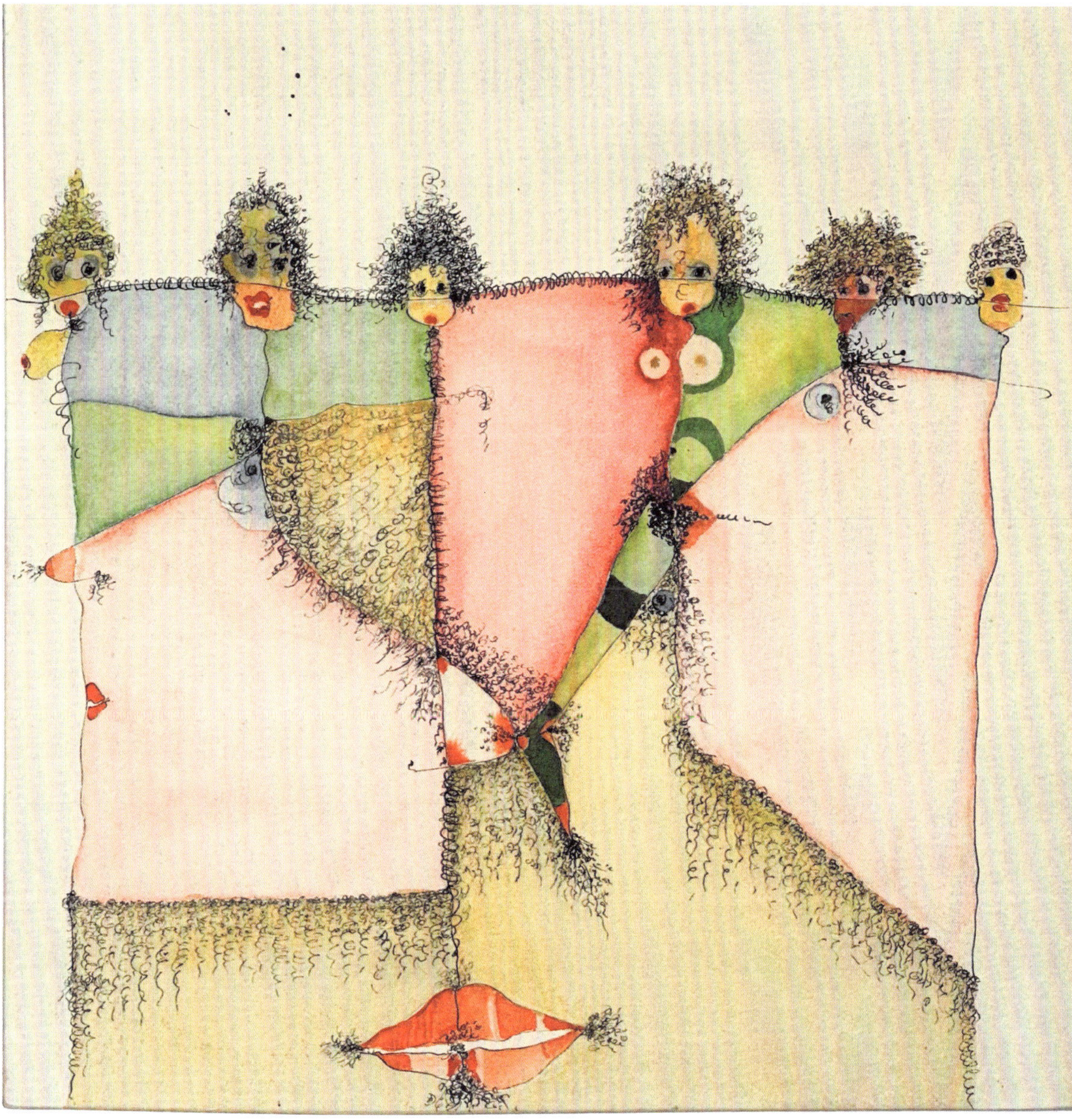

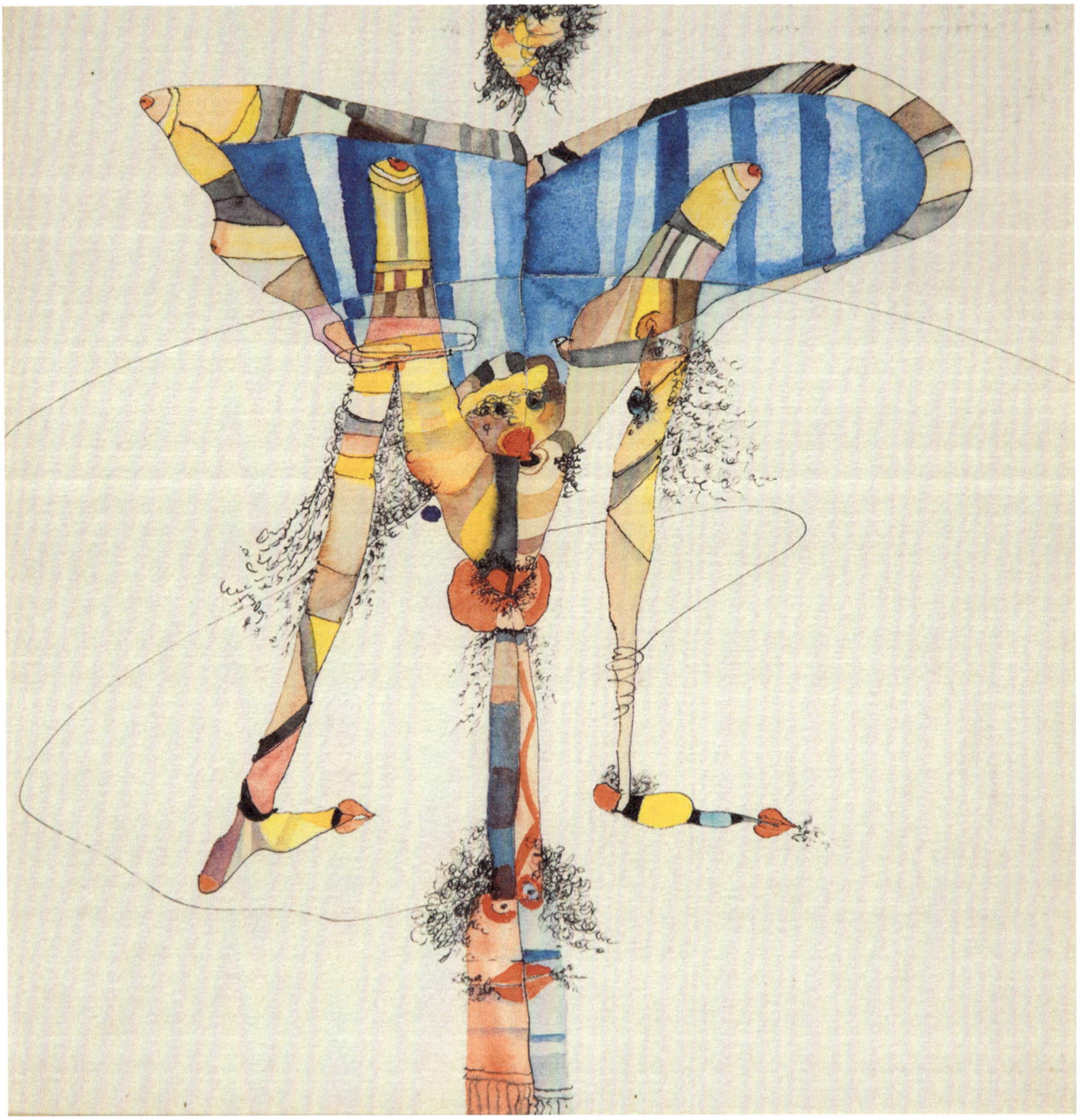

Homage to Pubic Hair, 1992
Mixed media on paper mounted on wood, 25.4 × 25.4 cm

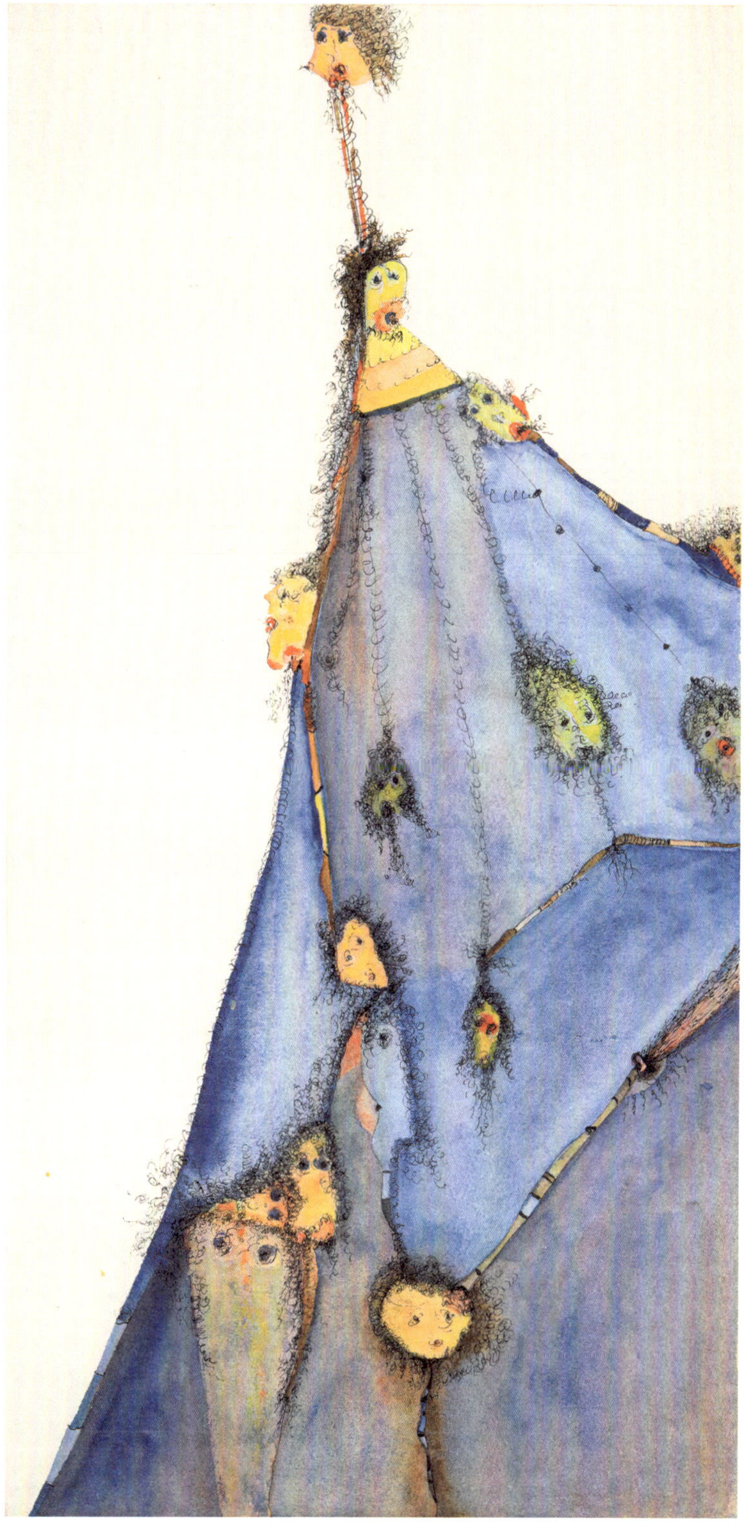

Homage to Pubic Hair, 1992
Mixed media on paper mounted on wood, 50.8 × 25.4 cm

Private collections, Los Angeles, California

In 1993, as Beirut began to emerge from the wreckage of war, Nadine Begdache invited Caland to exhibit at her newly opened Janine Rubeiz Gallery. The artist spent several months in Lebanon preparing her first exhibition there, titled *Faces and Places*. In 1997, a second exhibition under the same name followed, and the title was later reused in 2009 for two large paintings and again in 2010 for a series of ten sheepskin paintings. This repeated use of *Faces and Places* signals the enduring importance of both personal identity and geographic memory in Caland's life and work—an artistic reflection of places she had inhabited and the faces she had known since childhood[13] (see photos on p. 53-56). In 1994, she created a remarkable series titled *Money (Doesn't Bring Happiness, But It Sure Helps)*—365 works, one for each day of the year—prompted by the idea that "you need money every day." Painted on 25-cm-square canvases, these pieces wittily engage with financial themes, their titles capturing economic realities and social commentary with playful irony. Examples include: *Monetary Landscapes, Account Closures, Monetary Funds, A Golden Bridge, Old Money, Money Opens Many Doors, Fresh Cash Injection, Lost Funds, Sugarcoating the Pill, No Interest, Gold Coverage, Not a Dime, Belt Tightening, Bribe, Money in Perspective, A Good Tip, A Safe Never Follows a Hearse, Money Went to His Head, A Penny for Your Thoughts, Time is Money, Rolling in Gold, She Comes from Money, Rubber Check, Silence is Gold, A Heart of Gold*, and *They Killed the Golden Goose* (see photos on p. 64-65). A few years later, the paradoxical title *Nude Letters* would emerge, followed by another significant series with an oxymoron title: *Silent Letters*. Both series point to Caland's continued exploration of the interplay between language, visibility, and abstraction.

In 2006, Caland created *Rossinante*,[14] a series of drawings on paper that she later transformed into delicate sculptures made from wire, wool thread, and Japanese paper.[15] These works explore the contrasting malleability of wire and wool, as well as the variety of forms these materials can assume. The sculptures are so fragile that even the slightest pressure from a fingertip can pierce the paper (see photos p. 66-69). This fragility—balanced by the tension and resilience of the materials—mirrors the artist's own physical and emotional state at the time. Simultaneously, she painted a dozen vibrant canvases under the title *Rossinante Under Cover*. While referencing the whimsical, dreamlike world of Cervantes' novel, the title also subtly reveals a "masked" pain—an allusion to a body increasingly burdened by age and vulnerability.

Throughout her career, Caland titled the vast majority of her works in French, occasionally opting for English, particularly after she settled in California and her paintings began to reference specific locations such as *Topanga*, *Appleton*, and *Pasadena*. Only two titles that evoke childhood memories are in Arabic. The first, *Zikrayat toufoulati fi loubnan* (*Memories of My Childhood in Lebanon*), was handwritten by Caland on the back of a wooden panel; the piece is signed and dated 1998. The second, *Tarik el-Sham*[16] (The Road to Damascus), transliterated into French, was given to a painting created in 2010 for the exhibition *Mes jeunes années*.

13 *Warae elwoujouh* interview (see photos p 53-63)

14 "I feel like Rossinante, the aging horse of Don Quixotte" said Caland one day in 2006 during a visit to Ephesus.

15 These sculptures were from 2010-2011.

16 The original title is in Arabic, transliterated into Latin letters, translating to La Route de Damas in French and The Road to Damascus in English.

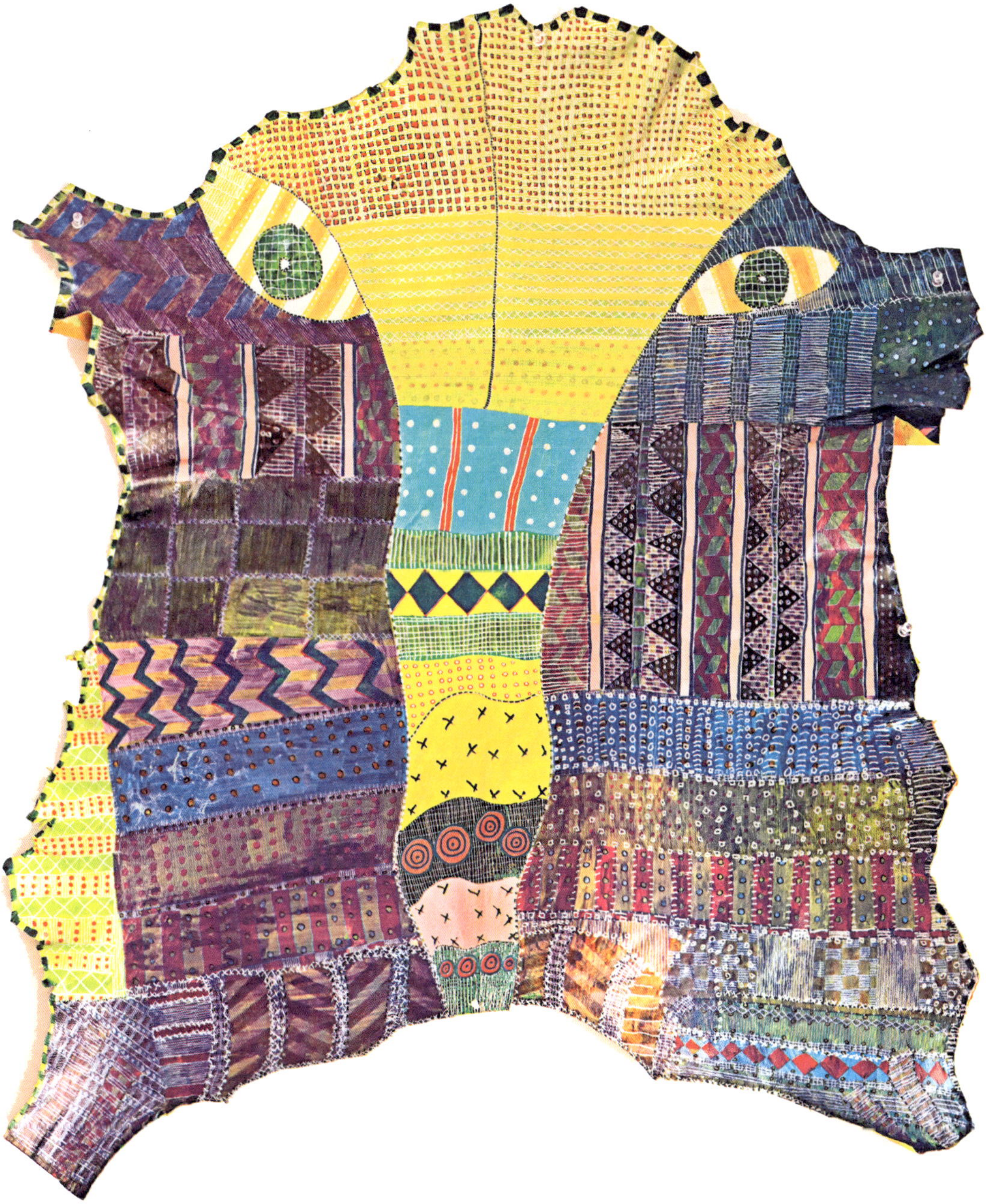

Faces and Places VII, 2010
Mixed media on sheep skin, 107 × 96 cm

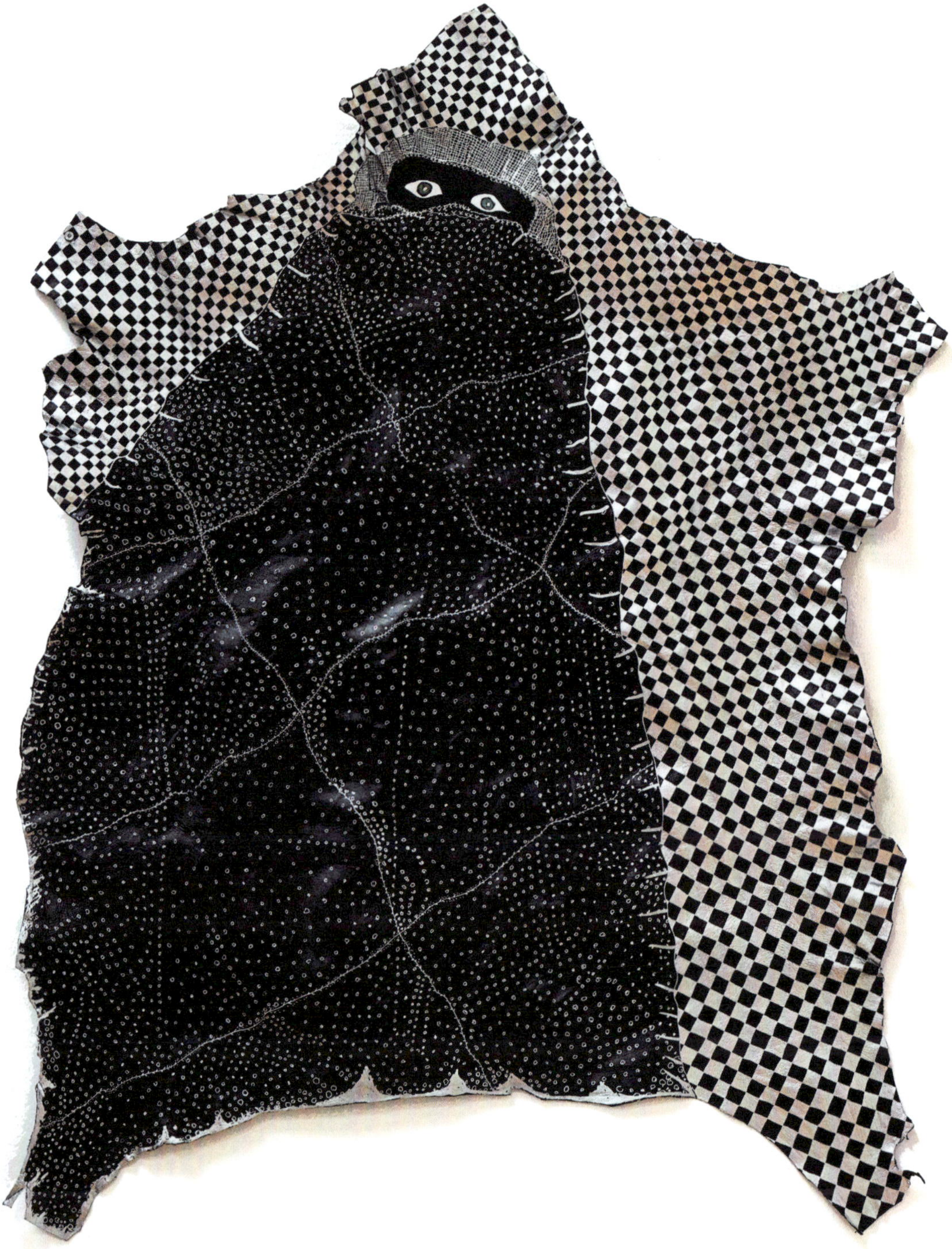

Faces and Places VI, 2010
Mixed media on sheep skin, 107 × 76 cm

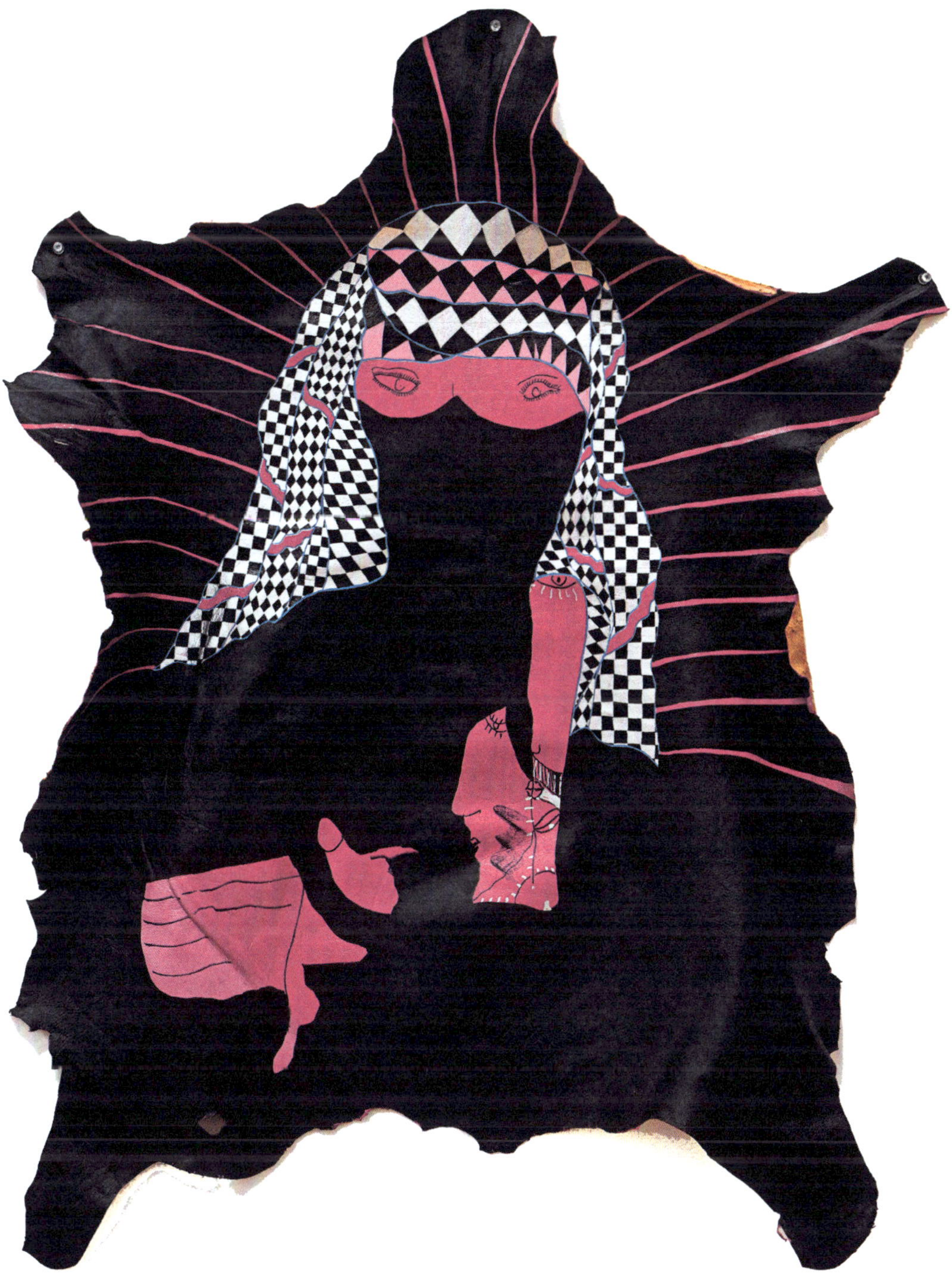

Faces and Places IV, 2010
Mixed media on sheep skin, 107 × 76 cm

Private collections, Los Angeles, California

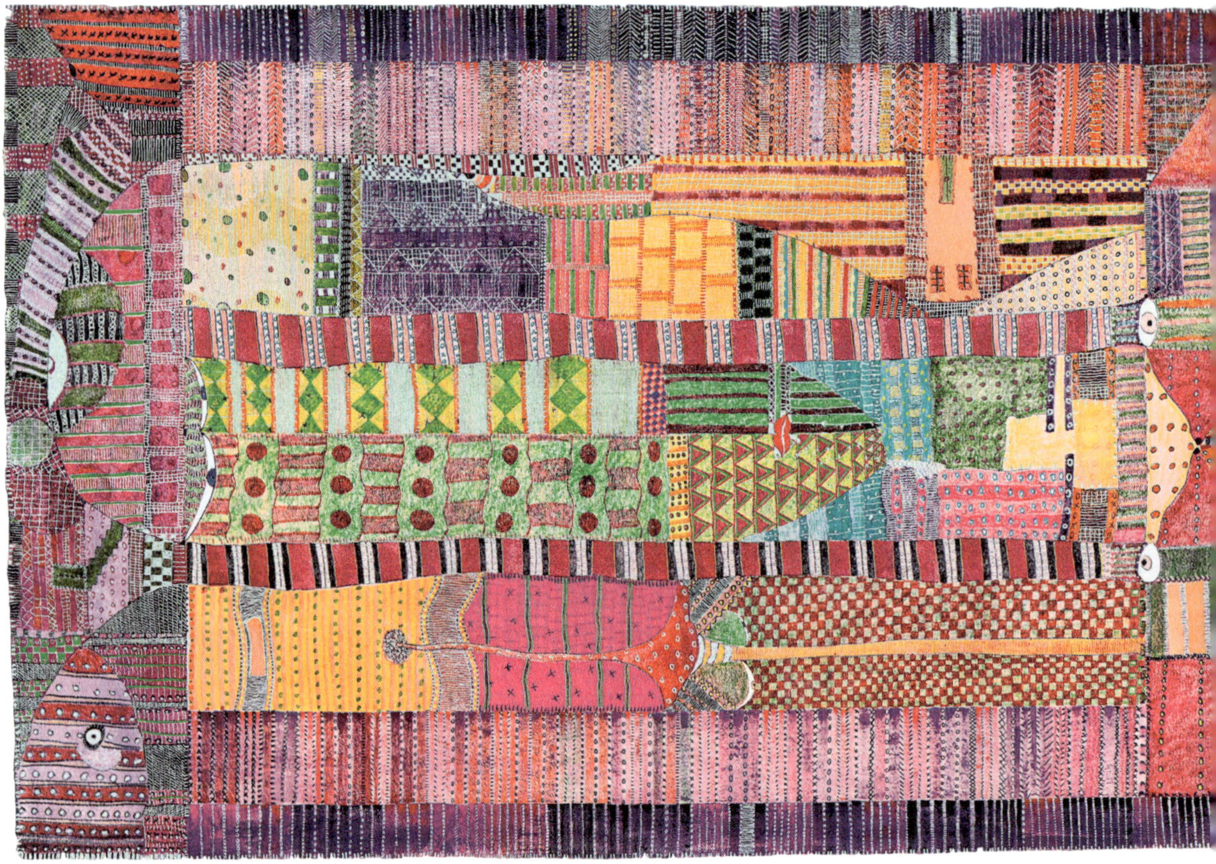

Faces and Places I, 2010
Mixed media on canvas, 91 × 288 cm

Private collection, Los Angeles, California

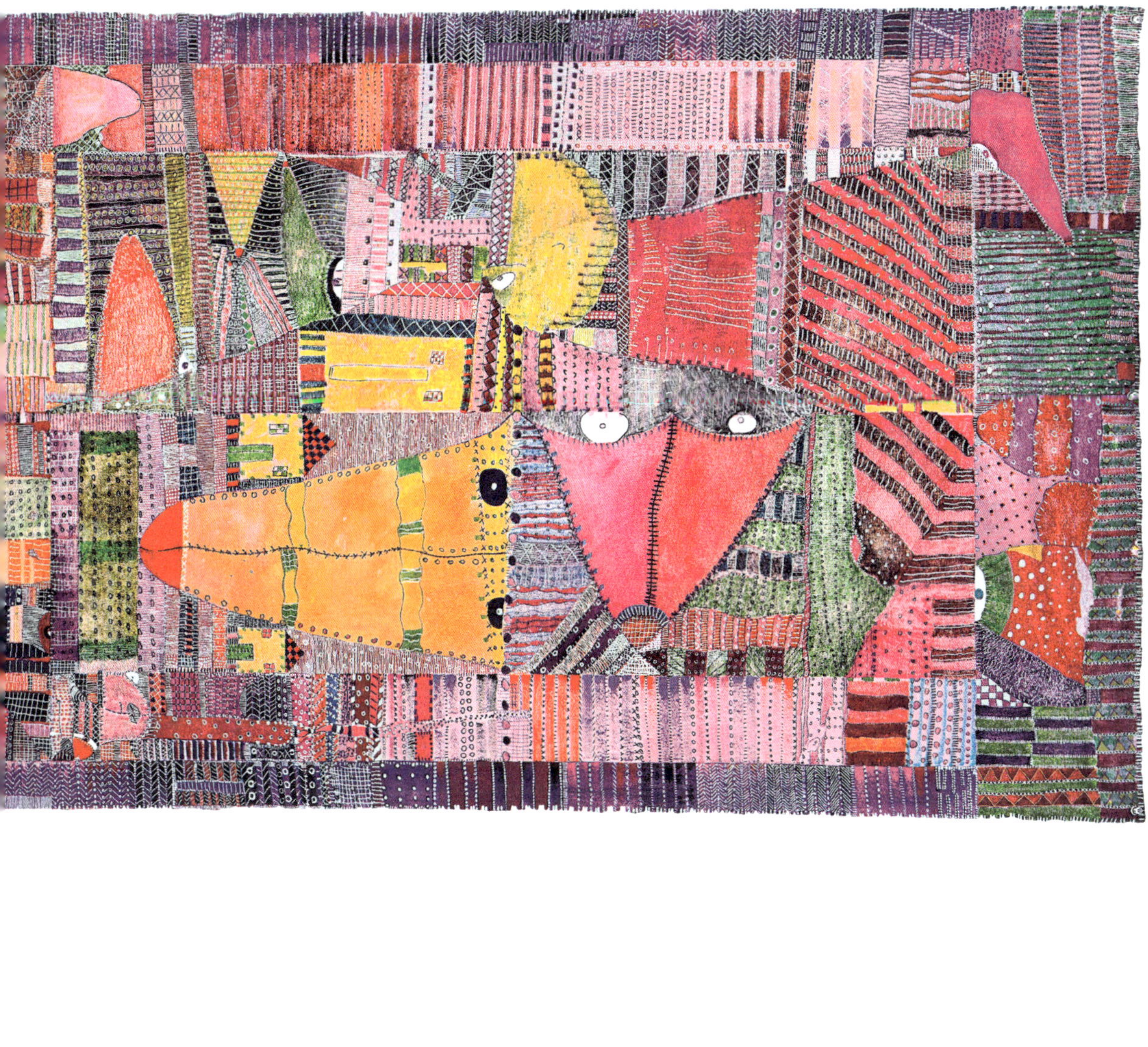

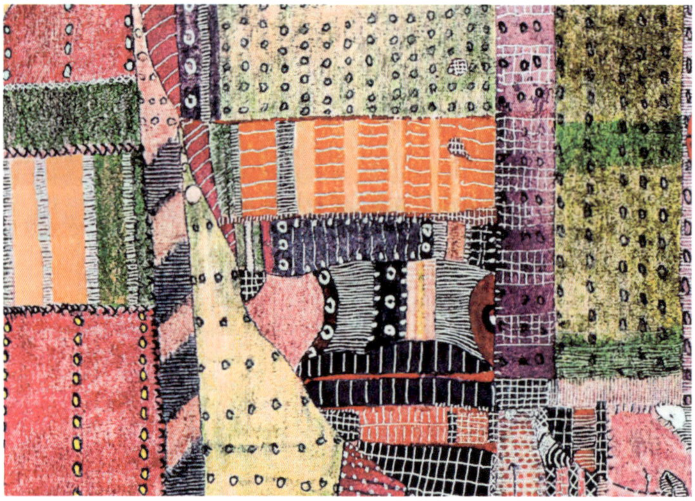

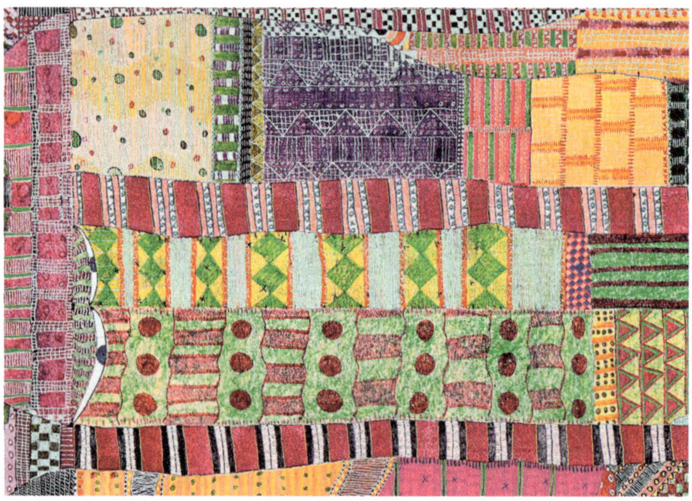

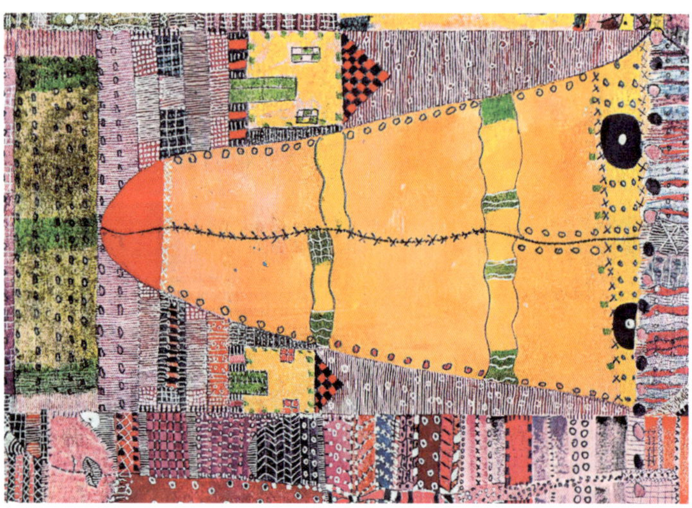

Faces and Places I (details), 2010
Mixed media on canvas, 91 × 288 cm

Private collection, Los Angeles, California

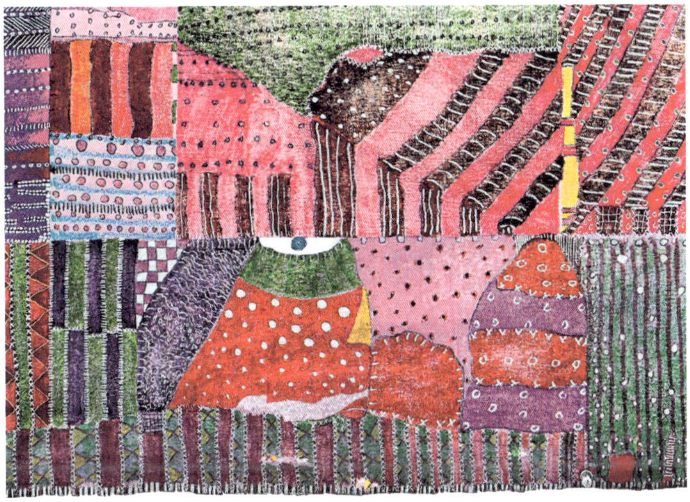

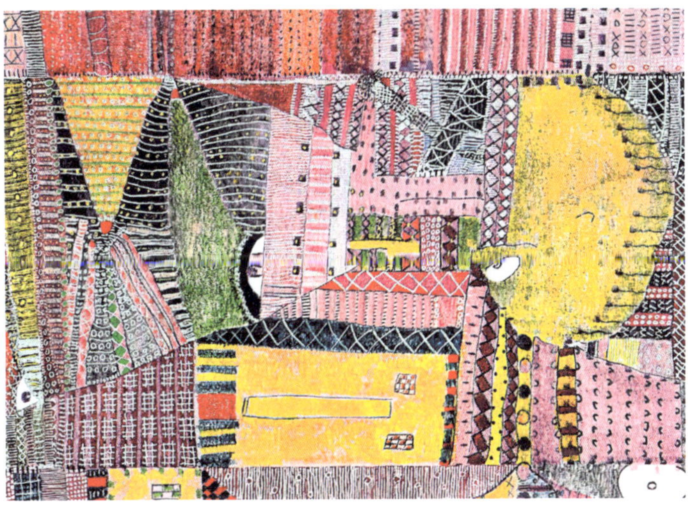

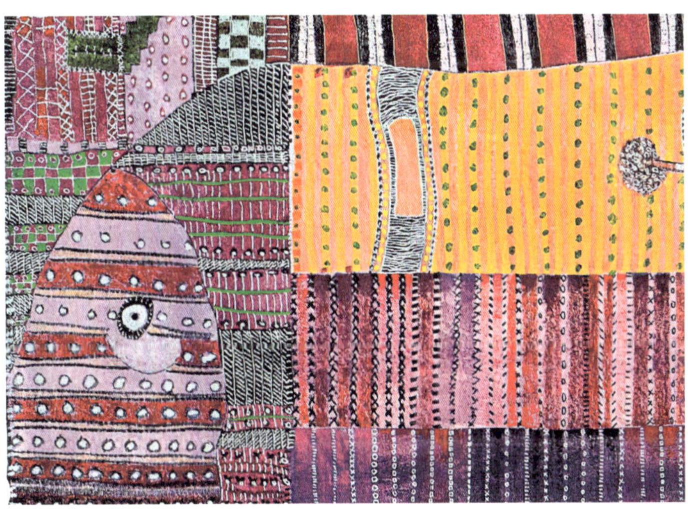

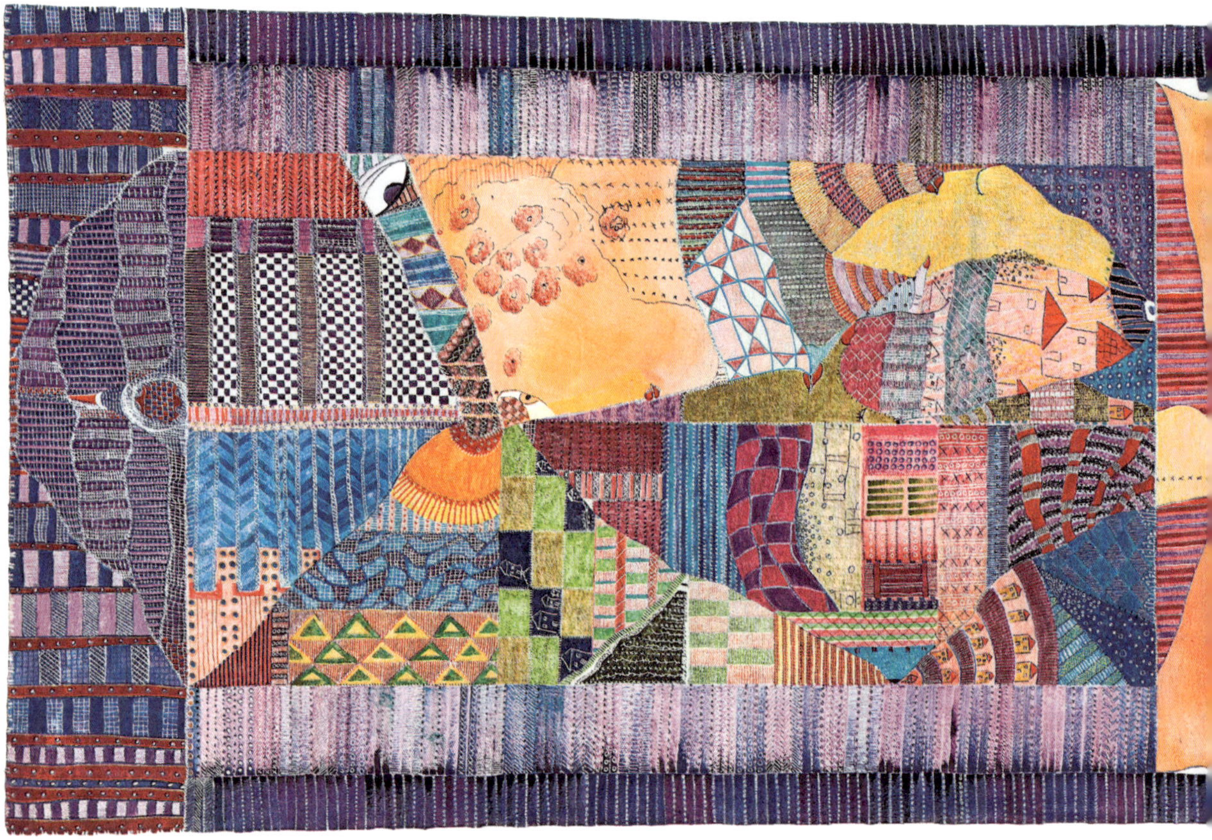

Faces and Places II, 2010
Mixed media on canvas, 91 × 288 cm

Private collection, Los Angeles, California

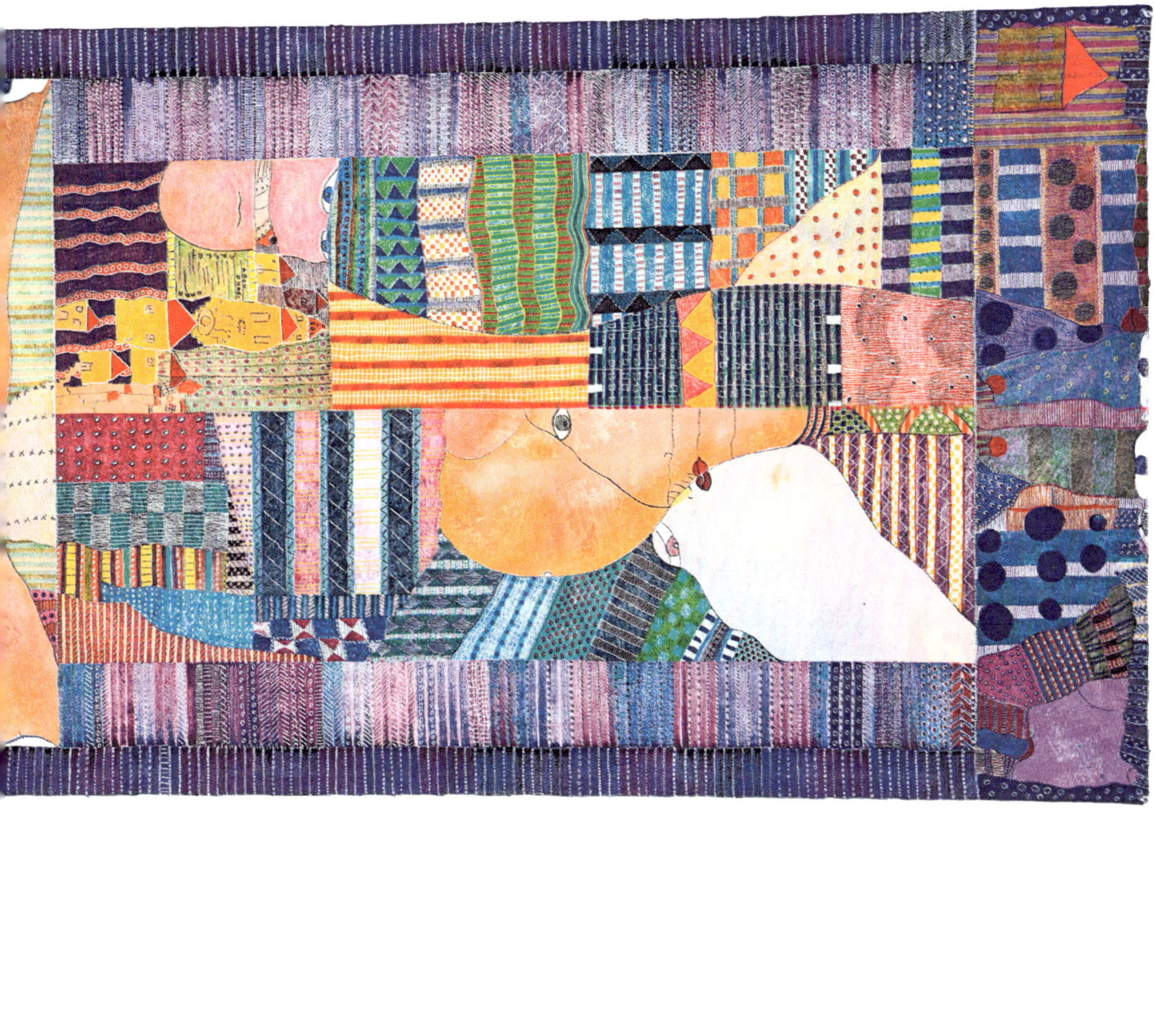

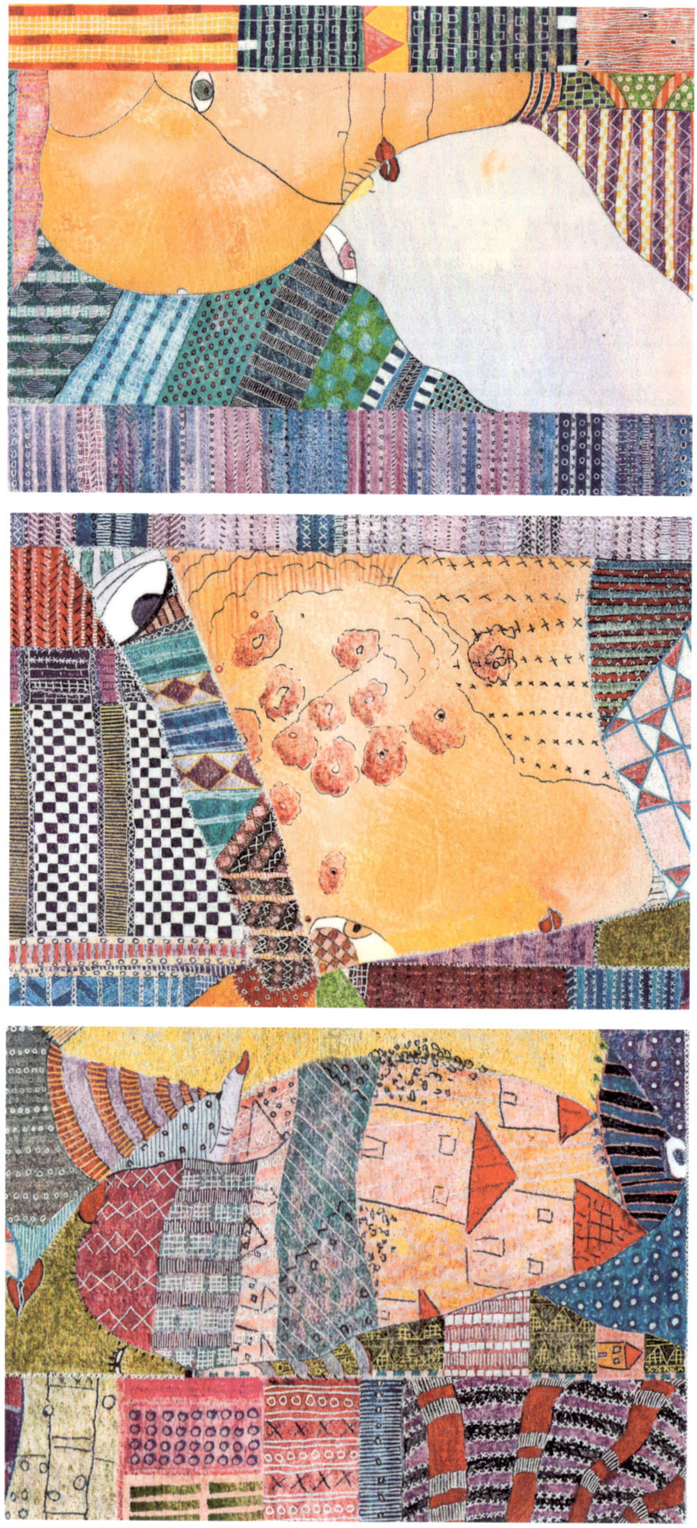

Faces and Places II (details), 2010
Mixed media on canvas, 91 × 288 cm

Private collection, Los Angeles, California

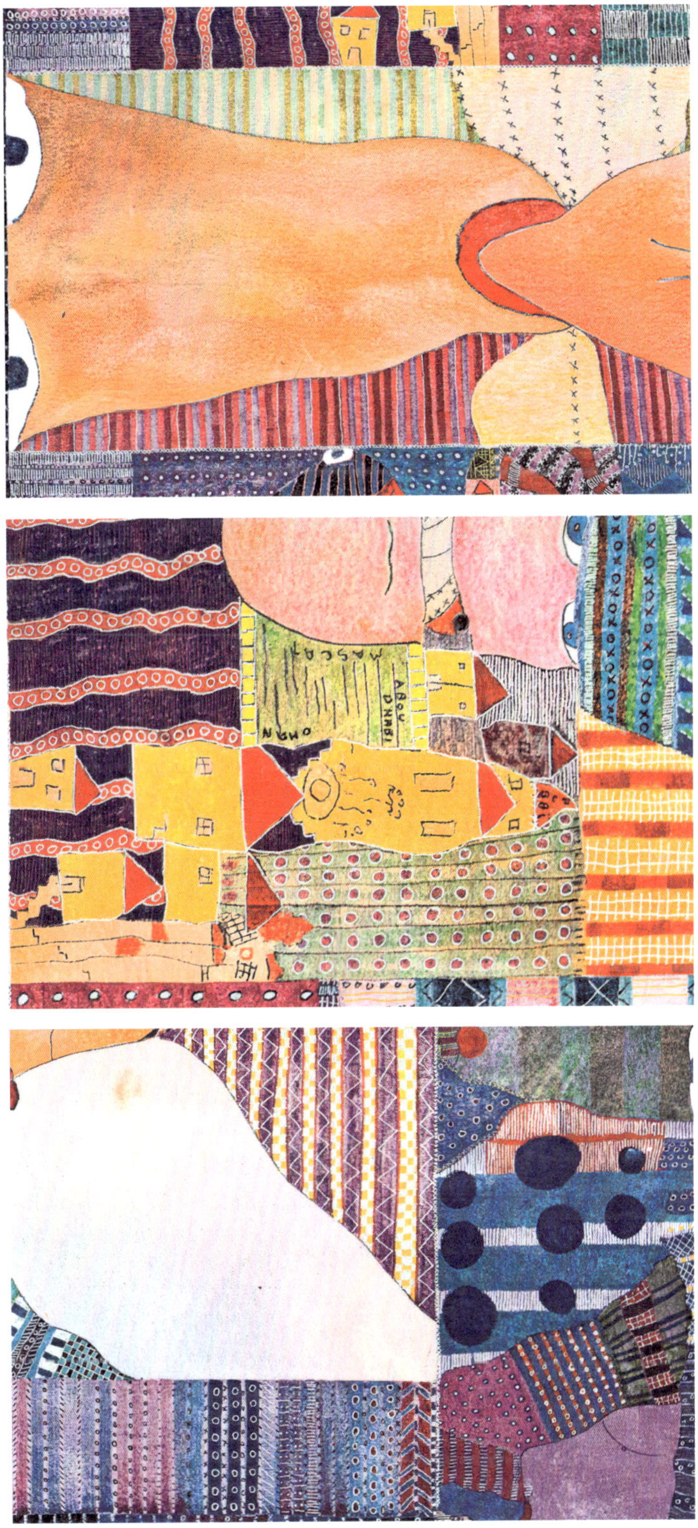

L'argent (Money Doesn't Bring Happiness, but It Sure Helps)

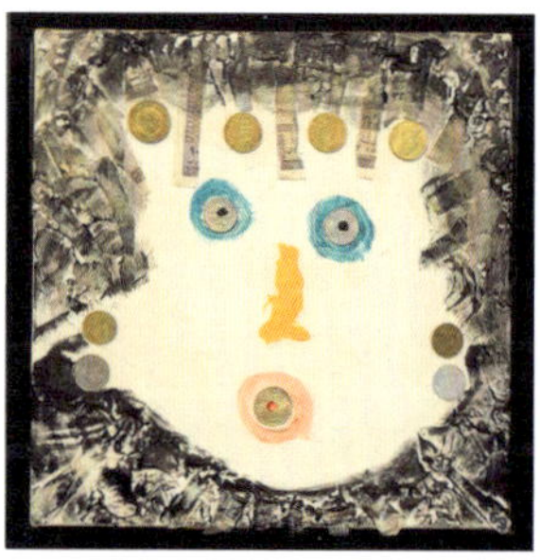
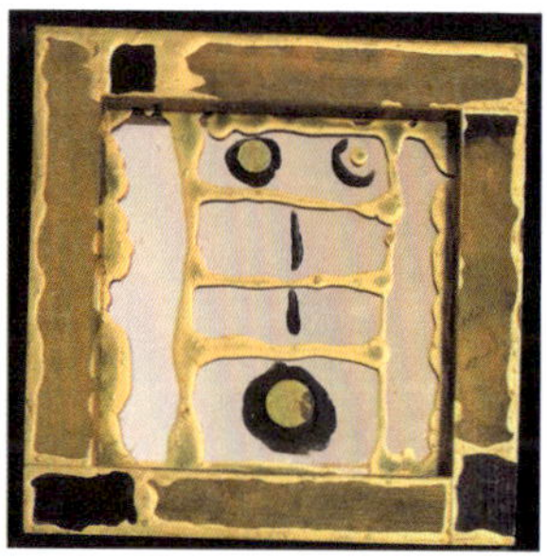
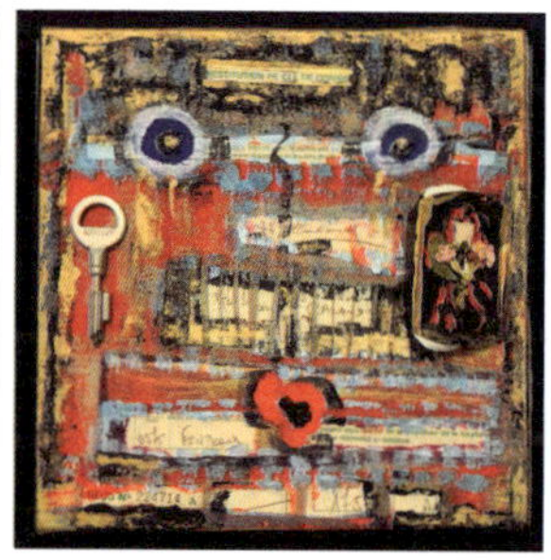
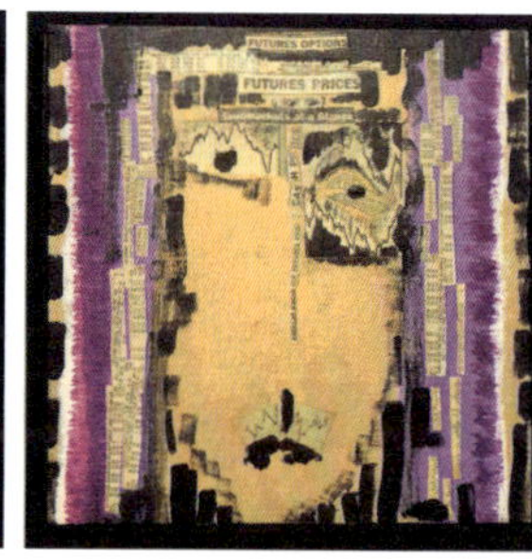
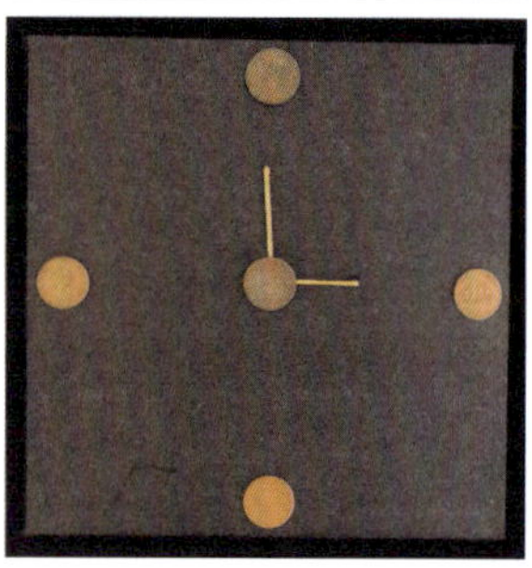
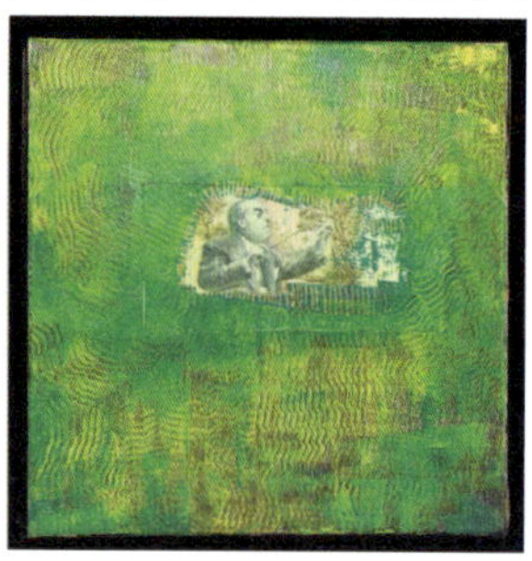
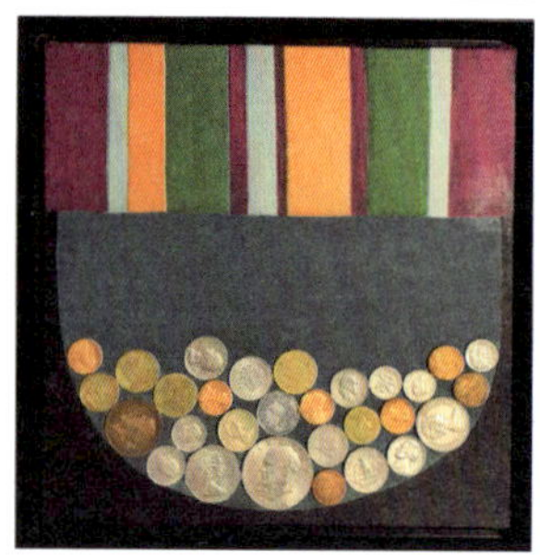
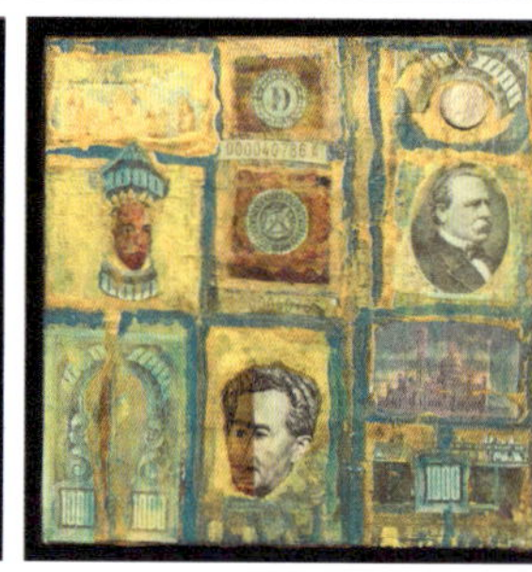

She Comes from Money
Fonds perdus quinquies
Un coffre-fort ne suit jamais un corbillard
Portrait sans intérêt
Time is Money
Paysage monétaire
Fonds monétaires
Old Money

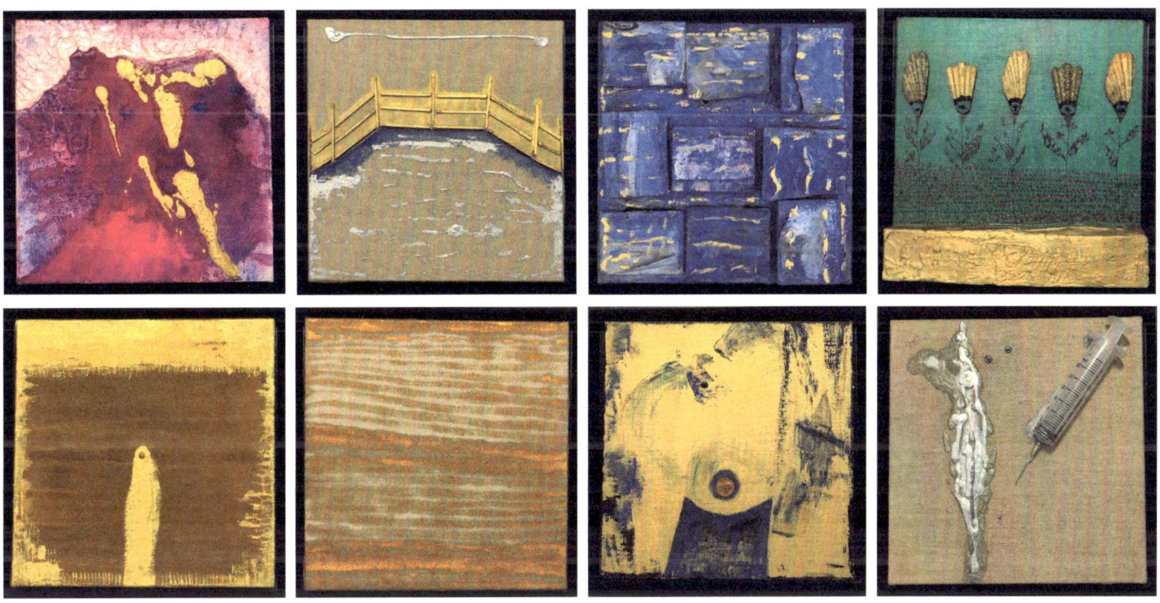

Le silence est d'or
Un pont en or
Fermeture de compte ter
Rouler sur l'or
Dorer la pilule
Pas le rond
A Penny for your Thoughts
Injection d'argent frais

Mixed media on canvas or on wood frame, 25 × 25 cm (1994-1995)

Private collections, Los Angeles, California

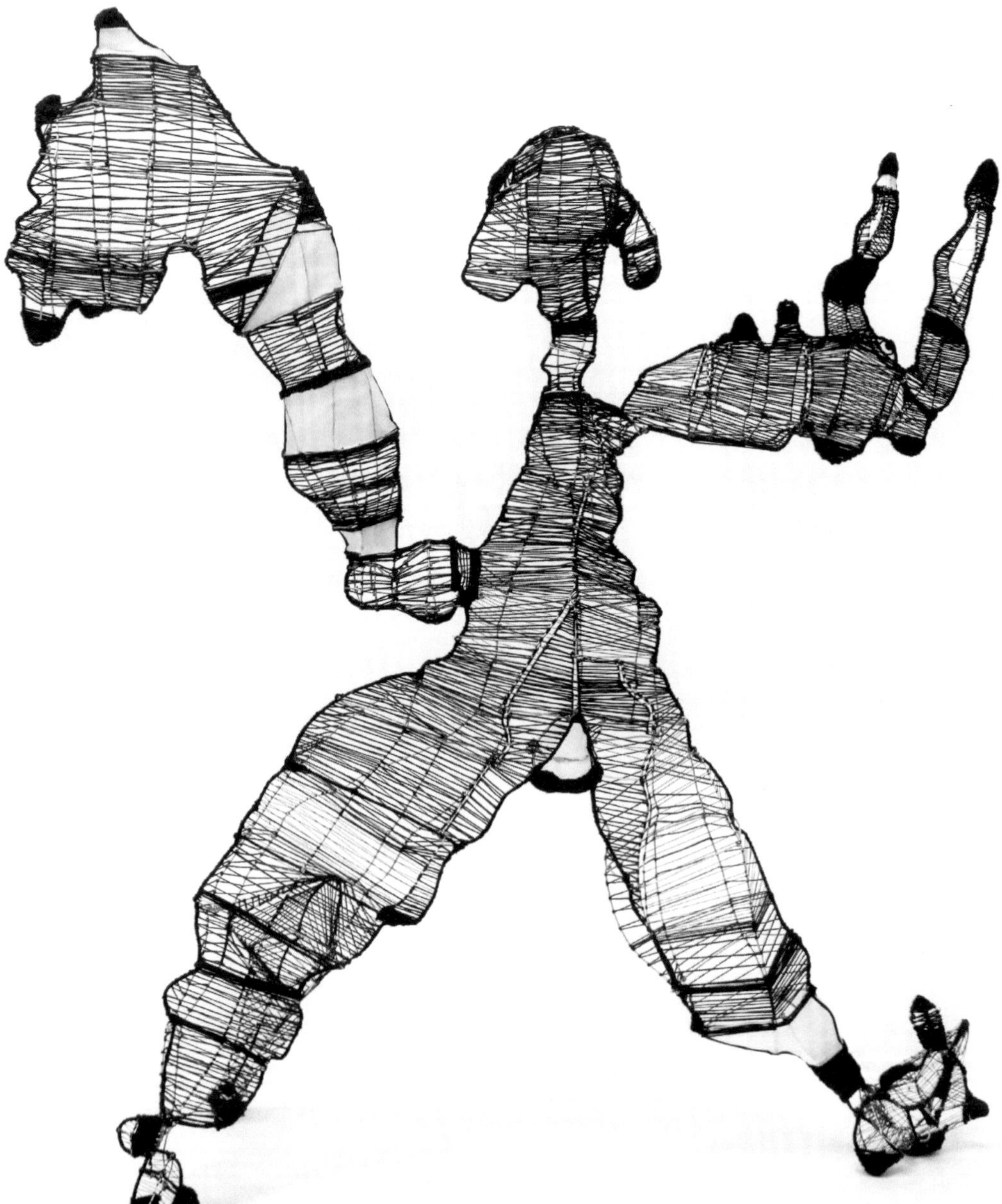

Rossinante #10, 2011
Wire, Japanese paper and embroidery thread, 94 × 86.4× 30.5 cm

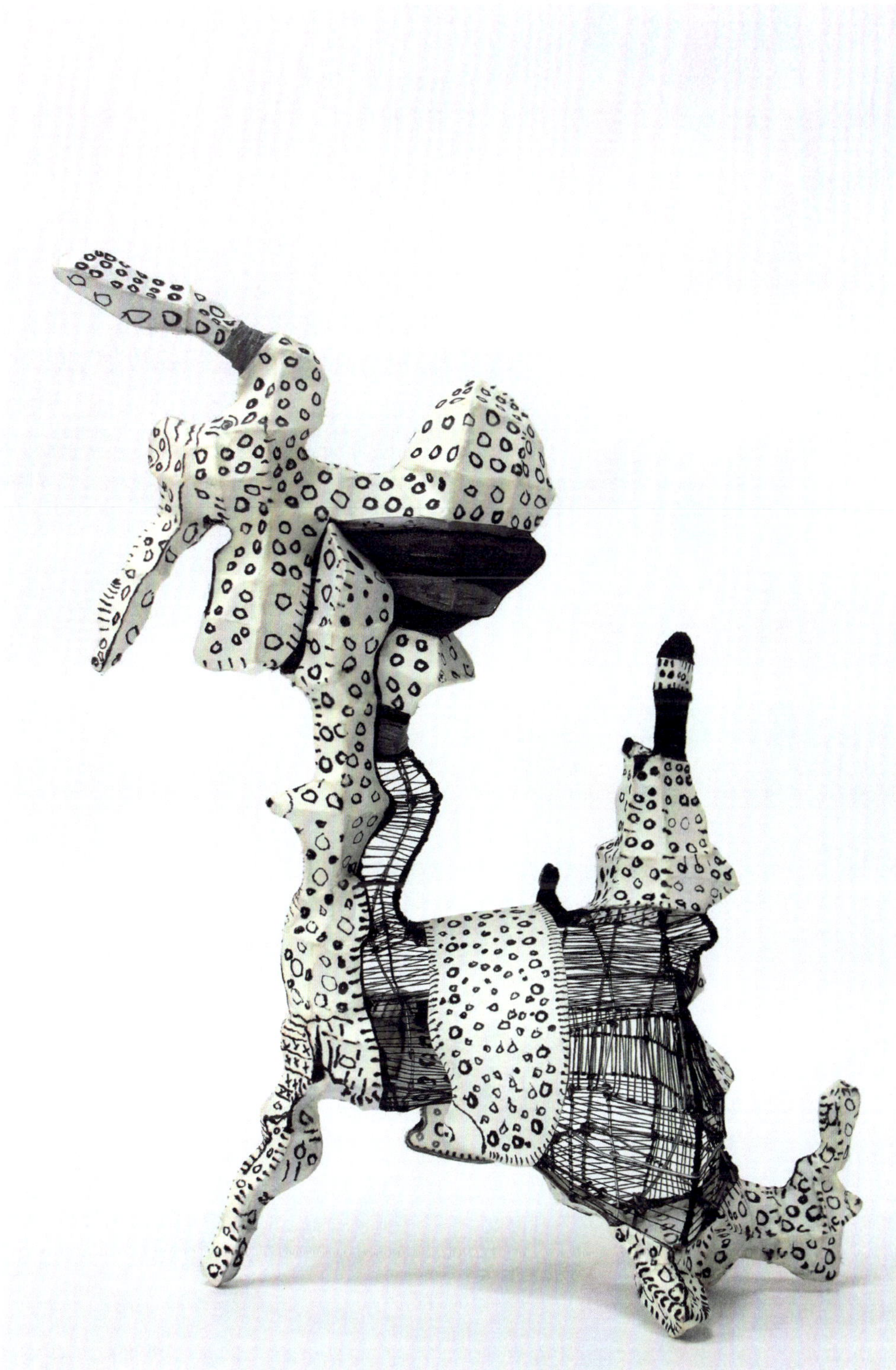

Rossinante #12 (Chihuahua), 2011
Wire, ink, Japanese paper, and embroidery thread, 40.6 × 38.1 × 22.9 cm

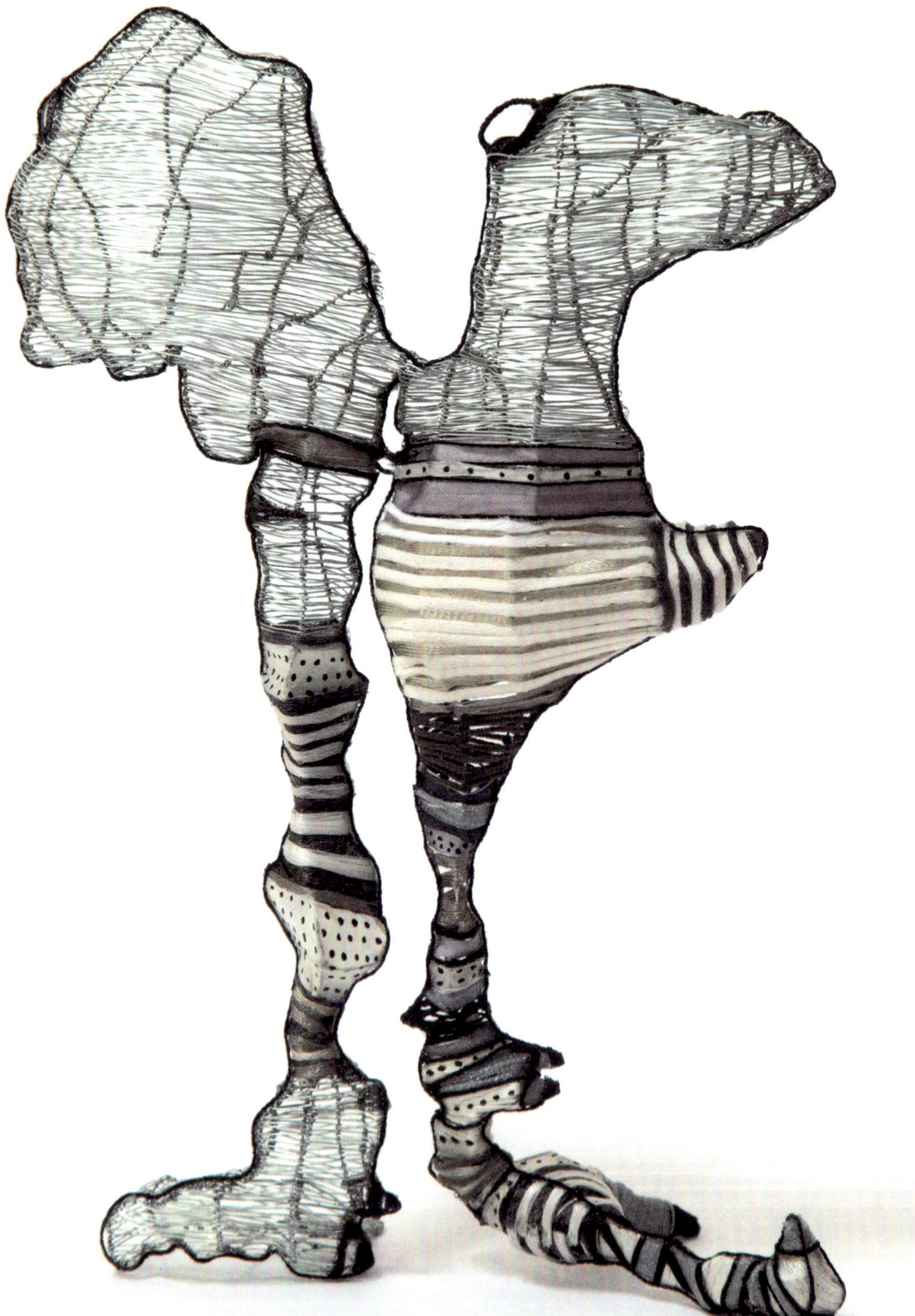

Rossinante #11, 2011
Wire, Japanese paper, ink, and embroidery thread, 30.5 × 22.8 × 7.6 cm

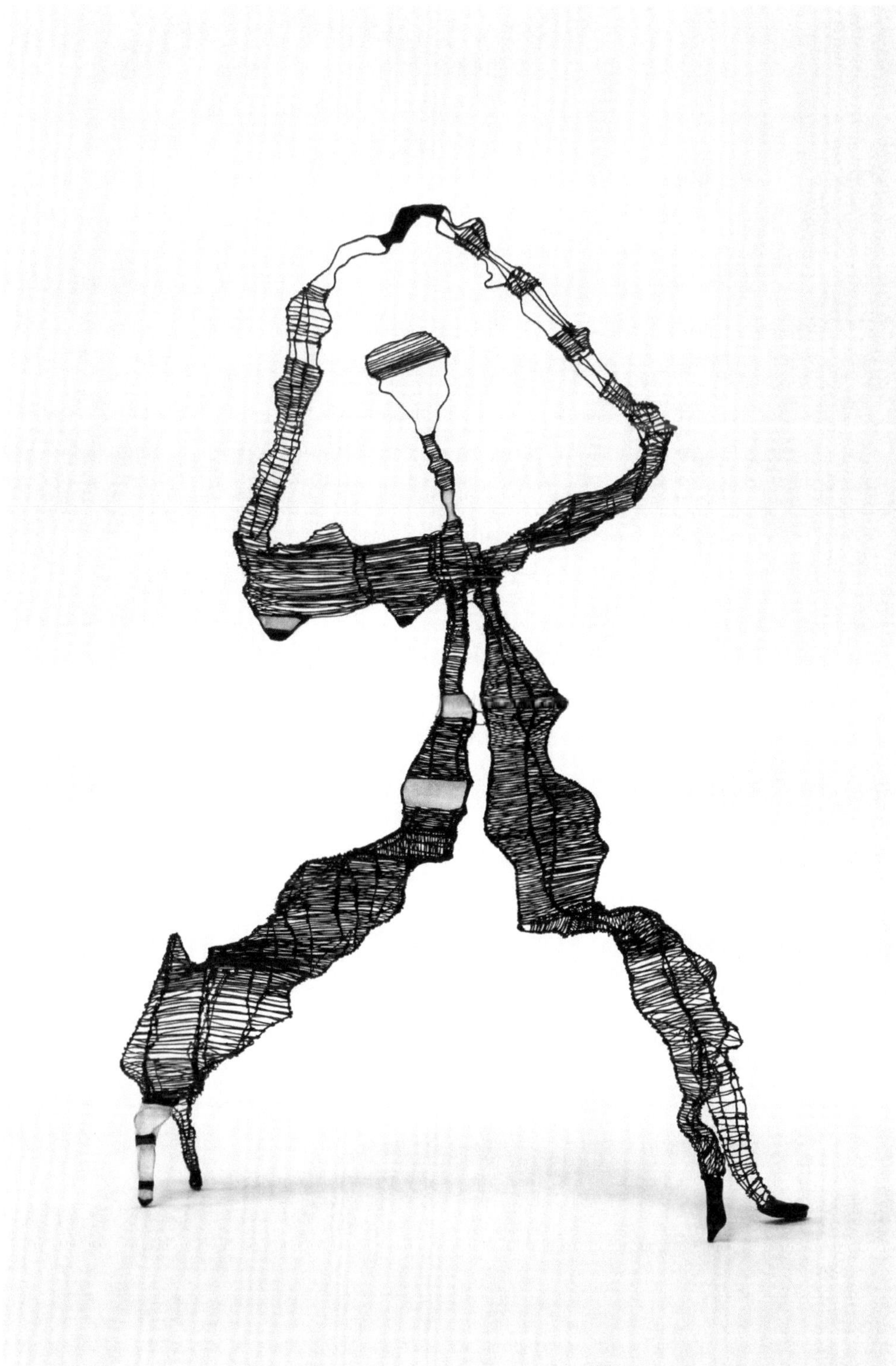

Rossinante #13, 2011
Wire, Japanese paper, ink, and embroidery thread, 25.4 × 40.6 × 7.6 cm

Private collection, Dallas, Texas

In 1968, amid a period of global cultural and political ferment, Caland—then 37 years old, married, and a mother of three—completed her studies at the American University of Beirut. That same year, she created an oil painting in the distinctive style of her early work. In it, Arabic letters intertwine with various symbols and references drawn from Middle Eastern culture and folklore. This relatively small piece,[17] signed on the back in Arabic, disappeared for over five decades before being accidentally rediscovered during research for the artist's catalogue raisonné (index of artworks). It was found in the home of a cousin who had purchased it at an exhibition held in Caland's Kaslik studio in 1970—likely drawn to its decorative quality, apparent legibility, and seemingly innocuous content.

On a prepared canvas, rounded forms—evoking the artist's own body—intertwine and overlap in places, lending the painting a subtle, almost imperceptible sense of depth. A black contour line stands out starkly against a white background, leaving visible voids that recede behind it. The surfaces, rendered in yellow, pastel pink, blue, mauve, green, and orange, evoke the garden at Kaslik, the family estate where the artist had her first studio. At the center, leaning against what might be a supple tarbouch, a warm brown oval—resembling sun-gilded skin—emerges as a kind of egg: a matrix of life and creation, a "space of the id and the formless, of asexual form with multiple possibilities." Within it appears the Arabic letter "ا" (alif), the first letter of the alphabet and of the singular personal pronouns in Arabic ("I," "you"). Below it, fifteen nearly straight black pegs are laid out in four lines, like an assertion. The composition seems to radiate from this central shape, expanding outward, rising and extending to the left and right. Beneath it, on a blue surface, a multitude of maddah signs—marks used above the alif to prolong its sound—evoke the undulating movement of a restrained yet restless sea. To the right, against a grassy green background shaped like firm, open legs, megalithic pillars joined at the top appears the letter "ش" (shīn), followed by a dash: a reference to a word deliberately left unsaid? It is, after all, the first letter of the Arabic word for "prostitute." Discontent in her married life, is Huguette Caland dreaming of other adventures... torn between the identities of "mother" and "prostitute"?

Other letters are present too: the "و" (waw), a binding letter (waw al-wasl)—perhaps an attempt to unify the many parts of the self? To reconcile Eastern and Western cultures? Or the multiplicity of lives she inhabited: wife, lover (to her husband's best friend), student, mother, engaged artist. There is also the "ن" (nūn), the first letter of the Arabic word for "we," and the "ي" (yā'), which, when added to the end of a word, denotes possession ("my"). But here, the letter is inverted—could this signal a refusal to belong, either to a place or a person? A resistance to claiming anything as her own? Triangles placed tip to tail suggest both the point

17 The work measures 49.5 × 64.3 cm.

of the kalam—the reed pen used for writing cuneiform in clay—and the pubic triangle. In the bottom left corner, against a yellow background, two lines of question marks. Might the painting itself contain the answer to this unspoken question?

Elsewhere, scattered across colored surfaces, symbols and motifs emerge: dots, wavy lines, and parallel lines forming new geometric shapes. To the left, lips appear against a purple background—suggestive of the female sex—and farther left, on a reddish-brown surface truncated by the canvas's edge, phallic symbols—at once referencing the male sex and cuneiform script. A pinkish phallic shape penetrates the top left of the canvas, while other forms spill out from the frame, vanishing from sight. Near the upper edge, on a blue shape resembling an animal, appear eyes with long, made-up lashes—talismans warding off the evil eye. In this work, the use of symbols, motifs, and letters functions like a visual riddle—a game with the viewer. It hints at the emergence of language in human societies and signals the beginning of an artistic journey in which writing would become a central element. The presence of Arabic script roots the painting in a Middle Eastern context, while the subtle inclusion of sexual symbols suggests a growing sense of personal autonomy and a nuanced assertion of identity. The canvas features isolated Arabic letters without clear connection, question marks, hyphenated forms, and a blend of primitive, sexual, and folkloric imagery. These elements reveal Caland—just embarking on her career—playfully and intuitively exploring a path of her own within the diverse worlds she was inhabiting. By adopting her husband's French surname while signing the painting in Arabic, she deliberately blurs cultural and linguistic boundaries. Through the incorporation of Arabic script into her visual language, she distances herself from the conventions of the French-speaking bourgeois milieu in which she was raised and from her French-born husband.

Sketchbook #2 (extracts pages 1, 2, 4, 7, 8, 9, 10, 19, 20, 26, 27, 29), 1990-1991
Ink and watercolor on paper, 27.9 × 35.5 cm

Private collection, Los Angeles, California

Venice, California - 11/19/1990.

I need to begin this book. Just because it is so scary
Scary to do any kind of inscription on a white page.
a beautifull white page of a precious book.
a white page is sometimes comparable to a certain quality of silence.
This silence that is so intense, that breathing becomes important.
Breathing in English on the silence of a white page, when English is not mine
Gives such big emotions, that my heart is beating so strong....
Will I ever be able to use words as well as in french?
Will I adjust to America as well as I did to France?
My wish is to make Venice my homeland, and my home in Venice.

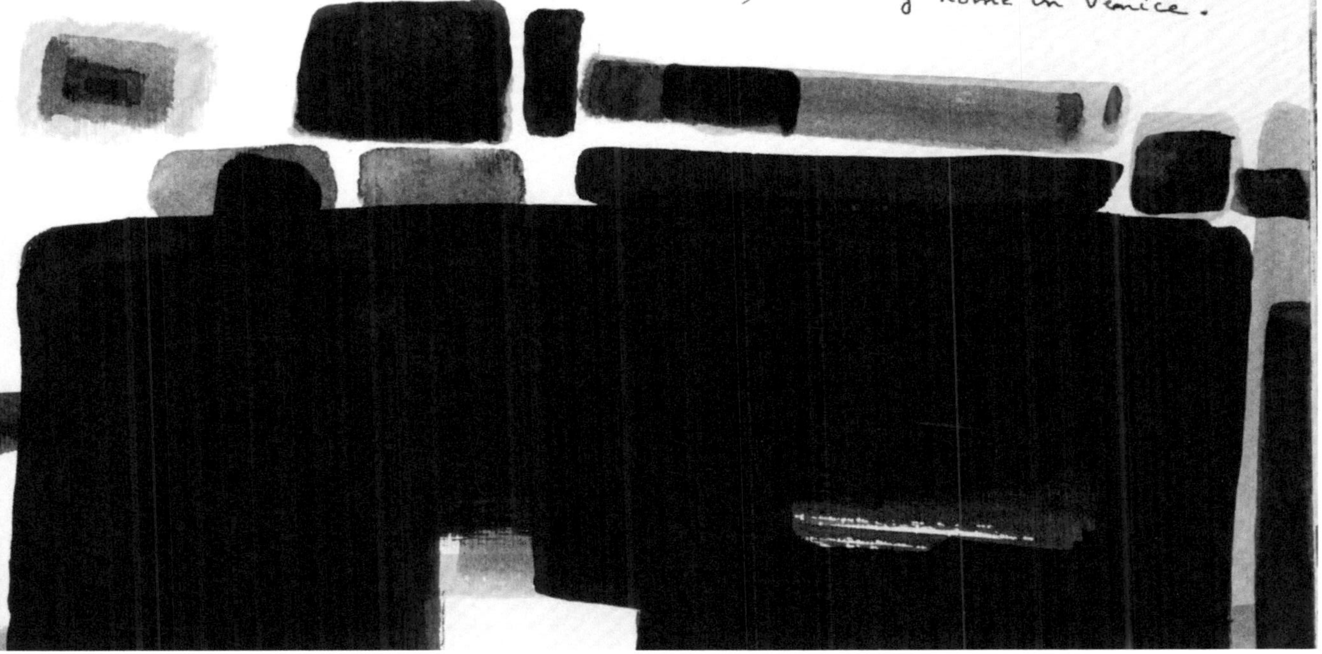

"If the first step to my adjstment to California is having a car, now I have it. Marc was the first passenger I took.

The car is an eleven year old Honda. I am quite happy to have it without having to make this important decision ~~myself~~ ... I still was in Paris when Pierre bought it for me. Thanks Pierre .... and thanks Suzanne who knew about the car. I was afraid to have more problems out of it than help ... Today after registration, I felt good about my new and nevertheless limited independance. I don't know if I could drive to the desert or to San Francisco - but defintely in the neighbourhood it's nice to drive .... and to be able to go to Standard Brands or to Lincoln Fabrics without wainting for Leila (precious Leila ...) to drive me around during the week-ends ....

The opening of Jimmy Heyward at the Ace gallery was the best I saw in a long time. I came back to my work with big energy - that only happens when you see good work ... And the space is one of the most interesting I ever saw. At the same time impressively big, with full-of-surprise corners and cosy little rooms. The only fact of imagining ones own work in such an environment must be so stimulating to the artist ... Thank You Mr. Xmas and Jimmy Heyward for providing us with such pleasure. Thanks for the colours & for the hanging ...

Moses was there, so were many others ....

Comments could come much later.

Actually silence is best.

Venice 11 | 29 | 90

Venice 12 / 6 / 90

This is the translation of a passage of a letter I once wrote.
I just shall do a partial translation, it was a hot letter.

" The desire of writing you unusual things, at the least unusual for me, is there
since a long time .... [redacted] I
sometimes I wake up with your hands all over me, I recognize them. They
also seem to be on a familiar ground, finding their way in the
landscape, climbing, escalating, slipping, penetrating, slowing down,
beginning again from scratch, then stopping immobile... .... and who knows, left then,
to their creativity and to your imagination .... " etc...

I needed to exercise my english in a field totally new to me.
But the reason I did it, is that it is so easy at a distance to feed a fire -
Another question is : to how many persons since then, could I have wrote this
letter. and what would a man do if he received today this letter from
me & out of the blues ?.....
I really don't think I am interested in trying.
But I cannot help thinking of Richard & Annie - and about the responsability
she (Annie) carries in this hole story, a hawaïan story .... "Love Annie"
I personally feel ethics in such cases, impose the responsability of facing the
other, at least in a public place and having the courage of reviewing the
image .... May be laughing at the whole story would then have been possible -
and that would result in killing the myth ....
But very few people can live without myths.

We have to get to terms as soon as possible, with our own life & death -
With a very strong taste for life & at the same time a total acceptance of death.
The taste for life helps postponing death -
And the omnipresence of death in each cell of our bodies gives our lives intensity.

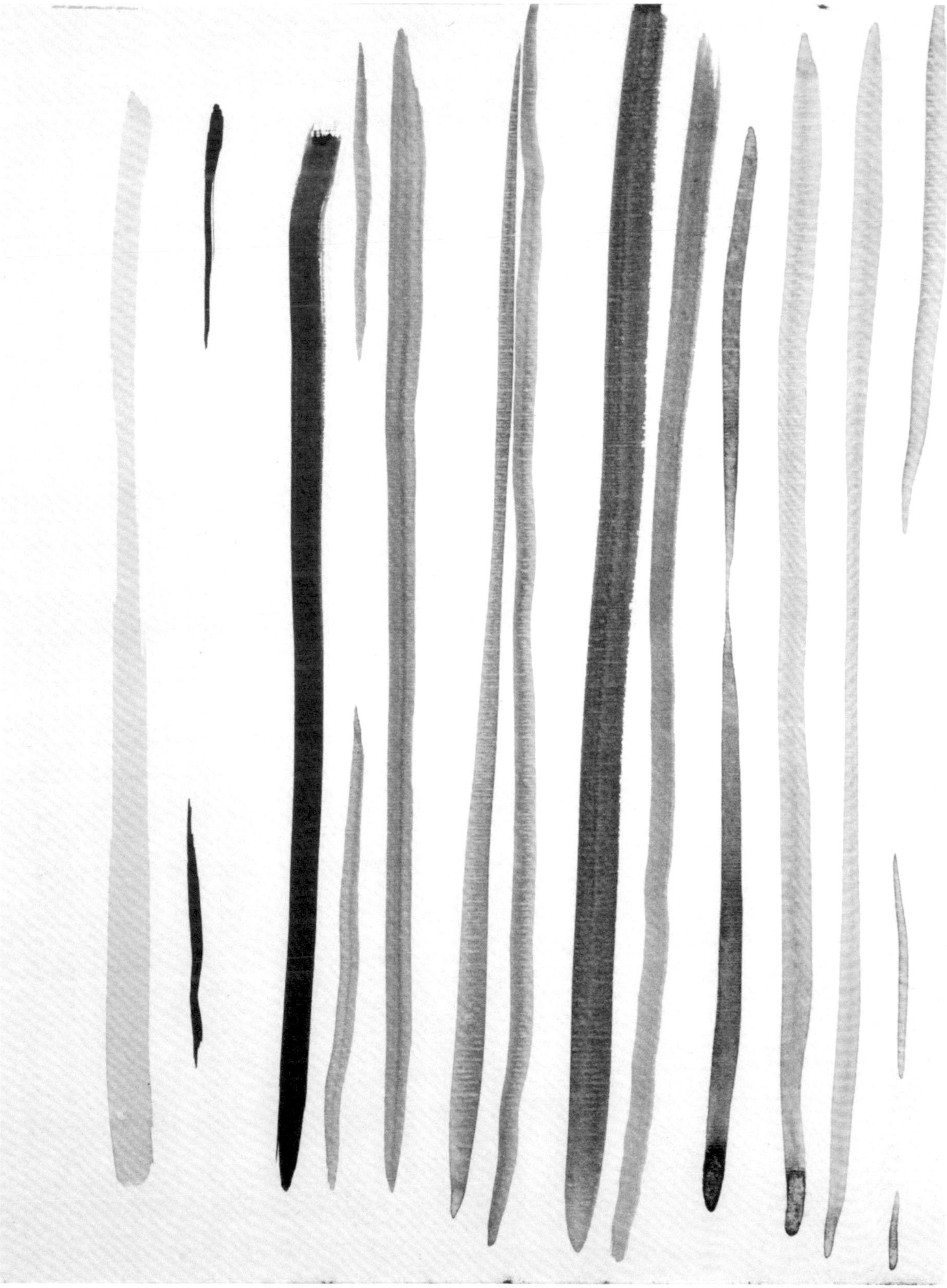

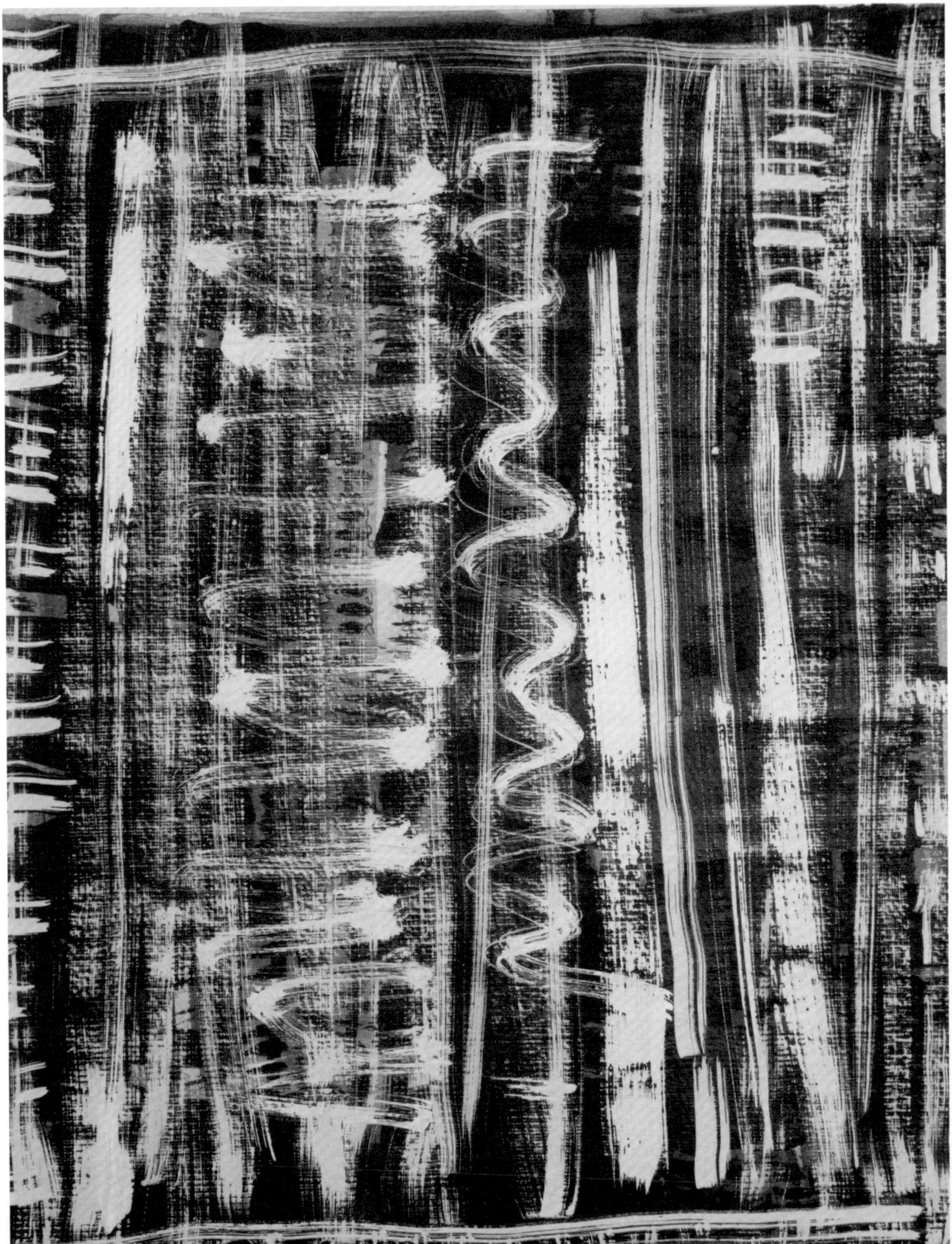

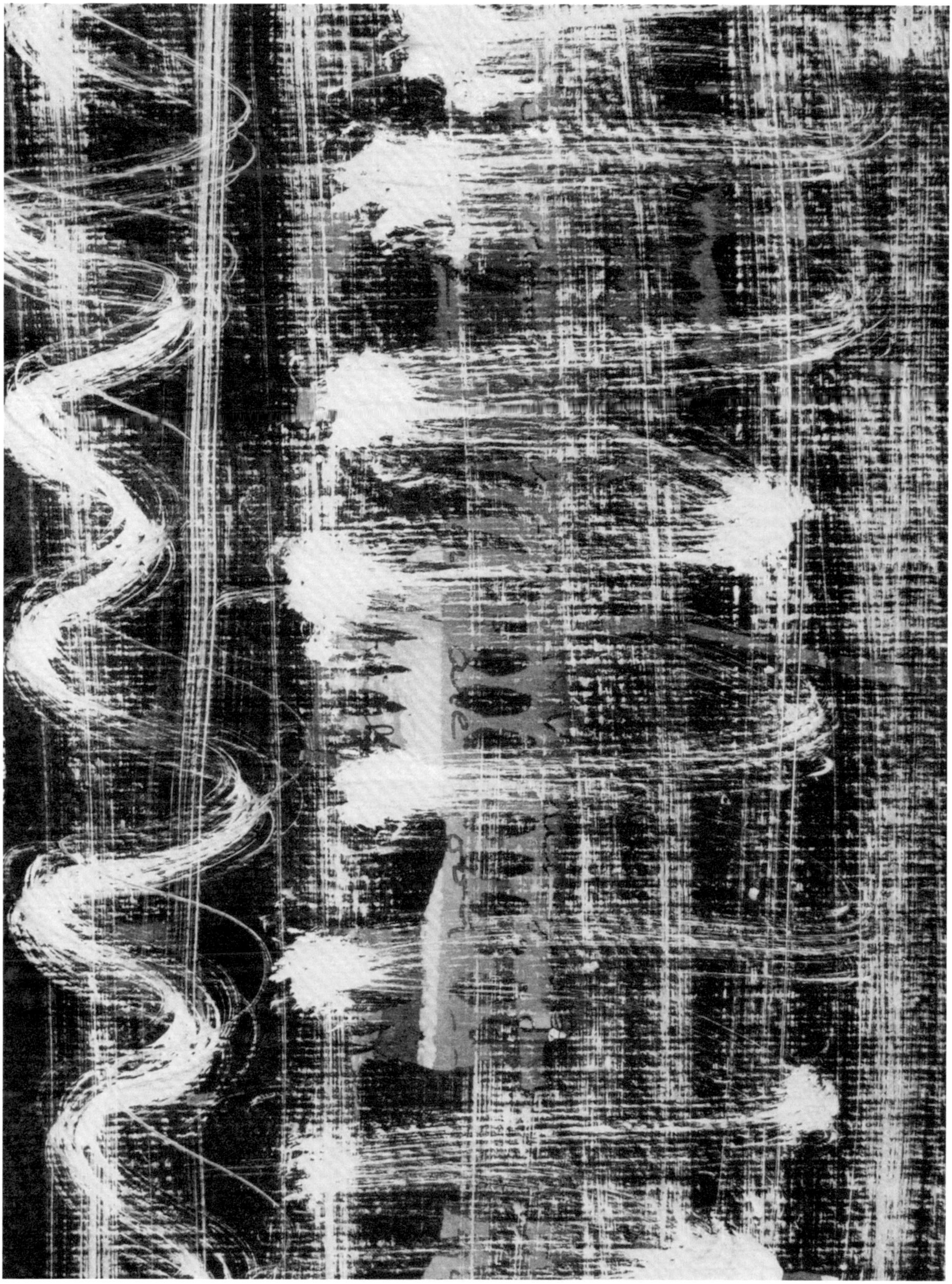

Venice 12/16/90

I heard myself saying 2 days ago: "If God exists he surely has no religion"....

I like this statement.

1/12/91

1/14/91

Rabiza came yesterday after noon for the 1st time - I like her. She is Seta's friend. Seta made the connection. that was nice.

We spoke a lot, also about minimalism and emotions.....

Do controlled emotions lead to minimalism? That is the question that was brought up to my mind about my own work in ~~#~~ relation to my emotions.

Once Moses told me to loose control. I cannot.
I cannot loose emotions. I hope I will not loose my control ~~in~~ in expressing them.
It would simply drive me where I do not want to be.
I feel a necessity to control ~~...~~ the expression of my emotions. That stops me of controlling others and keeps me in a certain kind of sanity....

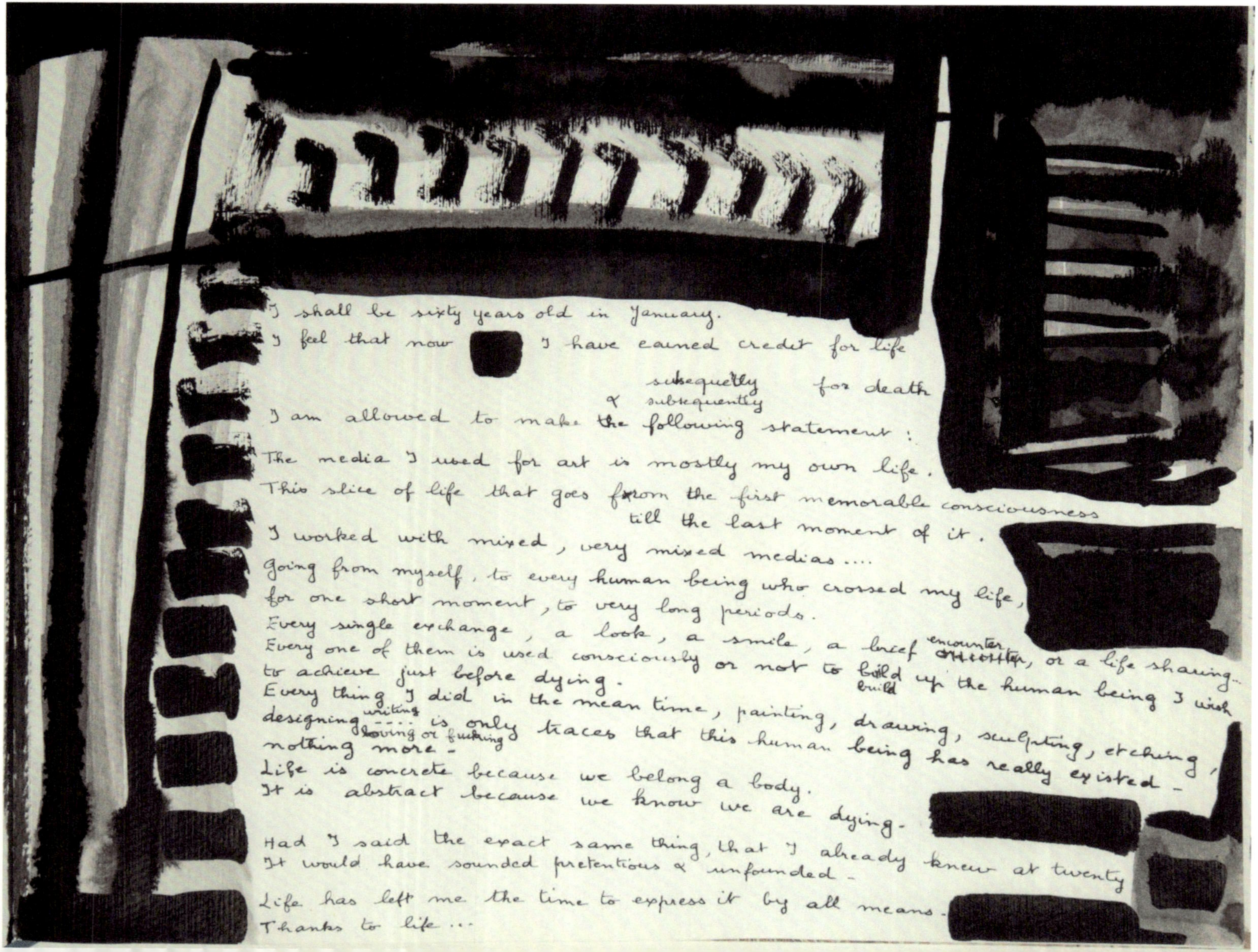
I shall be sixty years old in January.
I feel that now I have earned credit for life
& subsequetly subsequently for death
I am allowed to make the following statement:
The media I used for art is mostly my own life.
This slice of life that goes from the first memorable consciousness till the last moment of it.
I worked with mixed, very mixed medias....
Going from myself, to every human being who crossed my life,
for one short moment, to very long periods.
Every single exchange, a look, a smile, a brief encounter, or a life sharing...
Every one of them is used consciously or not to build up the human being I wish
to achieve just before dying.
Every thing I did in the mean time, painting, drawing, sculpting, etching,
designing, writing.... loving or fucking is only traces that this human being has really existed -
nothing more -
Life is concrete because we belong a body.
It is abstract because we know we are dying -
Had I said the exact same thing, that I already knew at twenty
It would have sounded pretentious & unfounded -
Life has left me the time to express it by all means -
Thanks to life ...

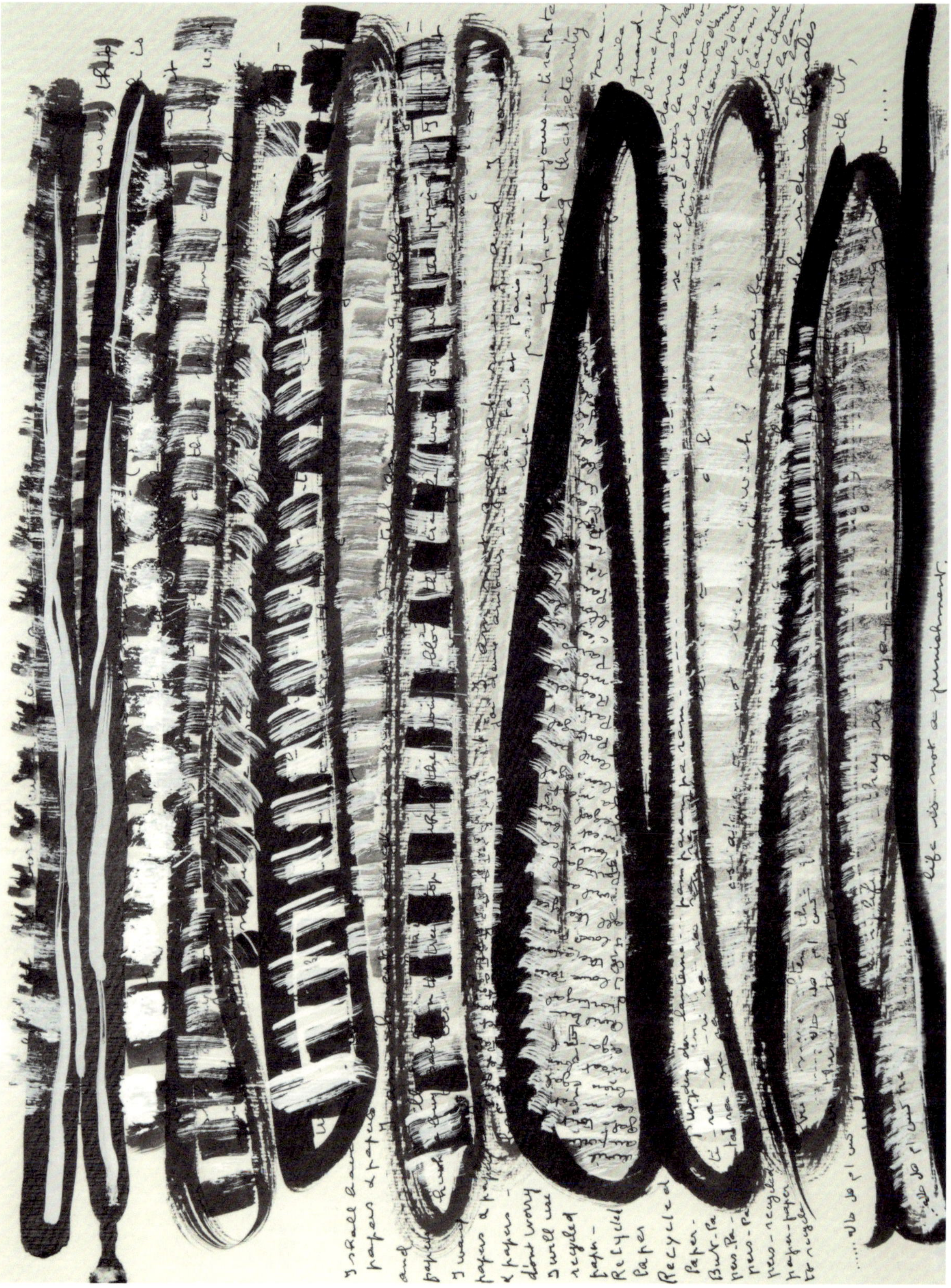

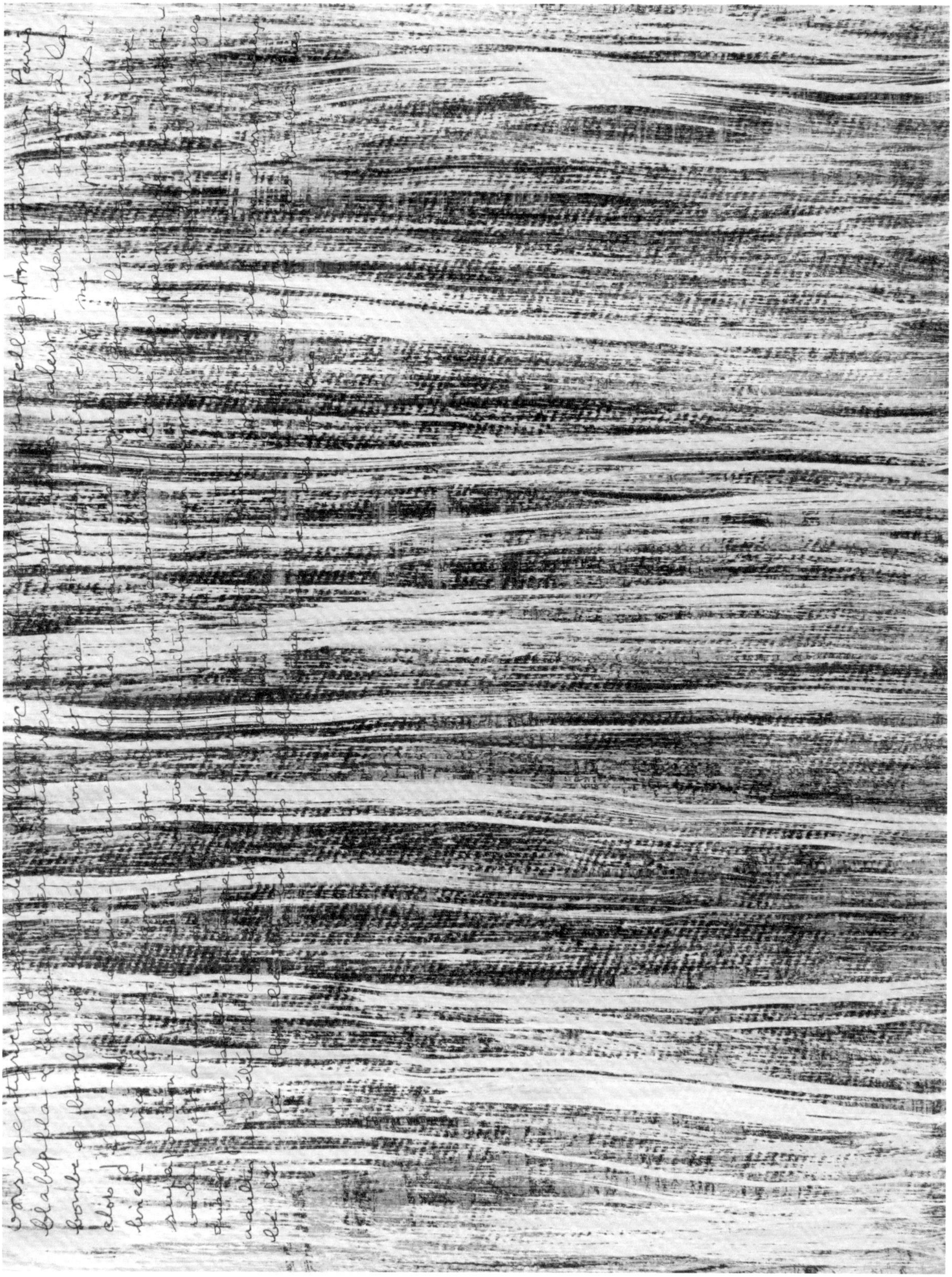

Happy week-end - sold work - went to many openings - met a lot of people - discovered a lot about "so called "friends".....

going to Paris soon - Brigitte is carrying her first child, my first grand.son -

I will leave L.A as I am beginning to enjoy it most.

Leaving it happily - I will be working in Paris on my first exhibition in California - hopefully when I will come back, in a few months -

I feel I belong here now - and that my home is really Venice.

I love Paris - it will feel good to visit there for the first time since I have no where of my own for the first time since 1970......

Callas is singing - I love Callas - I love life -

Venice.

4 / 30 / 91

Yesterday Paul & I were married 39 years -

Today I am sad and fed up.
May be I am tired of having no money.
Sure money helps - I would buy lots of paper - & canvasses & could use them without concern of waist. I miss large beautifull white Belgium linen - I would just go ahead without being scared .... even a few hundred dollars on paper - even a few dollars on paper ...... Merde . Merde et Merde

Venice 4/22/91.

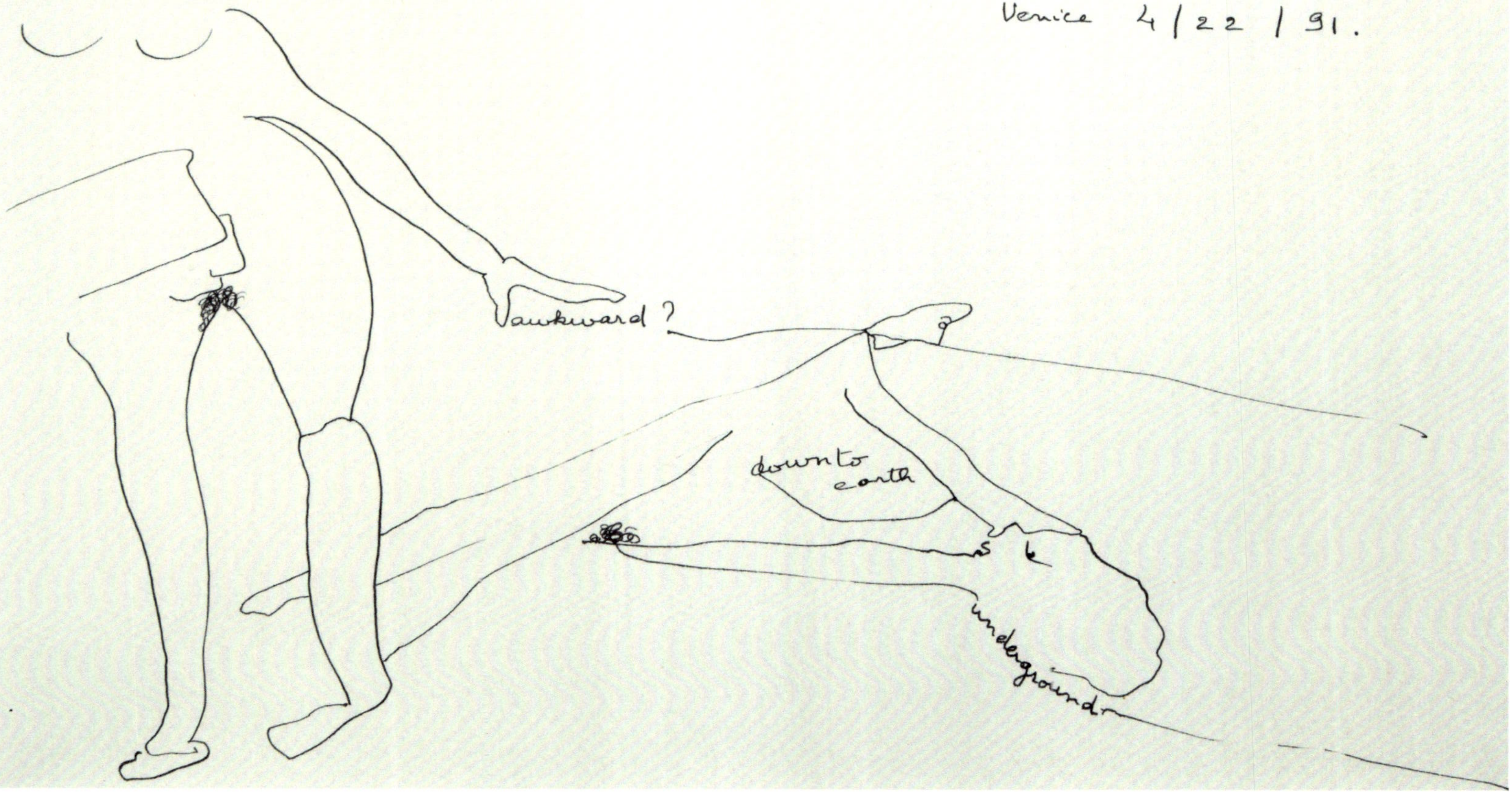

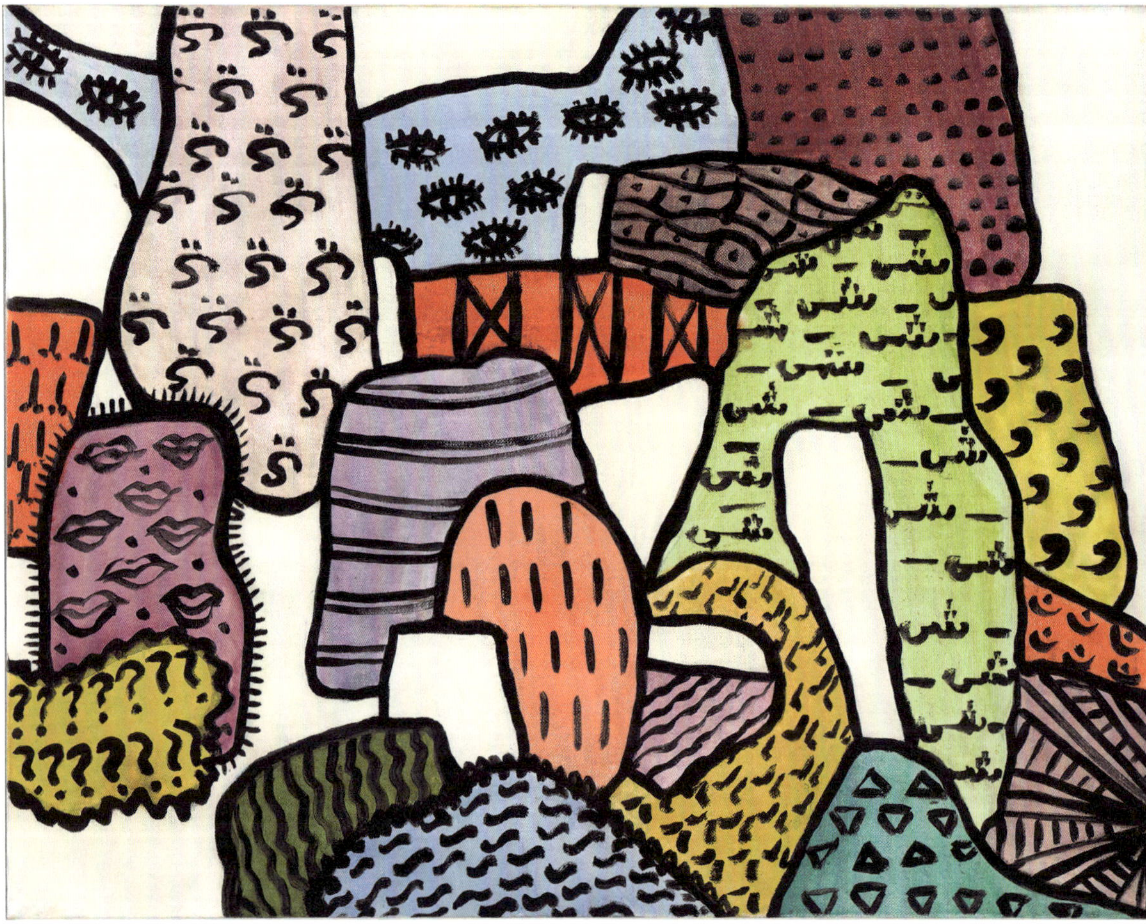

Untitled, 1968
Oil on canvas, 49.5 × 64.3 cm

Private collection, Beirut, Lebanon

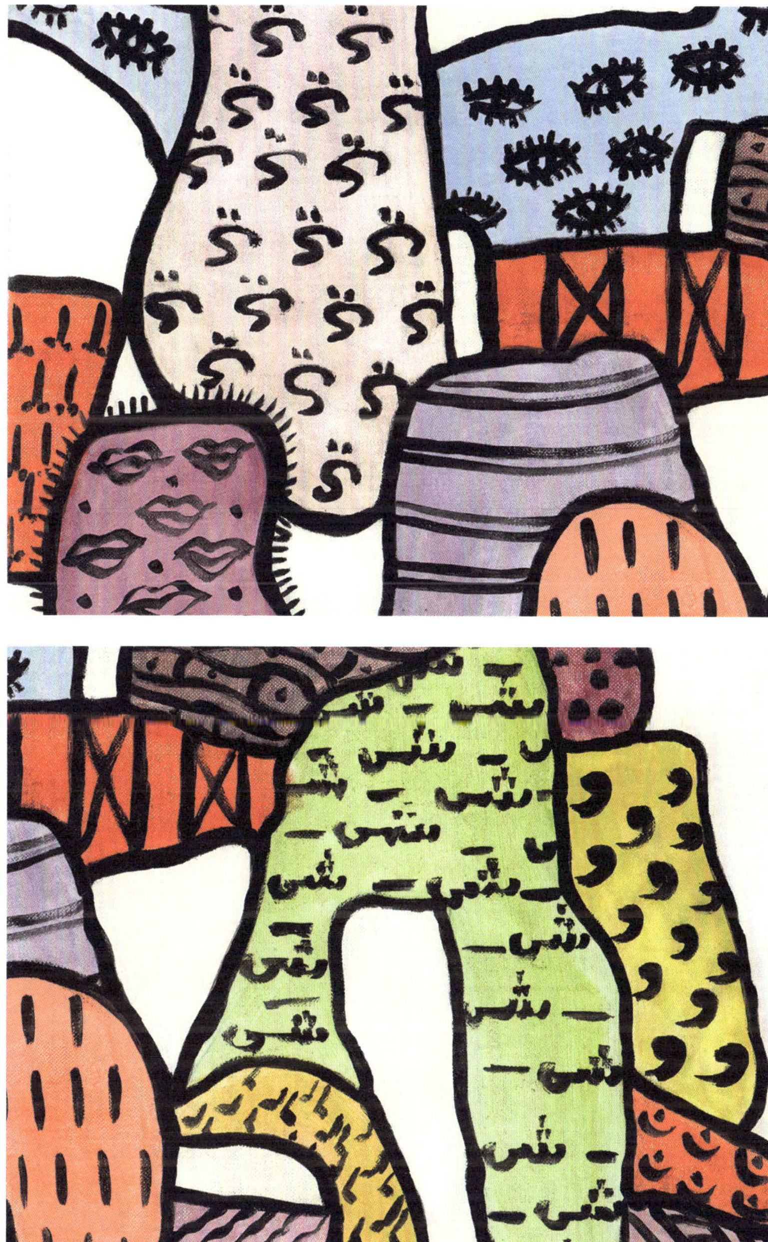

Untitled (details), 1968
Oil on canvas, 49.5 × 64.3 cm

Private collection, Beirut, Lebanon

At the same time, she gestures toward an emerging sense of *Arabité* or Arabness—a conscious identification with Arab culture and identity. This embrace is shaped by the presence of Moustafa in her life, her friendships with fellow artists and intellectuals she met during her time at AUB (such as Aref el Rayess, Helen Khal, and Waddah Faris),[18] co-founding Inaash[19] that same year.

Some fifteen years later, beginning in 1983, writing began to appear in notebooks where Caland combined text and drawing, marking the start of a new artistic practice. The artist's archives in Los Angeles contain nineteen such notebooks[20]—varying in size, with white or black paper of different textures. The ones dating from 1983 to 1986 recount, through sketches and brief texts, intimate moments shared with George Apostu, her companion during those years. When Apostu spent weeks working in the granite quarries of France's Limousin region, Caland accompanied him, bringing along her art supplies, including notebooks in which she drew and painted. Five of these notebooks contain both drawings and written reflections, but two in particular stand out: *Sketchbook #5* (1986) and *Sketchbook #2*(1990-1991).

In *Sketchbook #5* (see photos p. 72-73), ink drawings depict Apostu at work or resting, as well as scenes from their shared environment—the village, the house's interior, and the courtyard. The earliest drawings are dated July 1986. Then, after a months-long pause, new sketches and writings appear in December of that year, just weeks after Apostu's death. Most of the illustrated pages are annotated with a date, a location, and occasionally a signature, title, or note—for example: "*Christ au chapeau - Ars, 26/5/86 Huguette Caland.*" One sketch even includes a car's license plate number. While the earlier drawings serve as personal visual archives of their time in Limousin, the later texts, added after Apostu's death, read like a private journal.

Written in a delicate, rounded, flowing script, her sentences are short, spare, and devoid of punctuation—conveying intimacy through restraint. The reader is drawn into the private world of their relationship: a space of consensual vulnerability and tenderness. Caland records her partner's whispered words about sleep and the choreography of their bodies merging like spoons. She describes "a safe space, a space of inner security,"[21] a "momentary comfort" she creates to soften the final stages and struggle of his illness. In this environment, she sees herself as "a teddy bear," "a toy," and "a toy on the lookout." With Apostu, she allows herself to be "touched, moved, reached, disturbed."[22] She feels needed and valued emotionally, just as she did artistically

18 Aref el Rayess (1928–2005) was a Lebanese artist, painter, and sculptor who traveled between 1948 and 1957 to Africa and Paris, where he joined the workshops of F. Léger, A. Lhôte, and the Grande Chaumière, among others. Helen Khal (1923–2009) was a Lebanese-American artist who co-founded Gallery One in 1963, the first modern and contemporary art gallery in Beirut. Waddah Faris (born in 1940) is a photographer, art critic, and the founder of Contact Art Gallery in Beirut in 1972, as well as Faris Gallery in Paris in 1979.

19 In 1968, Caland co-founded the association, Inaash, with a group of Lebanese women from various backgrounds to enable Palestinian women in the Sabra and Shatila camps to earn a living through their embroidery work. Her work with Palestinian women was highly controversial socially, and many Christian clients boycotted the restaurant she and her husband owned in Beirut.

20 Two notebooks were written in collaboration with friends: one with Dominique Eddé and the other with Fouad Elkoury.

21 C. Marin, Ruptures, *Comment les ruptures nous transforment*, (Éditions de l'Observatoire, Paris, 2019) 109, quoting Winnicott.

22 C. Bensaid, J.-Y. Leloup, *Qui aime quand je t'aime*, De l'amour qui souffre à l'amour qui s'offre, (Albin Michel, Paris, 2005) 53.

during their years together.[23] Following Apostu's death, and amid the emotional turbulence of the Romanian community in Paris—so present during his final days—Caland turns to writing and drawing to fill the void. Through these two expressive practices, she brings the absent to life and gradually begins to process her grief. Writing gives form to what cannot be spoken; drawing recovers presence. Together, they become tools for mourning, memory, and healing.

23 When Apostu arrived in France in 1983, she helped him, through her connections, to find a studio in Paris and obtain a residency. Their close relationship led Apostu to create a small book of her works, and despite the turbulence of life (during this time, her partner would have other mistresses), Caland flourished and created a plethora of work such as the series *Limousin* and *Granite*, more than thirty terracotta sculptures, four bronze sculptures, and numerous notebooks. They traveled together; she worked not far away, and it was in her bed that he spent his final days.

From Paris to Los Angeles (1987–2013)

By the early 1990s, the Lebanese Civil War had come to an end, time had softened the grief of Apostu's death, and a new, complex relationship with artist Ed Moses had begun to take shape. At the same time, Caland found herself struggling to fully integrate into the Los Angeles art scene.[24] Despite these emotional and cultural challenges, her creativity remained unshaken. She produced a prolific number of works organized into different chronologically overlapping series: *Collages, Self-Portraits, Christine, Homage to Pubic Hair, Faces and Places, L'argent (Money Doesn't Bring Happiness, but It Sure Helps), Ed Moses, Silent Letters*... Each of these series is distinct in tone and theme—marked by humor (*L'argent, Homage to Pubic Hair*), eroticism (*Christine*), vulnerability and affection (*Ed*), and mystery (*Silent Letters*). These works draw directly from life—transmuting experience into art. "The material I use in my art is essentially my own life," Caland once said. "That slice of life that goes from the first memorable moment of consciousness to the last." Playing on the double meaning of the word "medium," she added in English: "I have worked with mixed, very mixed medias"—referring at once to her art and life.

In *Sketchbook #2*, a Florentine-covered notebook begun on November 19, 1990 (see photos p. 32), Caland reflects on her unease about writing in English. Yet, now living in Venice, California, she nonetheless commits to the exercise. Nearing sixty, she looks back on her life with a blend of gratitude and frustration—some of which she deliberately obscures with layers of ink, partially veiling the text. Only fragments of sentences remain visible, allowing just enough to be read, thus inviting the viewer to piece together what remains hidden. This visual-textual technique anticipates and helps contextualize her *Silent Letters* series, where a single line—placed just above the center of the page—traces the movement of a brush dipped in black ink, masking a written sentence. A few letters peek through, offering glimpses of meaning while maintaining a protective distance from the event itself. Yet, when Caland writes about her

24 A. Moshayedi, H. Walker, Sandy Lajer, Ed Moses and Robert Wilhite in conversation with Aram Moshayedi, in Made in L.A. 2016, catalog published by the Hammer Museum for Made in L.A. in 2016. On page 51: "I know I used to give her a bad time, and everyone would say, "Why do you give her such a bad time?" She had a view, but it was not my view about what art was and what a painter was. She had a different point of view, which I thought was a little bourgeois, and so I gave her a bad time about that. I thought I was educating her so she would know what was happening. I don't know if it did any good or not. She would show a few tears at times out of frustration, and her friends often said, "Why do you put up with him giving you that trouble all the time?"
The story of Moses begins when Caland first spots him at an exhibition opening in Paris in 1987. Obsessed and infatuated by his physique, she creates numerous portraits of him on canvas and paper after returning to California (the first four portraits of Moses date from 1988, and she continues to paint them: three in 1989, two in 1990, one in 1991, one hundred twenty-five in 1992, ten in 1993, three including a massive diptych in 1994, another three in 1999, and two in 2012). These vary in size, color, and texture, ranging from small intimate formats to monumental works that are comparable to impressive mural art; some are very dark (reflecting bad days), others are joyful with vibrant or soft colors.
A few years later, the two artists met in Los Angeles during exhibition openings and other art events. In 1997, when Caland built her studio on Appleton Way in Venice, Moses and Caland became neighbors; only one street separated their houses/studios. One day, when Moses visits her, he discovers the portraits Caland has painted of him. Surprised, he threatens, "I will inform all the galleries that if any of them display these portraits, I will never work with them again." He does so, and since he's a local star, the threat is taken seriously. From that point on, gallery owners, artists, famous or less famous neighbors frequently visit Caland, but for decades, no one makes the short walk that separates the studio from the room where they gather around a table full of abundant food and all kinds of drinks, wines, and spirits... often in the company of international friends with fascinating backgrounds.

relationship with Ed Moses,[25] the texts become fully legible. Moses, a prominent figure in the California art scene, who lived just two blocks from her home, appears more and more frequently in her life—dropping by for coffee, wine, lunch, and dinner. He was also regularly invited to dinners to celebrate art openings or birthdays, and other social gatherings that Caland hosted in her home, which became a welcoming hub for friends, neighbors, and visitors alike. In her writing, Caland confesses that, in her sixties and caught off guard by renewed emotional and physical desire, she felt like "an animal... but an intellectual animal" in Moses's presence. She compares her attraction to Moses with the one she had for Paul—her husband—at age twelve, and writes, "I knew immediately that I wanted Paul, and I succeeded." But with Moses, she says, "I knew I had to avoid him. And yet..." Despite her better judgment, she lets him into her life. "I don't even think I like Moses," she admits. "I like the way he looks." Paul and Ed both had slightly pointed chins, similar stature, and a preference for a certain kind of woman. Moses, however, kept their relationship discreet. In public, he was always seen with glamorous, often famous, younger women—"bimbos,". This situation reawakened the narcissistic wound first inflicted by Paul, leaving a lasting mark. Adapting to the Los Angeles art world was not easy. Language was not a barrier, but cultural differences were. In the same notebook, Caland notes the significance of buying her first car—essential in a city where life without one is almost impossible. She marvels at the space of a gallery she discovers, surprised as much by the architecture as by the artworks on display.[26] She writes about an opening she attends, saying: "Moses was present, as were many others... comments may come later. In fact, silence is more appropriate," dated simply: *Venice, 11/29/90*; and silence, here, is synonymous with repression.

As the pages of the sketchbook unfold, Caland records her new encounters, noting, for example, how a baby smiled at her, and that this is her fourth Christmas in Venice. Despite life's challenges, she seems to face them with optimism. Yet, frustration occasionally breaks through. One day, she vents her anger after someone she had been waiting for failed to show up or cancelled—an act of rudeness she finds unforgivable. To make matters worse, the person calls her from Moses's house—her neighbor—to say he is there with his entire family. Caland loses her temper, and in this rare instance, she does not conceal a single word. The page becomes a therapeutic space, a raw outpouring of emotion that helps her release anger before regaining composure. In this same sketchbook, at the start of 1991, she reflects on the looming possibility of a war "in the name of God" in the Middle East, recounts recent visits, and expresses, as her birthday approaches, a deep wish for the future: "I don't want to understand, I want to feel."[27] Paul appears again,[28] as does a humorous, affectionate written portrait of a homeless man

25 For over a decade, Caland painted portraits of Moses.

26 The paintings were James Hayword's, an artist of the Los Angeles community that she will invite to Morocco with his girlfriend, four years later (they are the couple mentioned on *Smock #31*).

27 Huguette Caland, *Sketchbook #2*, p. 32.

28 Written in English: "I was with Paul and I said: Paul I hope you will have nothing to regret marrying me, I am twenty today but I know that I will be better at thirty than at twenty, at forty than at thirty, at fifty than at forty, at sixty than ever, and more in peace with myself than ever. And after sixty, I don't know! I am happy I could keep my word."

living on her street. She writes about solitude, communication, and the mundane events of daily life—family moments, street encounters—frequently mentioning her lack of money, which prevents her from buying art supplies. A few pages later, she rejoices at having sold a piece. That good news is soon followed by another: the birth of her first grandson. She shares her desire to be with her daughter, her plans to leave California for a few months, and her excitement about returning afterward.

Writing about Moses, she admits, is "a way of exorcising him." To write something is to acknowledge it,[29] she notes—tapping into the psychoanalytic process and "the magic of words," that helps release the unconscious[30] (repressed). Through both writing and visual art, Caland establishes a dual mode of communication—a double treatment of the subject, and a double therapy. "Imagination was probably my only country of birth,"[31] she acknowledges in one of her notebooks. Elsewhere, she writes: "My energy comes from the earth and gives me wings to fly—I need it more than roots to which I would identify."[32]

This need to exorcise the presence of Moses, combined with the ongoing difficulty of integrating into her environment, gave rise in 1991–1992 to a new kind of visual "writing." Rooted in imagination and driven by her unique inner force, this emerging language plays with concealment. While the fluid lines, characteristic of her earlier work, remain, they are now joined by more rigid, broken, and varied marks. These lines form grids or fields—sometimes densely packed, sometimes spaced out—tracing diamonds, rectangles, squares, and checkerboards. These compartmentalized surfaces recall aerial landscapes or woven textiles and are filled with color. Amid these formations, she introduces new symbols:[33] cross-stitches,[34] small circles like champagne bubbles rising in a glass, slightly larger circles, and recurring motifs that have become signatures in her work—houses with red-pointed roofs, climbing vines, abstract or stylized flowers, palm trees, sailboats, veiled women, and human figures. These repeated lines, cryptic symbols, and motifs—along with the spaces between them—form a kind of silent language she continues to refine.

Returning to the cross-stitches[35] (*points de croix* in French), and free association. A point—"a tiny space, a fixed location"[36]—becomes a movement when linked to another. The cross, in turn, evokes Christian iconography: suffering, contemplation, and sacrifice. A humble embroidery stitch formed by two intersecting threads, the cross-stitch both strengthens the

29 Huguette Caland, Sketchbook #2, p. 17: "Maybe having to write this is a way of exorcism. Once you have the courage of writing down things you know are there it must have a purifying effect on the spirit... just by the formulation."

30 M. Arrivé, quoting Freud in *Linguistique et psychanalyse*, op. cit., 7.

31 Written in English in the text: "Imagination was probably my only homeland."

32 *Sketchbook #2*, p. 32.

33 M. Arrivé, *Linguistique et psychanalyse*, op. cit., On page 2: "It sometimes happens that the term sign is used by Freud as an equivalent of symbol..."

34 This brings to mind the work of the embroiderers of Inaash, thus pointing to a form of exile and discomfort, the necessity of earning a living, and laborious work.

35 Probably originating from Central Asia in the tenth century with the return of the Crusaders.

36 French dictionary Larousse was consulted https://www.larousse.fr.

fabric and decorates it. Once used by noblewomen to pass the time while waiting for their husbands' return, the stitch becomes Caland's meditative act; is she waiting for someone too? In this environment that fosters creativity and *lâcher prise* (letting go), the liberated unconscious begins to surface, and repressed content emerges, transformed but still imbued with mystery.

Out of this visual language—born in the early 1990s through weaving lines, interlaced symbols, and layered color—a sense of density and depth emerges in the work. And, much like written language evolving over time, this symbolic system also develops. At moments, it becomes lighter, less opaque—though never fully legible. Caland, the "scribe of her unconscious,"[37] uses this symbolic alphabet, composed of marks that are both "rational and emotional,"[38] to narrate a story while preserving her inner world. This visual weaving expresses the present and echoes of the past, and sometimes, when she chooses, Caland incorporates fragments of more decipherable language—on paper, canvas, or her smocks, the paint-streaked work dresses that bore the traces of her process.

37 M. Safouan, *L'Inconscient et son scribe*, (Le Seuil, Paris, 1982).

38 M. Safouan, La Parole ou la Mort, (Le Seuil, Paris, 2010), 9, quoting Dante.

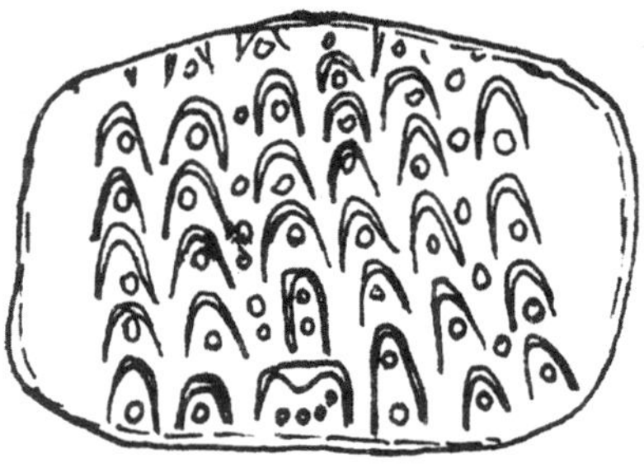

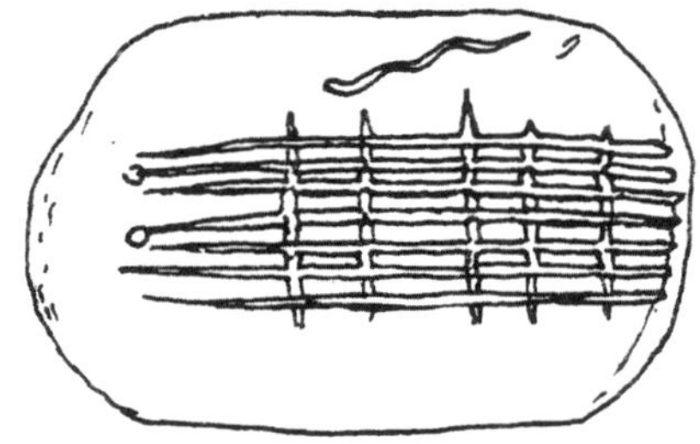

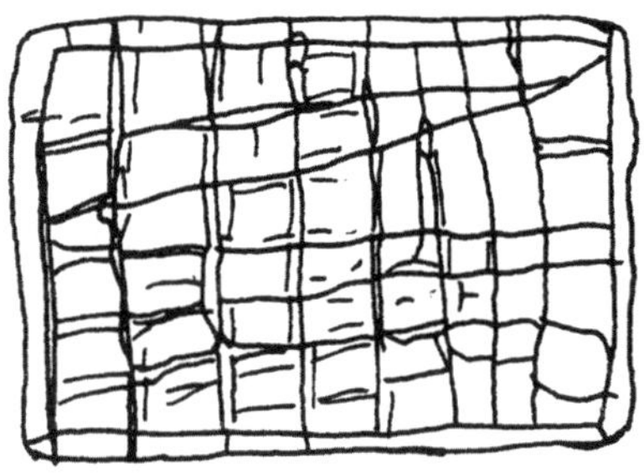

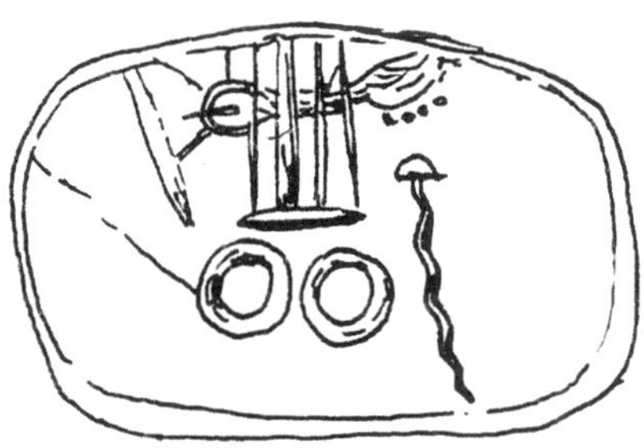

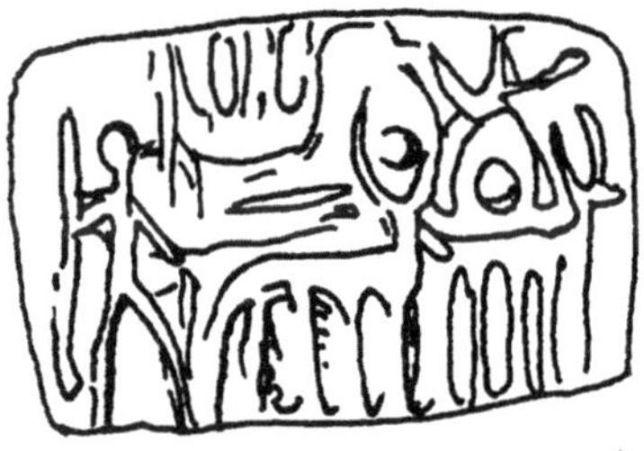

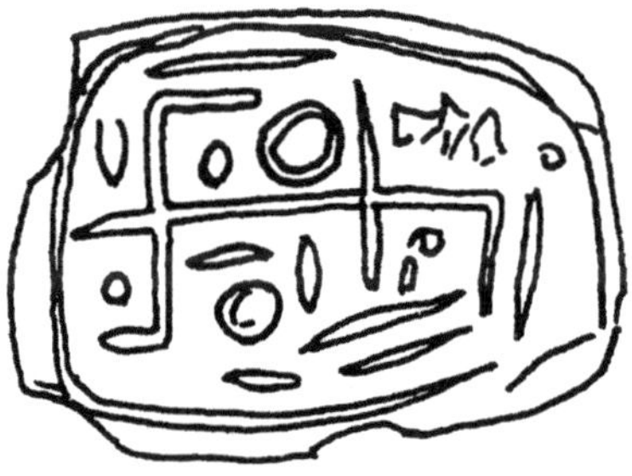

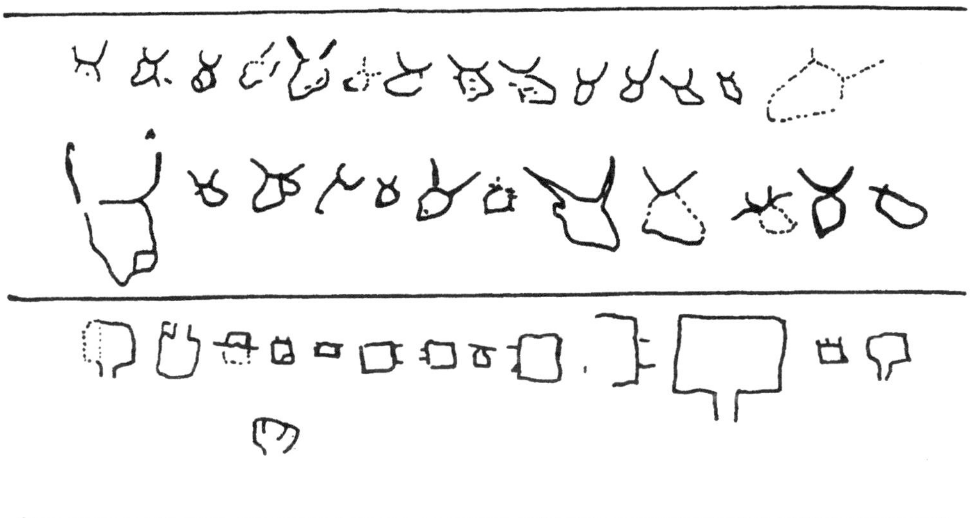

Photos from the book *L'Aventure de l'alphabet (2002)* by Hubert La Marle, Geuthner, Paris, 2002

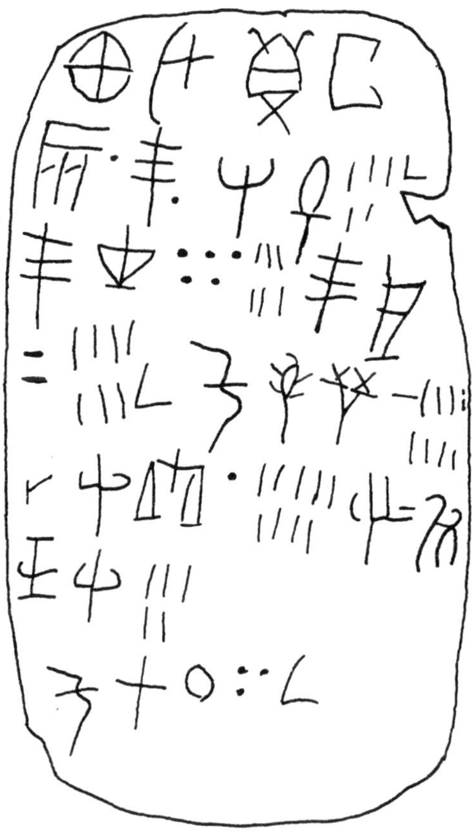

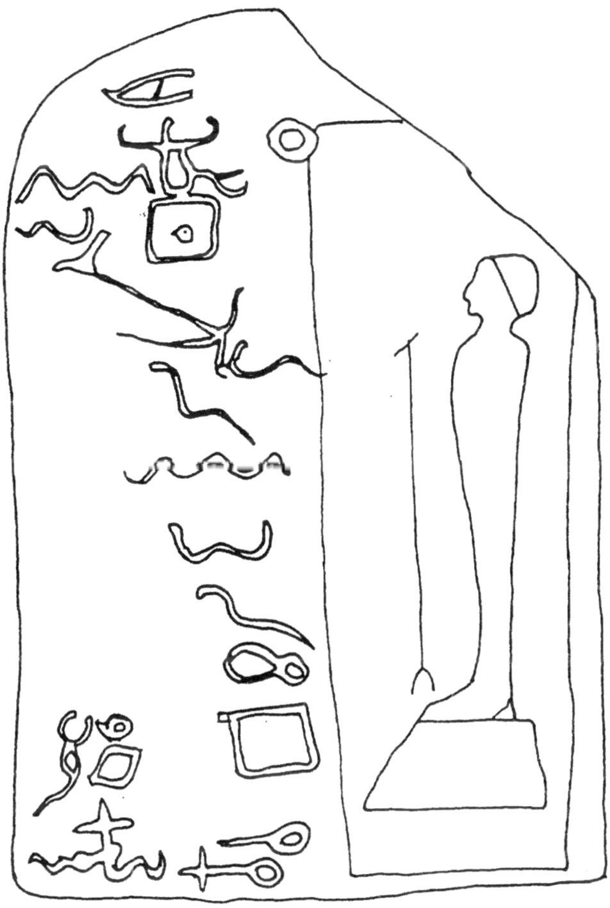

Photos from the book *L'Aventure de l'alphabet (2002)* by Hubert La Marle, Geuthner, Paris, 2002

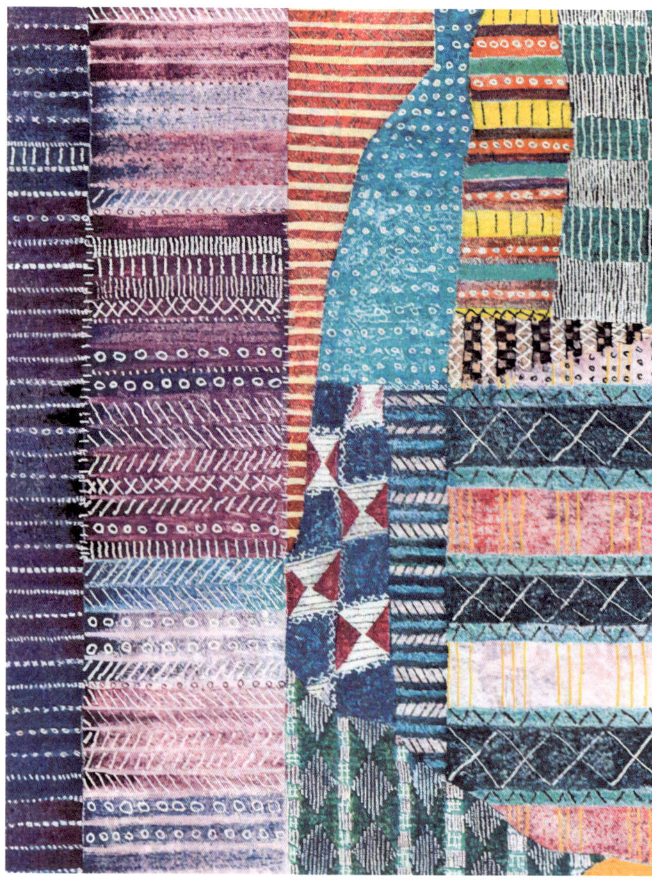

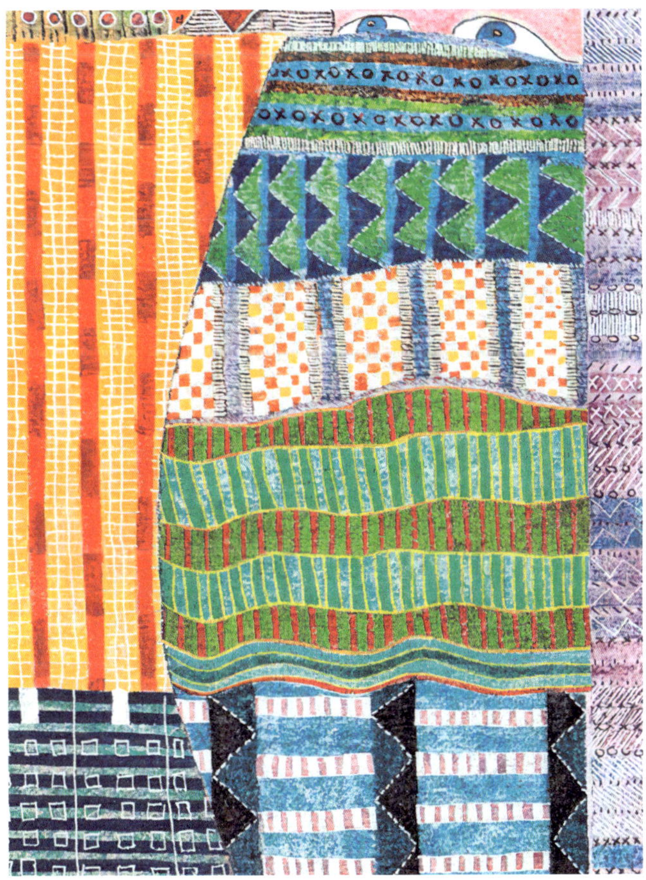

Faces and Places II (details), 2010
Mixed media on canvas, 91 × 288 cm

Private collection, Los Angeles, California

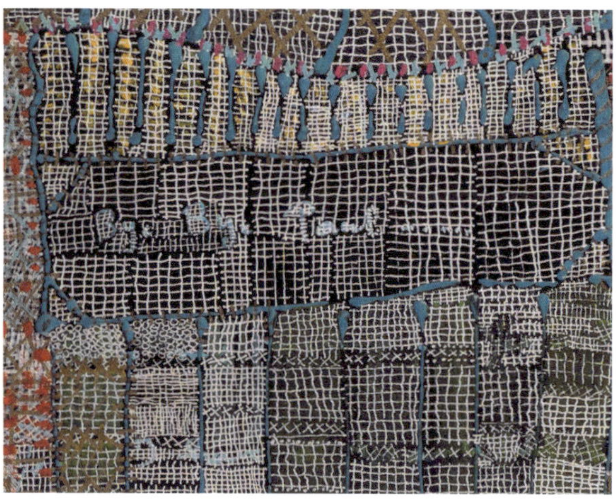

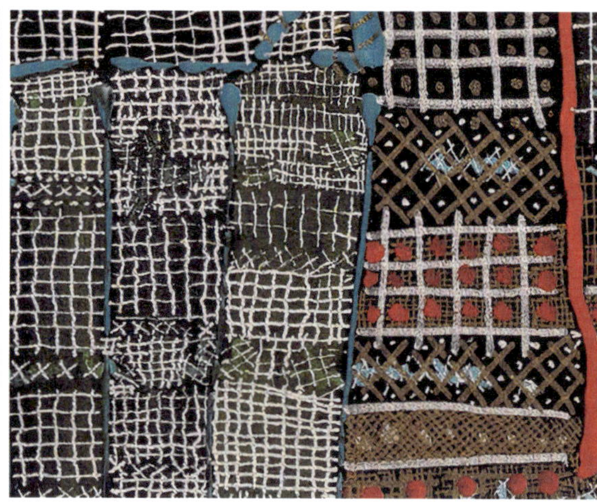

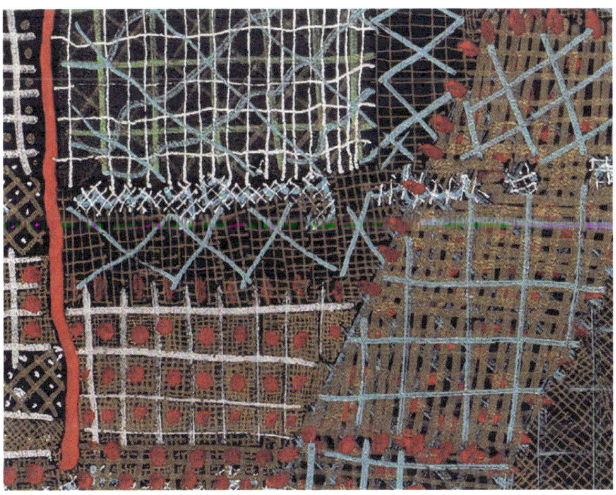

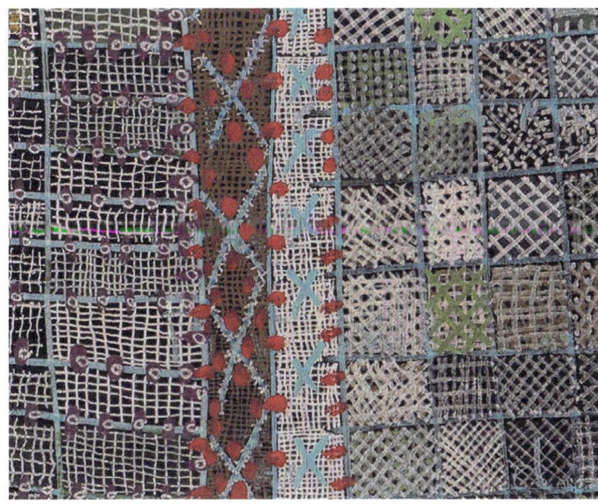

Zikrayat toufoulati fi loubnan (details), 1998
Acrylic on panel, 244 × 122 cm

Private collection, Beirut, Lebanon

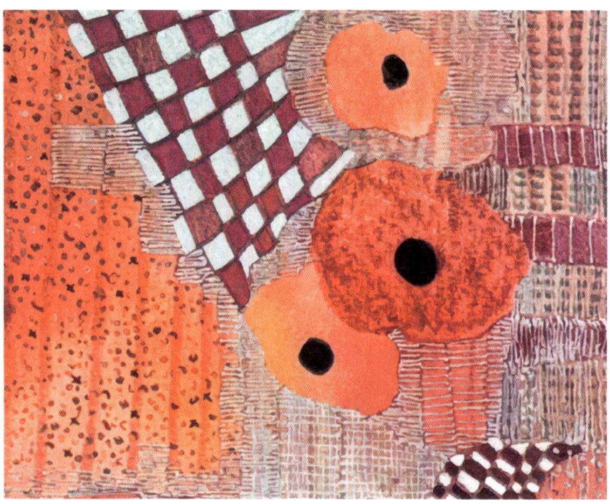

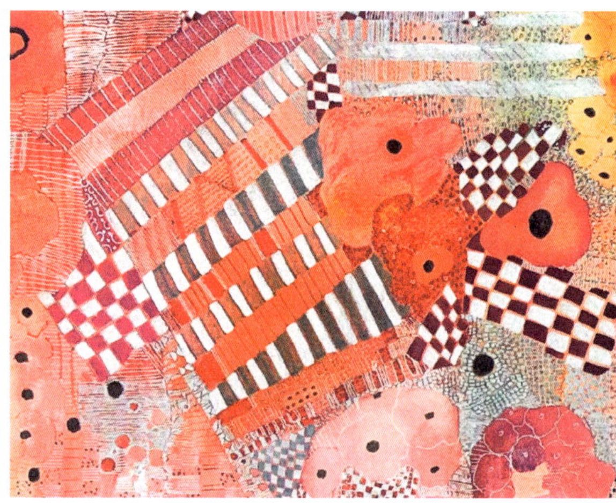

Appleton II (details)
Mixed media on canvas, 145 × 162 cm

Private collection, Beirut, Lebanon

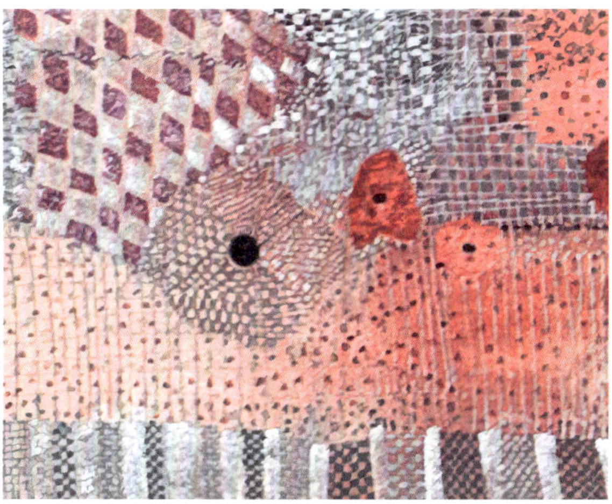

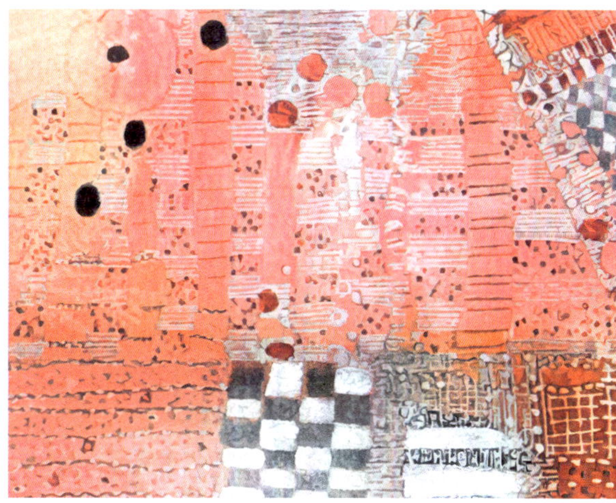

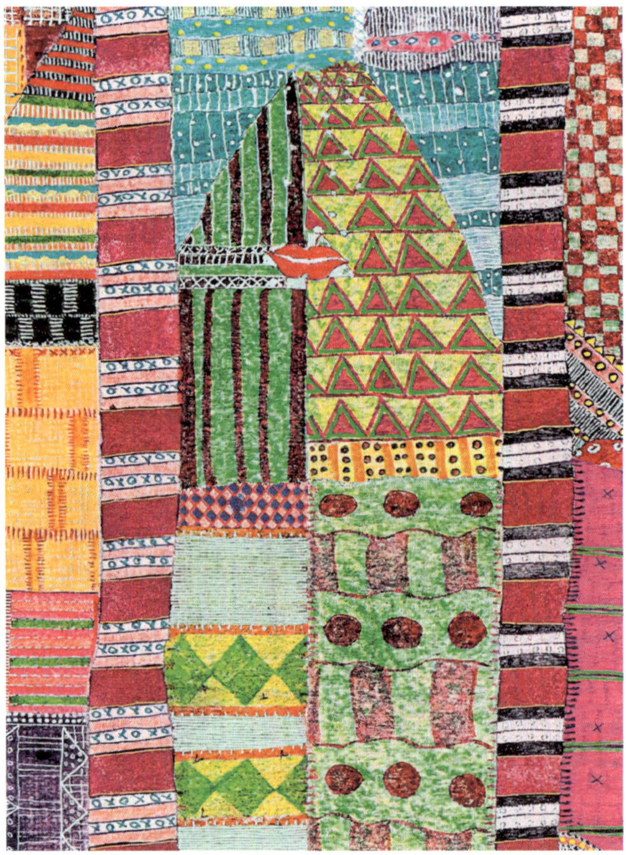

Faces and Places I (details), 2010
Mixed media on canvas, 91 × 288 cm

Private collection, Los Angeles, California

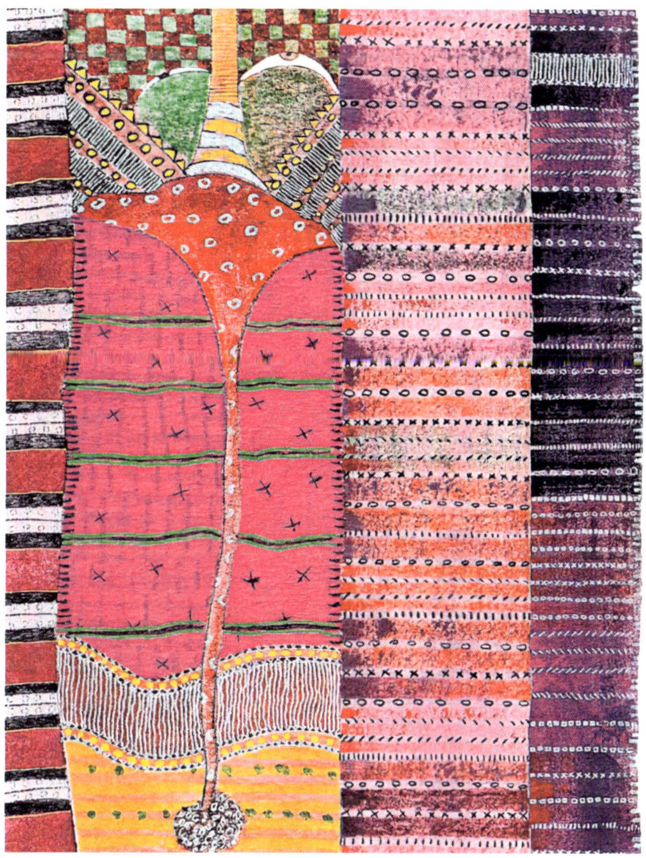

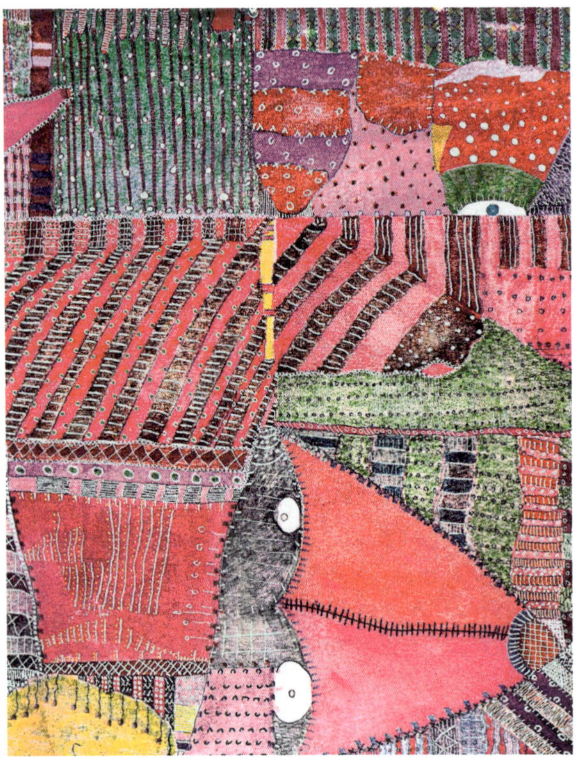
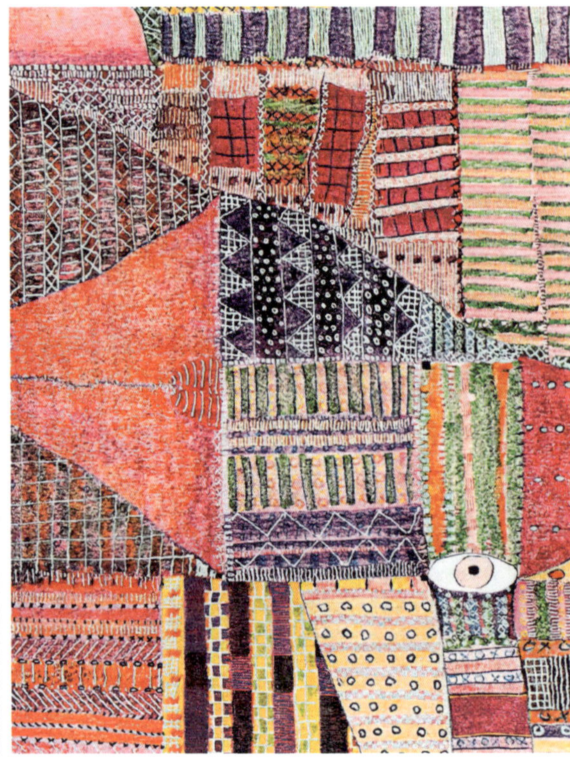

Faces and Places I (details), 2010
Mixed media on canvas, 91 × 288 cm

Private collection, Los Angeles, California

Caland once said, "There is no difference between my life and my art—the two are intimately connected," and even the clothes she wore became part of that fluid continuum. After her father's death, liberated from social and formal constraints, Caland gave away her entire "Western" wardrobe and began wearing abayas or caftans—loose-fitting robes inspired by traditional Middle Eastern dress. Although such garments had appeared in haute couture collections by Christian Dior and Yves Saint Laurent, within Middle Eastern bourgeois circles, they were still seen as regional cultural symbols rather than fashion statements, and certainly not as emblems of modernity.[39] These rectangular garments, while physically comfortable, also concealed the contours of a body that had carried extra weight since childhood. They offered protection—both from judgmental or pitying glances, and from the emotional sting of others' comments.[40] Though her decision to adopt this style was not politically motivated, it nonetheless expressed a quiet refusal to conform to Western standards—standards that often reflected forms of cultural and social colonialism, which Caland increasingly questioned.[41] On an unconscious level, this sartorial shift also marked a break from her husband's aesthetic ideals—his preference for slim, "Europeanized" women. Her choice of clothing, which likely crystallized deeper tensions in the marriage, was understood by her husband as a "serious problem" and became the only moment in their unconventional union when divorce was mentioned. Still, Caland stood firm in her decision, later reflecting: "These clothes changed my life. I could finally live it fully."[42] Unbound by fashion cycles and shielded from the pressures of seasonal change,[43] her clothing blurred gender norms and offered her both creative freedom and a timeless sense of continuity.

Caland's personal archives contain ninety-one abayas[44]—over thirty from her *Nour* collection—and fifty-nine smocks (work dresses), twenty-nine of which bear writing: names, addresses, appointment times and dates, notes, comments... written in Arabic, French, or English. Some abayas are elegantly embroidered, while the smocks, loose and utilitarian, feature large pockets (24 × 17 cm) that could hold pencils and the small-format paper that Caland always kept close at hand. These smocks bear the marks of daily artistic labor—traces of paint, brushstrokes, and handwritten musings. One example, *Smock #31*, worn in Asilah, Morocco,

39 N. Tamraz, "*Jouer, déjouer, transformer le corps comme performance*," in the catalog of *Faces and Places*, Mathaf/Doha, (forthcoming).

40 In the early days, when Caland started to wear her abayas and went to the American University of Beirut, people looked at her and said: "The president's daughter lost it."

41 N. Tamraz, "*Jouer, déjouer, transformer le corps comme performance*," op. cit.: "In his *History and Sociology of Clothing*, Roland Barthes adopts Saussure's theories to show that clothing, like language, is both an individual act and a collective institution. He suggests calling 'costume' what, for Saussure, corresponds to language, and 'dress' what corresponds to speech. Thus, dress would be a 'dress act,' just as there is, for Saussure, a 'speech act.' Huguette Caland's wearing of abayas would therefore be a pure dress act, a true speech act, the refusal of costume, of the imposed language, the affirmation of a garment, even a brand, a signature."

42 O'Connor, "*Her Magical World*"

43 *Warae elwoujouh* interview.

44 In addition to this number, there are seven "art" dresses created between 1970 and 1975 in Lebanon. On thick silk or linen, defying the social and religious norms of the time, she drew on the fabric erotic zones—the chest and pubis (Miroir)—arms embracing a body hidden by the garment (Tendresse), faces (La Foule), and then asked an artisan from Basta, a Muslim working-class neighborhood in Beirut, to embroider them according to her instructions, adding texture to the original design.
These dresses, some of which have been incorporated into collections at institutions such as the Tate and Hammer Museum, are mostly housed in her studio in Los Angeles.

in 1994 (see photo p. 97-99), stands out. Unlike most smocks, which served primarily to wipe brushes or catch spontaneous notes, this one was treated like a canvas. Its front is saturated with chaotic, almost aggressive colors—perhaps a reflection of disappointment: Is it because Moses, who had accepted the invitation to Asilah, cancels his trip at the last minute? The only writing on the front is a single sentence on the left shoulder. The back, which is sparsely painted, has fine-line traced characters: round, beaded eyes, red heart-shaped lips, bodies intertwined in orgiastic scenes. Despite being washed numerous times, the colors and texts have endured remarkably well. Caland's two artist friends from California, who joined her in Asilah, indulged in cannabis and alcohol—"ritually stoned, religiously drunk,"[45] she wrote. Yet, she says nothing about how she felt. The repression is so complete that she wryly echoes an English idiom, writing: "a penny for my thoughts? No! A million dollars for the embryo of a thought."[46] Her remarks about her American friends appear in English, but it is in French that she allows herself to play with rhythm and rhyme: "une limousine pour le harem… une limousine pour salem… et puis…"—a sentence that trails off and disappears beneath the names of her first two grandchildren, "Guy Karim & L'Or Iman," inscribed twice in quick succession. On another smock, *Smock #30* (see photo p. 101-100), new and unused, Caland initiated an impromptu performance during one of her exhibition openings in Lebanon, where she invited all the attendees—artists, collectors, gallerists—to write a comment and/or sign their name directly on the garment. She later repeated this spontaneous happening at a group exhibition in Washington, D.C., and gifted the abaya to the organizers.[47]

45 Written in English: "ritually stoned, religiously drunk," "happily drunk."

46 Written in English: "a penny for my thoughts No! A million dollars for an embryo of a thought."

47 The abaya Caland donated to APEAL was framed and hung in their office in Beirut.

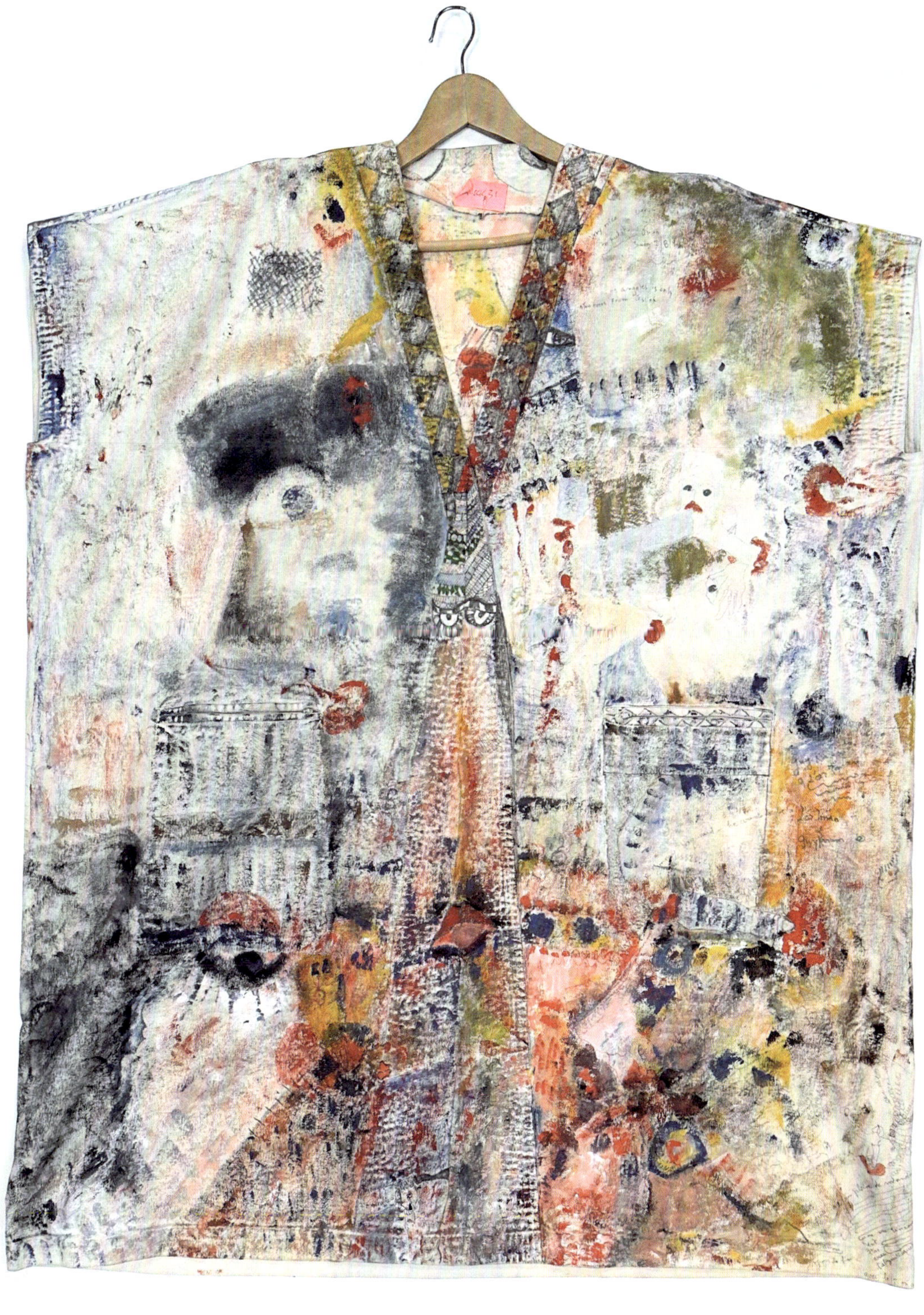

Smock #31, 1994
Mixed media on white denim, 110.8 × 92.8 cm

Private collection, Los Angeles, California

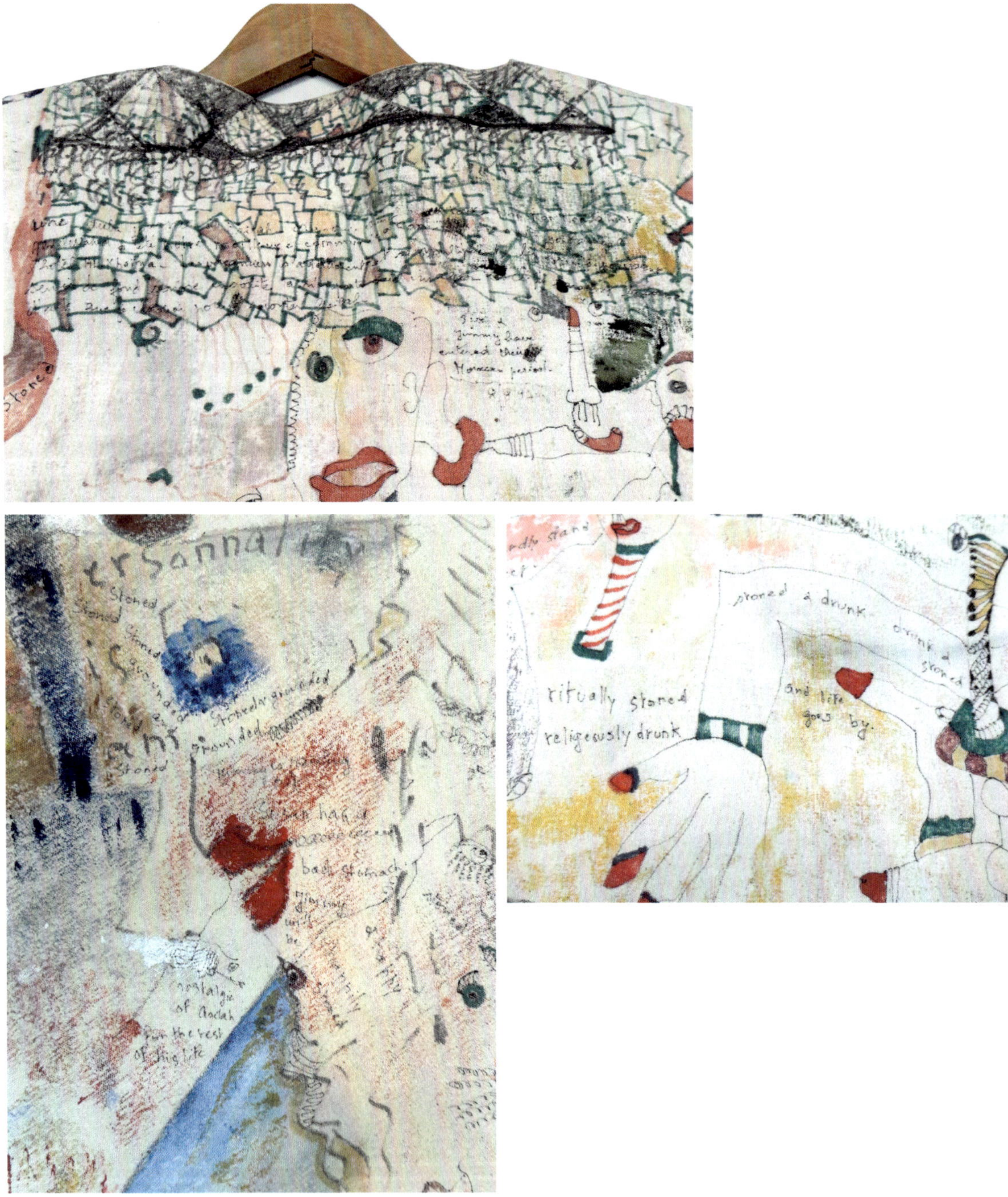

Smock #31 (details), 1994
Mixed media on white denim, 110.8 × 92.8 cm

Private collection, Los Angeles, California

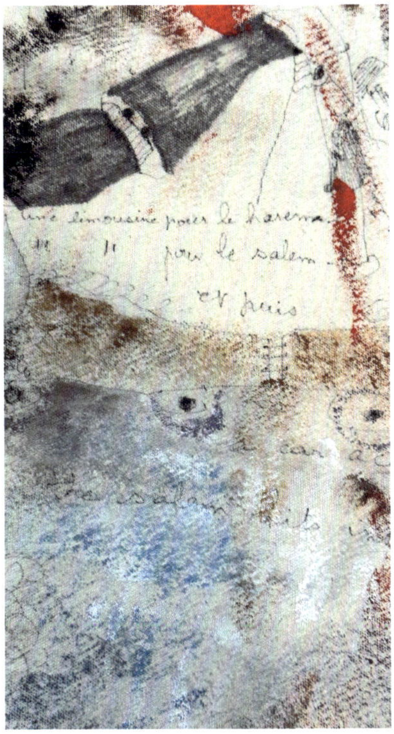
pour le salem
et puis

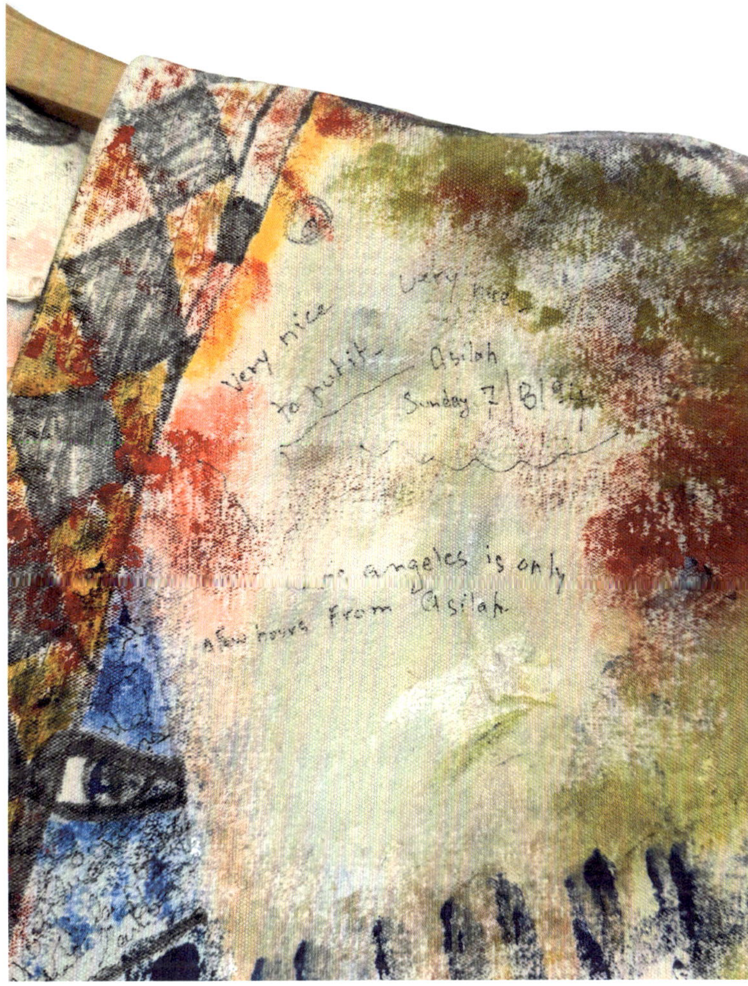
Very nice very nice
Asilah
angeles is only
a few hours from Asilah

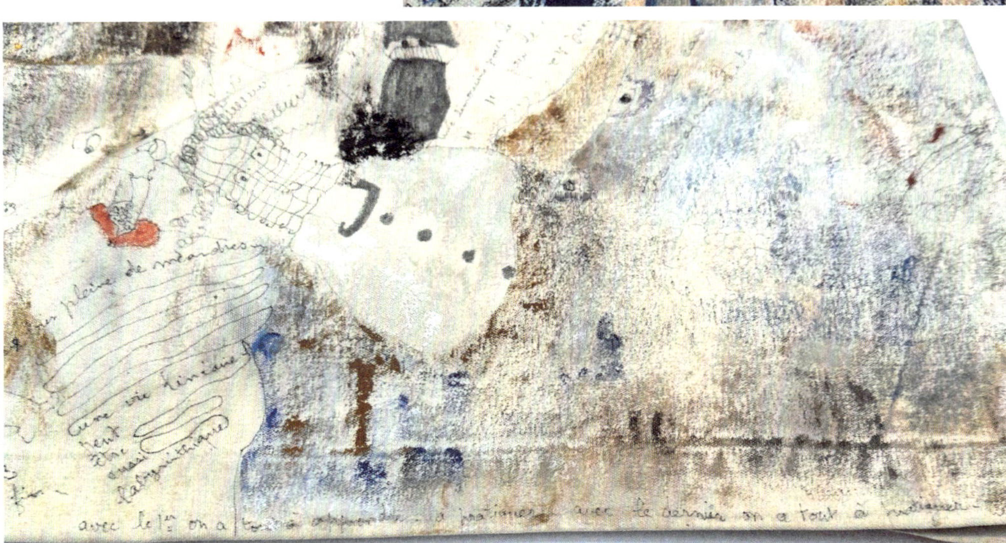

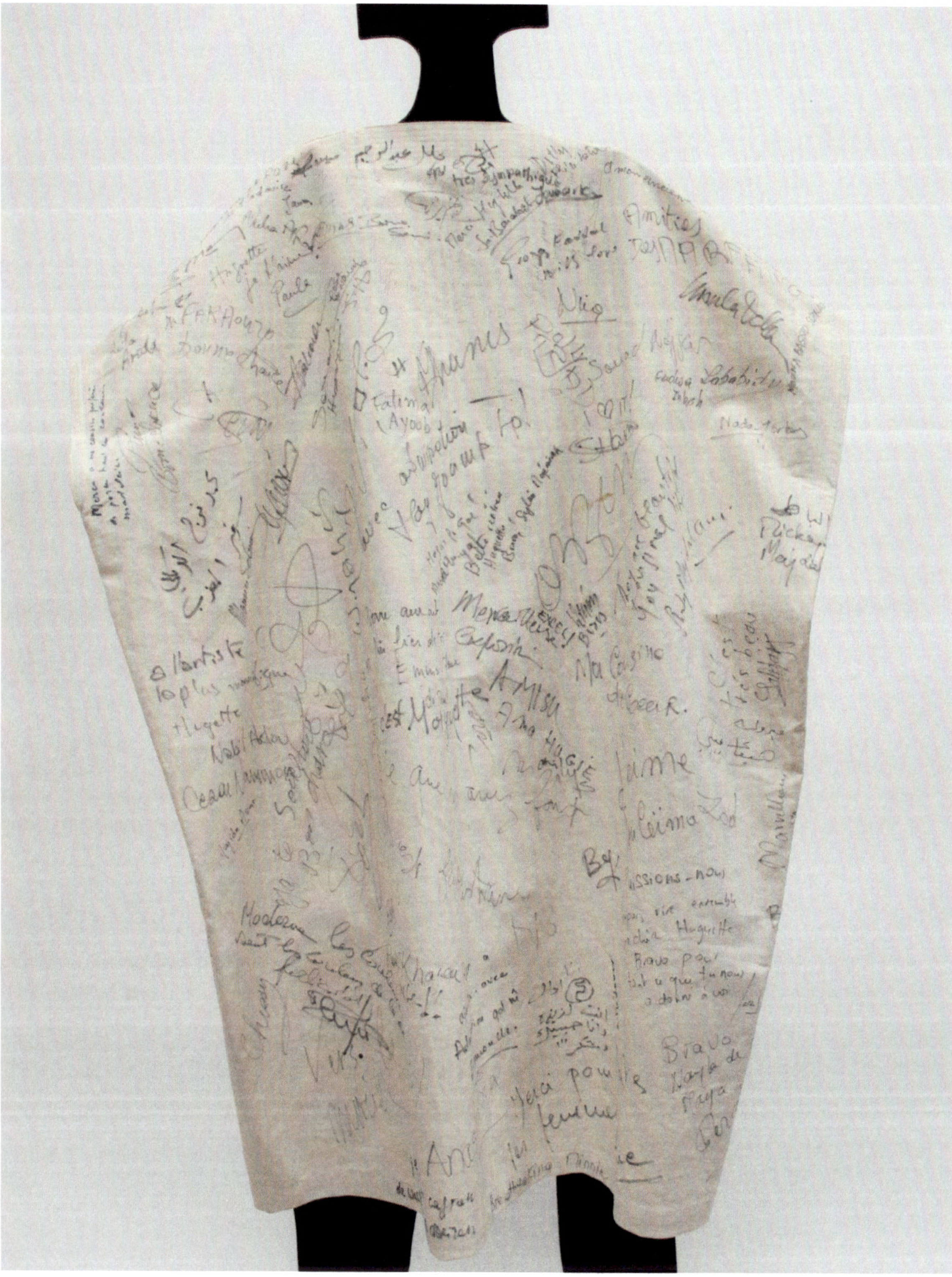

Smock #30, 1997
Ink on white denim, 90 × 103 cm

Private collection, Los Angeles, California

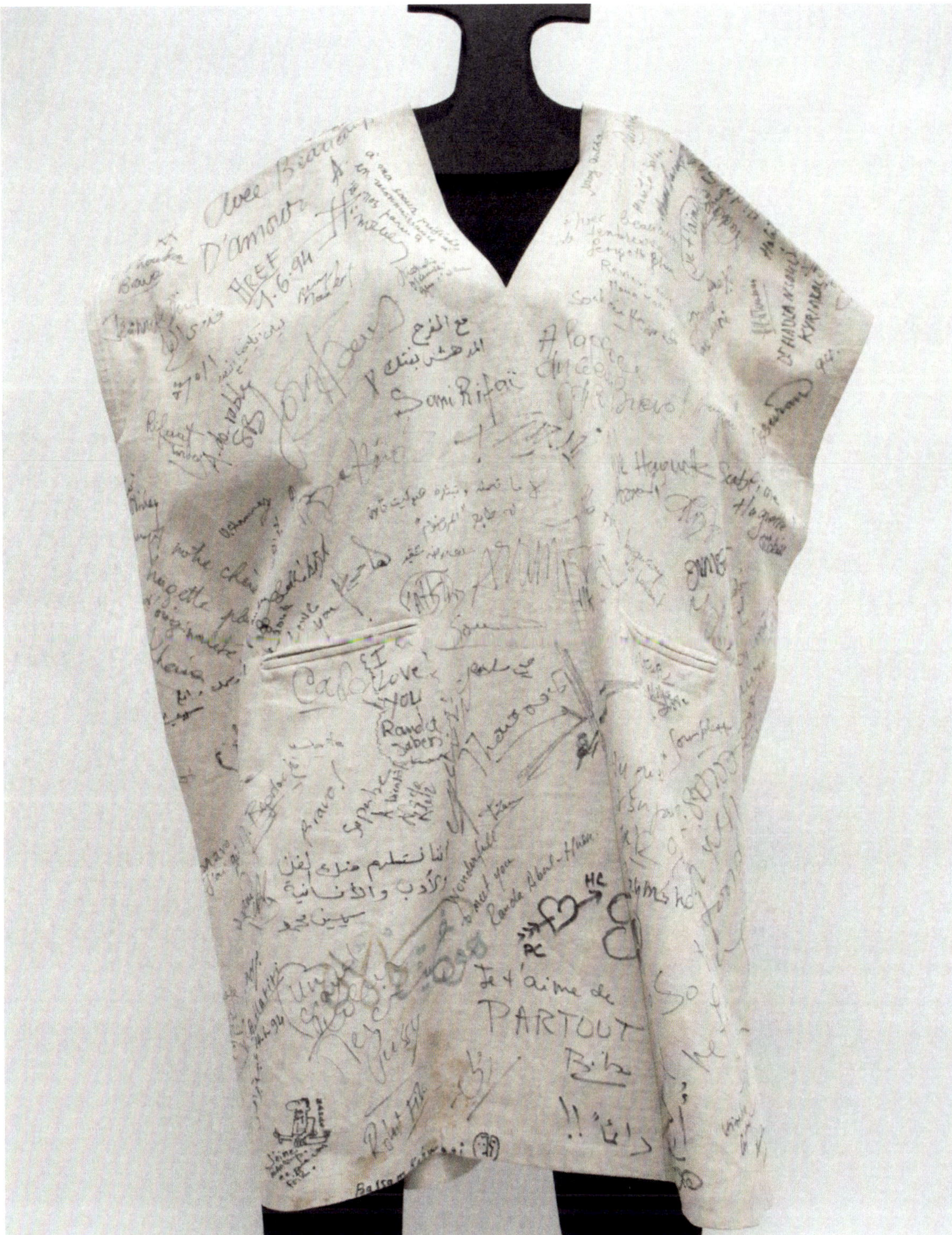

Smock #30, 1997
Ink on white denim, 90 × 103 cm

Private collection, Los Angeles, California

In the 1990s, Caland began incorporating text in many of her drawings, merging visual and written expression. Two works from 1993 (see photos p.104-105),[48] created during her stay in Lebanon while preparing for her first exhibition at Galerie Janine Rubeiz, stand out for both their form and content. Returning to Beirut after a fourteen-year absence, Caland encountered a city still bearing the scars of war—a reality both harsh and unfamiliar. The city was in the midst of reconstruction, its wounds still visible.

In these primarily monochromatic pieces, words immediately catch the viewer's eye, drawing them into subtle visual landscapes rendered in diluted black ink, tones of ash and dust. These muted hues evoke the grey ruins of a post-war Beirut. The ink, lightly applied, allows the texture—and at times even the grain—of the white paper to show through. On these raw surfaces, primitive shapes emerge in the background, alongside a text written in French—Caland's preferred language, which allowed her to be poetic and precise. In the first works of this series, slightly below the center of the page, an open circle appears on the right. The brush, soaked in ink, leaves behind a full and fluid trace—an "O" that recalls both the bullet and shell holes dotting the city's buildings and the bodily orifices associated with pleasure. On the third line, the word *exsangue* (meaning bloodless or drained) is written, corrected, and then repeated above and below—emphasizing the extreme fatigue of a nation wounded socially, politically, psychologically, and spiritually. The word "dangerous" is truncated, perhaps to stay within the page margins—or to symbolically prevent its full invocation, as if writing it in full might summon misfortune.

The phrases continue freely across the page, line after line. Written in fine black felt-tip pen, the text follows nearly straight, imaginary horizontal lines—some gently sloping downward to the right, a gesture that suggests weariness. This visual pessimism contrasts with the underlying hope expressed in the words. "Blood is dangerous," writes Caland. Blood is both the symbol of life and a signifier of death when spilled.[49] This moment coincides with the contaminated blood scandal in France—a major public health crisis implicating members of the Fabius government[50]—further deepening the work's resonance. And yet, amidst this bleakness, Caland suggests the possibility of recovery and rebirth: "beings healed by war—by suffering."[51] Her fragmented sentences, broken by dashes and punctuated with ellipses and periods, mirror a psychological attempt to process trauma, to come to terms with the new reality she found in Lebanon. Despite choosing to build her life and career far away, in the American West, Caland's emotional connection to Lebanon remains intact. That distance—between her homeland, torn and complicated, and the manicured predictability of American suburbia—is

48 Caland created four drawings in the same spirit: two have been located and there are visuals of the two missing drawings in the archives of MACAM-Aalita.

49 The casualties of the Lebanese Civil War are estimated between 130,000 and 250,000 dead; 17,000 people who disappeared; and thousands of people in exile.

50 In April 1991, the blood transfusion scandal erupted in France. It affected 2000 hemophiliacs between 1984 and 1985.

51 Caland, Detail of *Tout est possible dans une ville démolie*, 1993, ink on Canson paper, 21 × 29.7 cm, private collection, Beirut.

quietly captured in her wry reflection: "in the American Far West, with mowed lawns, clean and boring gardens, out of which boredom oozes."[52]

The second piece features zigzagging "W" lines (a reference to the word "women") set against a wash of gray tones. The variety of angles and the opacity of the ink create a layered background, giving the work a sense of depth. The text, written in a similar style to the previous drawing, offers a brief yet heartfelt tribute to the women of Beirut. Having left the city in 1970, the artist returns to reclaim her roots and express her admiration for Beirut's women, celebrating their resilience, beauty, as well as their emotional and mental strength. The series also evokes the repetitive alignment of windows in brutalist architecture, with a light source coming from the right, backlighting the forms. In these two drawings, ink is both the sole medium and writing tool, creating a striking yet simple visual. By using black ink to emphasize the words against the gray background, Caland directs the viewer's focus to the content, rather than the form—a contrast to other works where the pictorial and written elements are more seamlessly interwoven.

At times, in some pieces, after carefully examining the rich symbolism, a single word unexpectedly emerges—barely visible, sometimes even hidden beneath patterns or paint. In *Untitled* (2005), the word *vasistas*[53] (a small window) appears, a single small word lost within the vast expanse of the canvas. Here, the word acts as a mise en abyme (a story within a story): the central pink area seems to represent what one might see through a window—perhaps a pink island viewed from above, or a bed of flowers spreading over spring grass. The overall composition resembles a carpet, its borders filled with symbols. When the painting *Rossinante Under Cover VI* (2010) is hung on the wall (see photos p. 107), two nearly invisible words, "une larme" (a tear), written in fine black marker and reversed, emerge like a Freudian slip.[54] These words disappear into a sea of small circles surrounding a phallic form—a swollen red penis encircled by a blue band. These words, though subtle, contradict the piece's visual lightness and affirm the latent meaning of the title *Under Cover*.[55] In another painting, *Faces and Places* (2010) (see photo p. 108), if one looks closely, they'll notice different locations—*Dubai, Abu Dhabi, Oman, Muscat*—written in capital letters. "Dubai" is subtly inserted into the red roof of a house, nearly invisible at first glance. These scattered words appear like fleeting thoughts, hidden emotions, or references to places that emerge in the artist's mind for unknown reasons.

52 Ibid.

53 Used in France starting in the seventh century, *vasistas* has German origins. It comes from *Was ist das?* (What is this?). A vasistas in French is a window that opens toward the inside of a room with a lock on top, usually found in attics, basements, or even in a door.

54 S. Freud, *Psychopathologie de la vie quotidienne*, (Gallimard, Paris, 1997), 109-188. Mainly page 117: "verbal images 'vagabondantes' (wandering) located below the threshold of consciousness and not meant to be spoken."

55 "I feel like Rossinante, the aging horse of Don Quixote," says Caland one day during a visit to Ephesus in 2006.

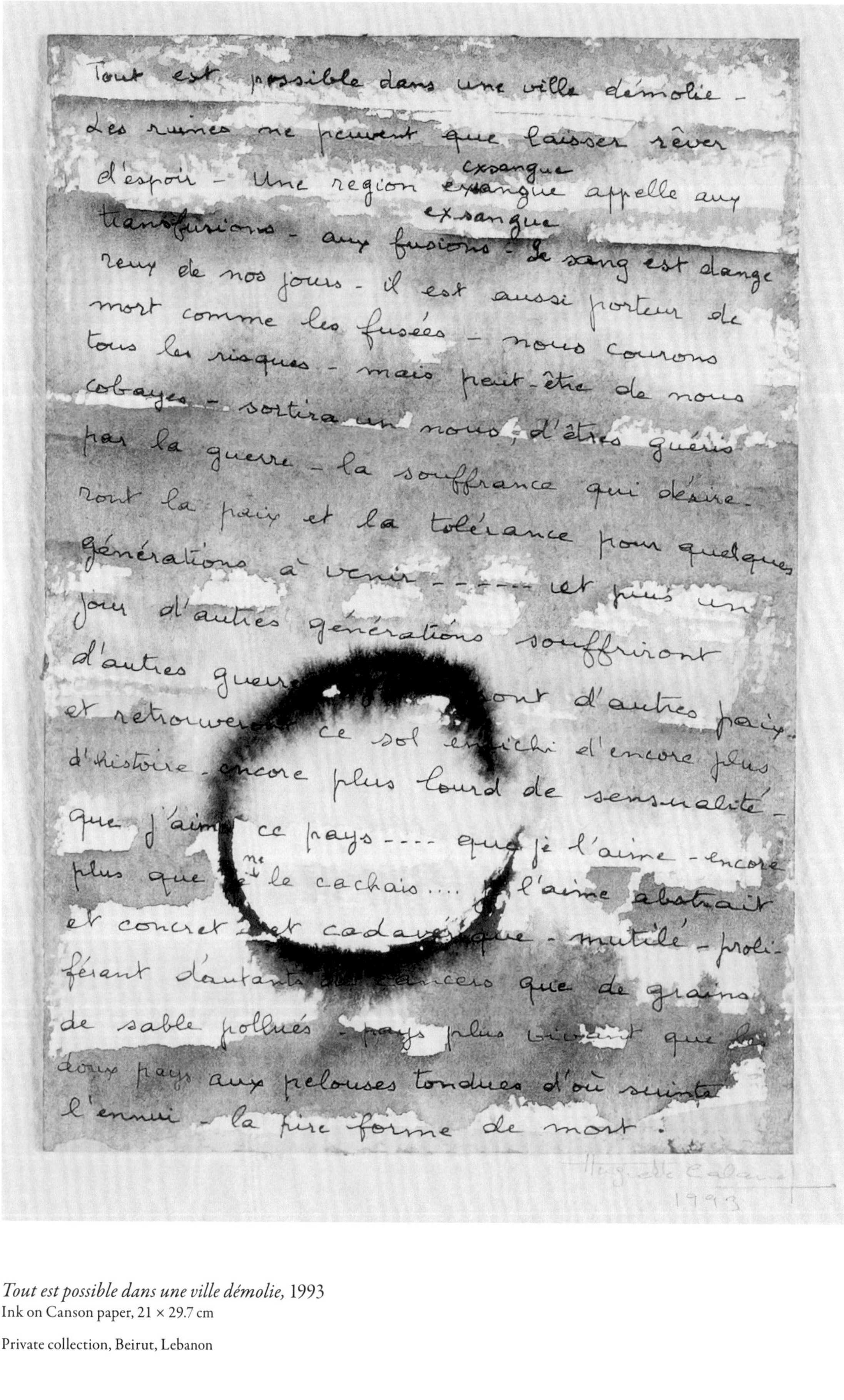

Tout est possible dans une ville démolie, 1993
Ink on Canson paper, 21 × 29.7 cm

Private collection, Beirut, Lebanon

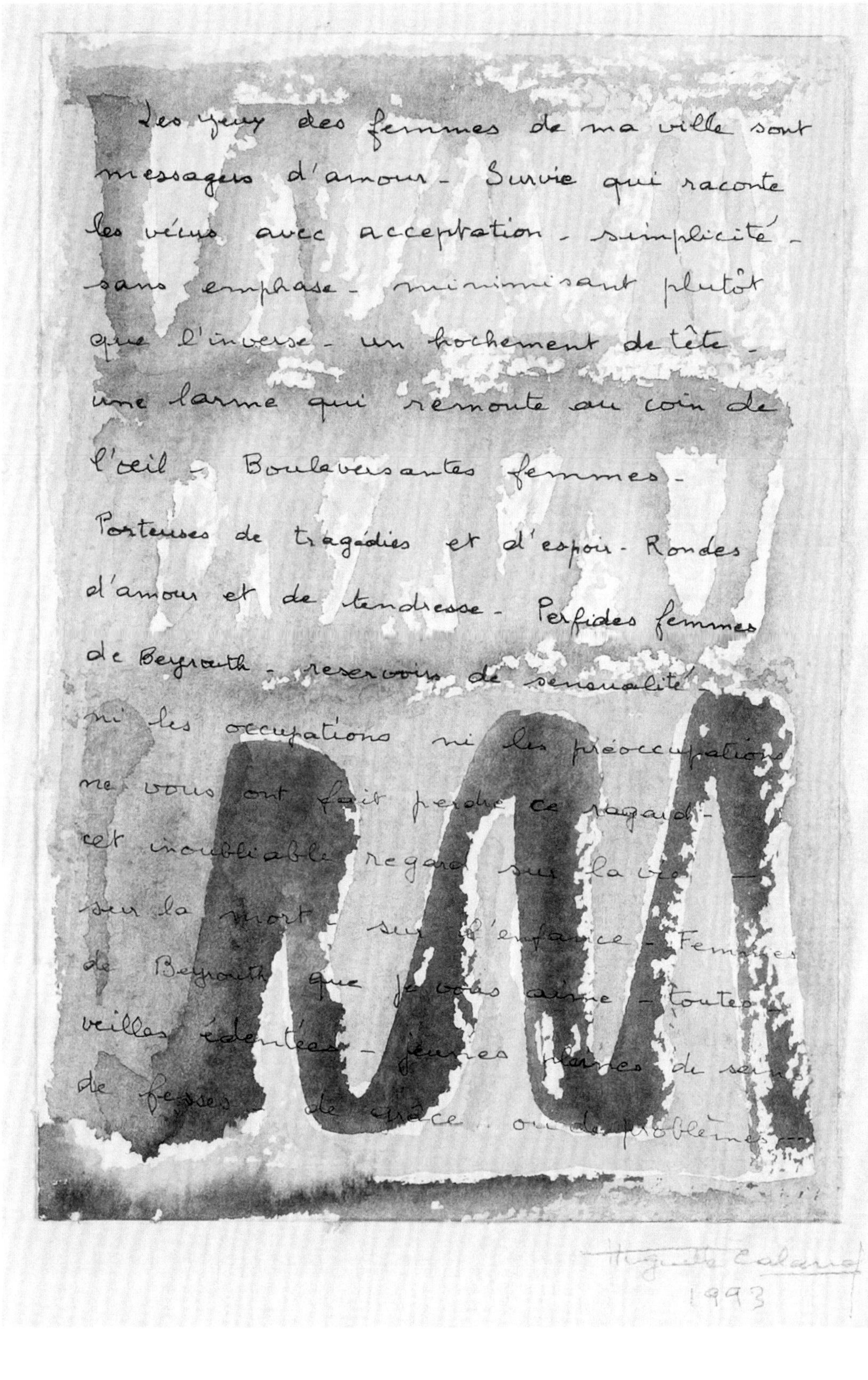

Les Femmes de ma ville, 1993
Ink on Canson paper, 21 × 29.7 cm

Private collection, Paris, France

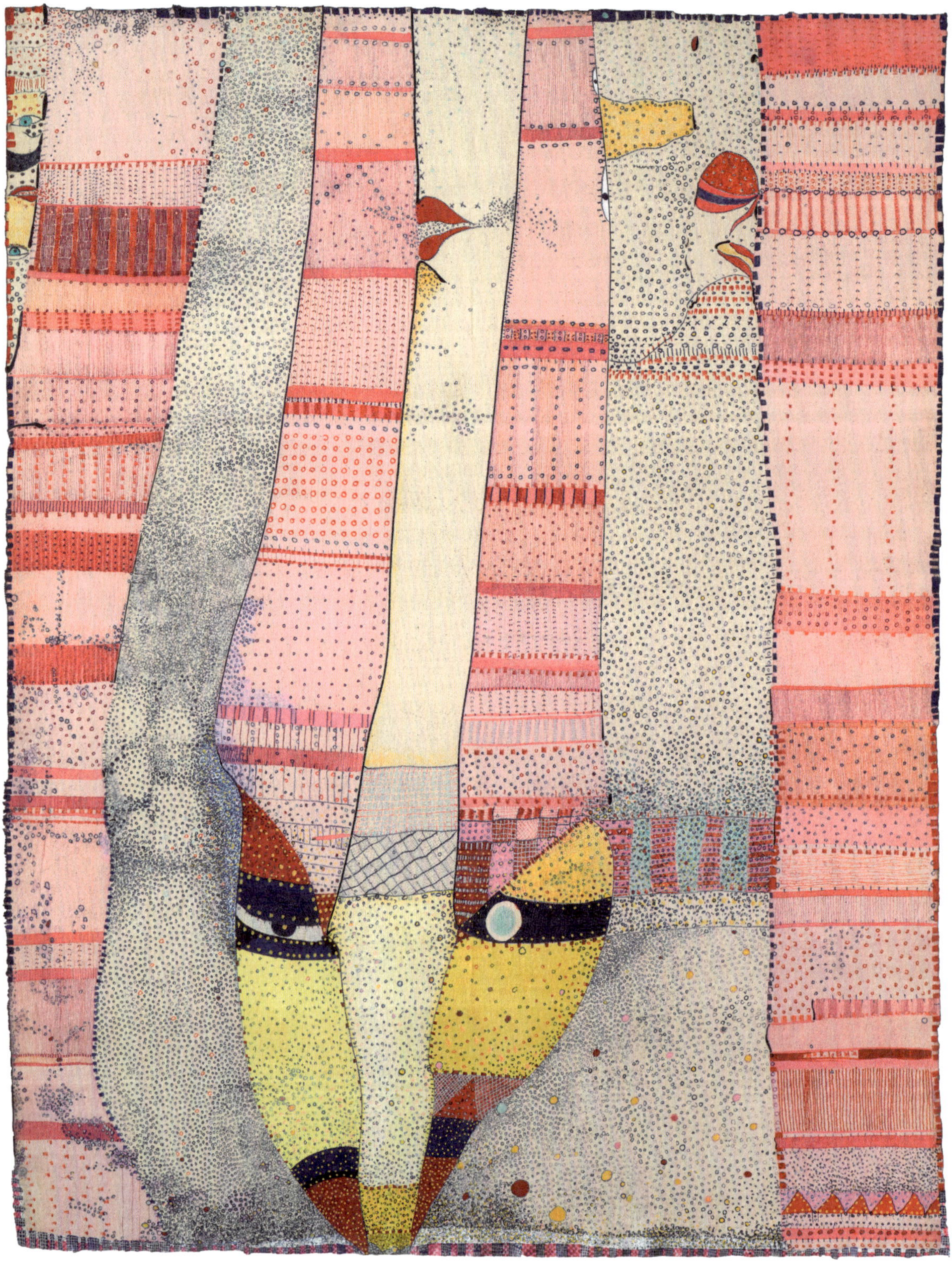

Rossinante Under Cover, 2010
Mixed media on canvas, 132 × 104 cm

Private collection, Dallas, Texas

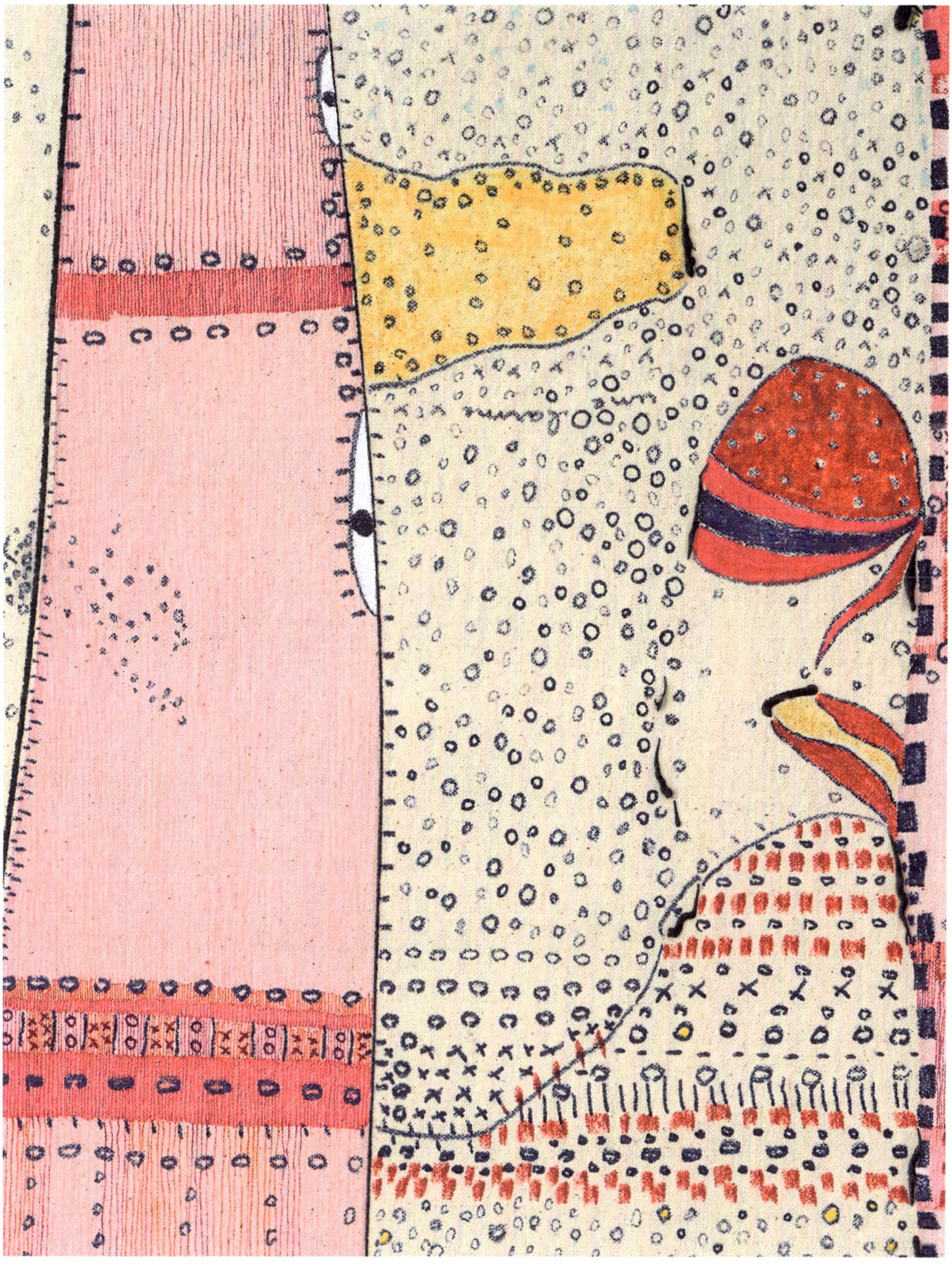

Rossinante Under Cover (detail), 2010
Mixed media on canvas, 132 × 104 cm

Private collection, Dallas, Texas

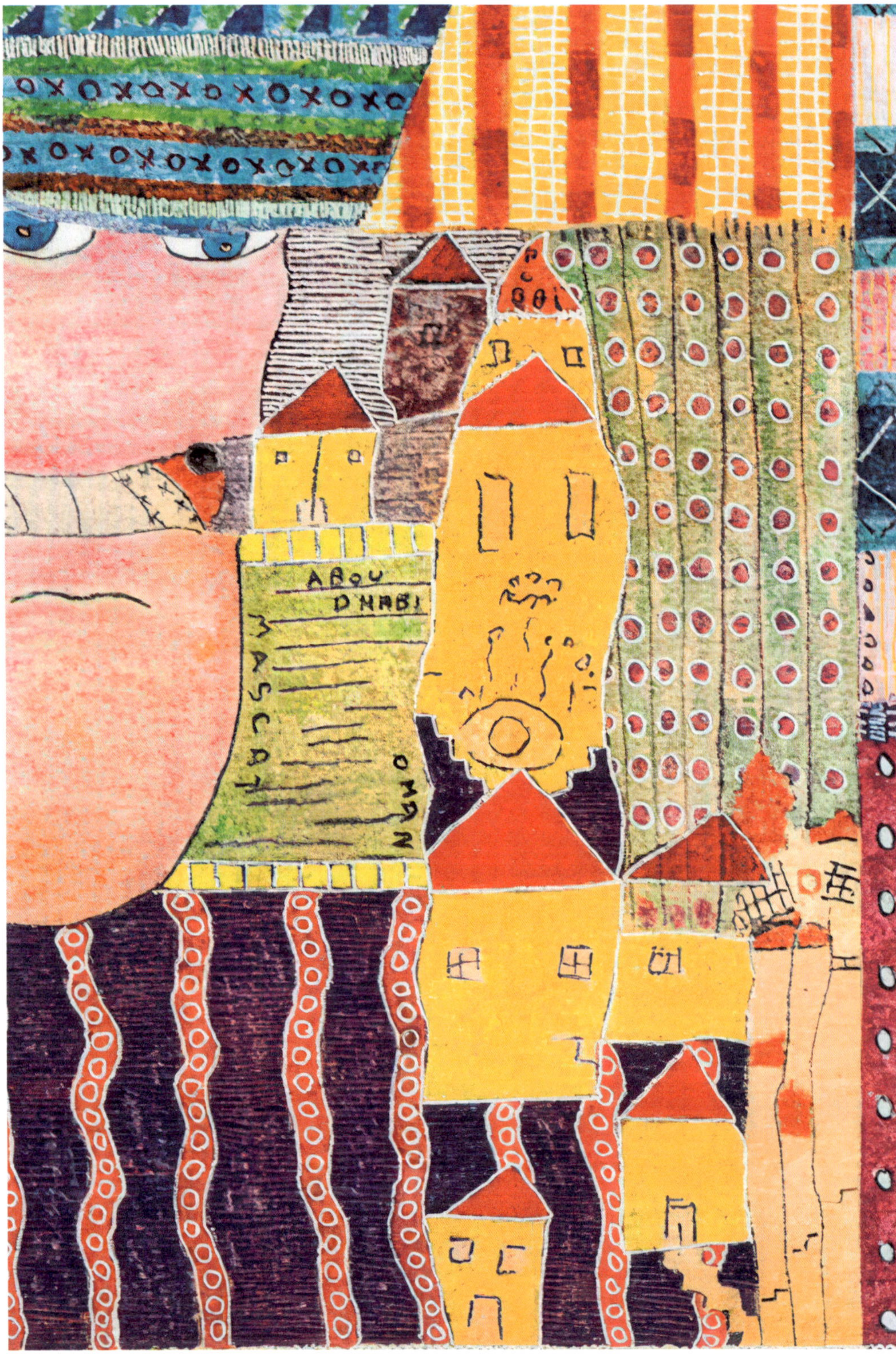

Faces and Places I and II (detail), 2010
Mixed media on canvas, 81 × 288 cm

Private collection, Los Angeles, California

The theme of women—whether veiled or naked, dressed, wearing a hat or not—is a recurrent subject in Caland's work, as seen in *Apple Green and Green Tomato* (2010), a painting she created while sailing in the gulfs of Turkey and completed later that year in her Los Angeles studio (see photos p. 110-113). Approaching eighty years old, the artist was deeply moved by the condition of women around the world, and here she reflects on Iranian women and men. The piece is a vibrant tapestry of colors and symbols, a patchwork of checkerboards and geometric patterns interwoven with softer, organic shapes, including marine and celestial motifs, as well as abstract representations of the human form, scattered across the canvas in varying degrees of visibility. Amidst these elements, faceless black silhouettes of enigmatic women emerge "that offer no intellectual, emotional or sensual hold"[56] as well as mysterious veiled women.[57] The canvas is adorned with recurring motifs such as red-roofed houses, palm trees, flowers, and sailboats, alongside a profusion of symbols like circles, zigzag lines, and cross-stitch patterns—elements Caland frequently used in her work. Scattered across the canvas are short phrases in Arabic, French, and English, many of which are subtle and nearly lost within the composition, some written horizontally, others vertically as Caland folded these large canvases several times to facilitate the work.[58] At first glance, only two words stand out: "Oh!"—an exclamation of surprise, written in black ink on a background of green, yellow, and white that evokes a sunlit spring landscape; green—"... a non-violent and peaceful color"[59]; yellow—often associated by Caland with sulfur and negativity;[60] white— at once the color of purity, innocence, and missing[61] also worn in certain countries for funerals and mourning.

At the bottom of the piece, the word "Santorini" appears on a yellow background, referencing the Greek island and its mythological significance. In a black rectangular area, a few other words written in French and in gold pencil surround an image of a figure hanging from the gallows in the center, drawing the viewer's attention: "Thank you for the gallows, thank you and thank you" (on the left); "Thank you, thank you, and thank you" (on the right). The additional text scattered across the canvas requires time and patience to uncover, inviting the viewer to engage more deeply with the piece.

56 Bensaid and Leloup, *Qui j'aime quand je t'aime ?*, 42.

57 K. Tranberg Hansen, *Anthropology of Dress and Fashion, Bloomsbury Academic*, accessed online June 2023: "The art historian Laura Fair suggests that the recent use of the niqab is more about following a trend than following religious fundamentalist beliefs."

58 *Apple Green and Green Tomato* is 159 × 435 cm and was folded eight times at the beginning of the work process.

59 M. Pastoureau, *Le Petit Livre des couleurs*, (Éditions Panama, Paris, 2005), 64.

60 Ibid., 82.

61 Ibid., 48-49.

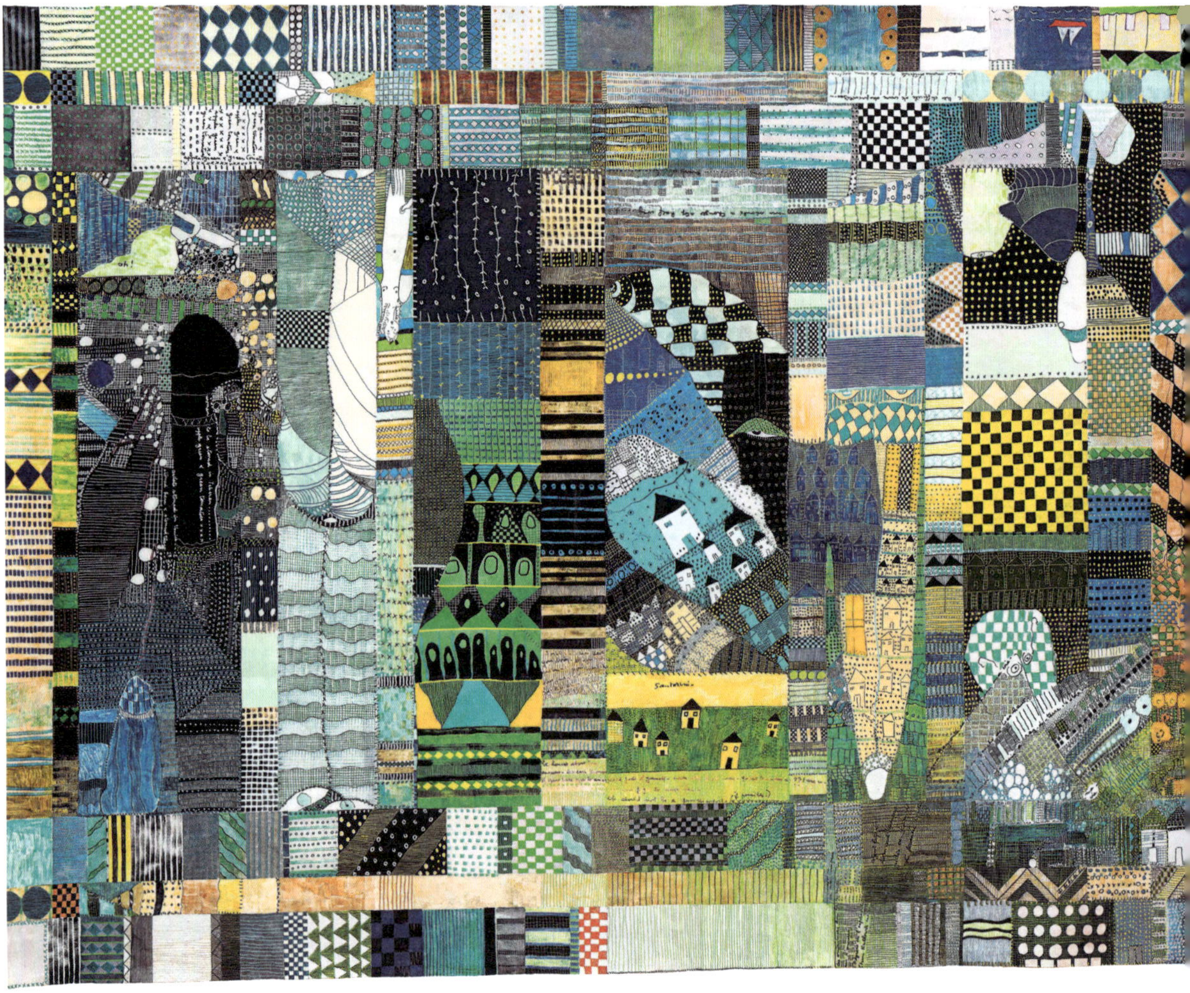

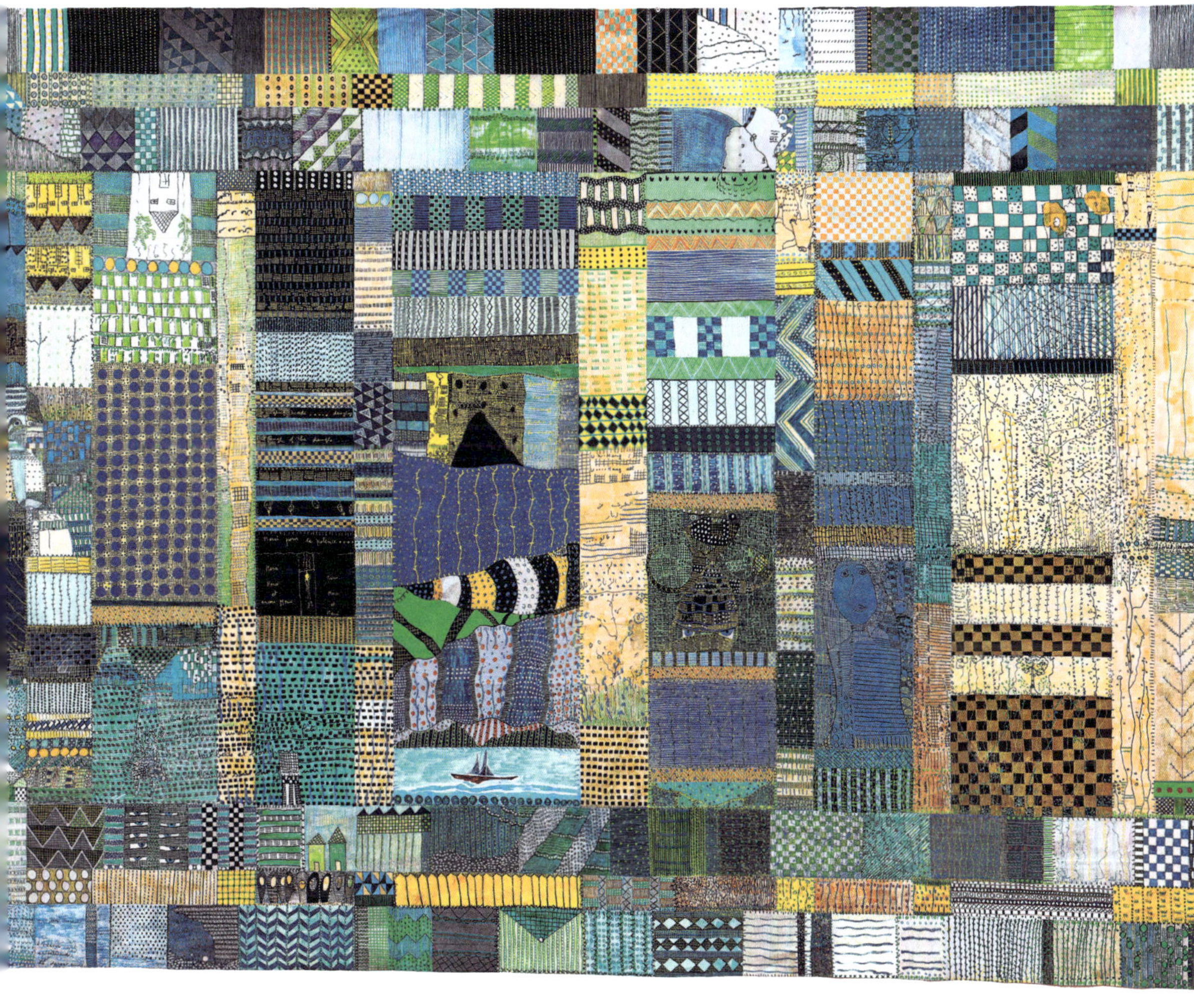

Apple Green and Green Tomato, 2010
Mixed media on canvas, 159 × 435 cm

Private collection, Los Angeles, California

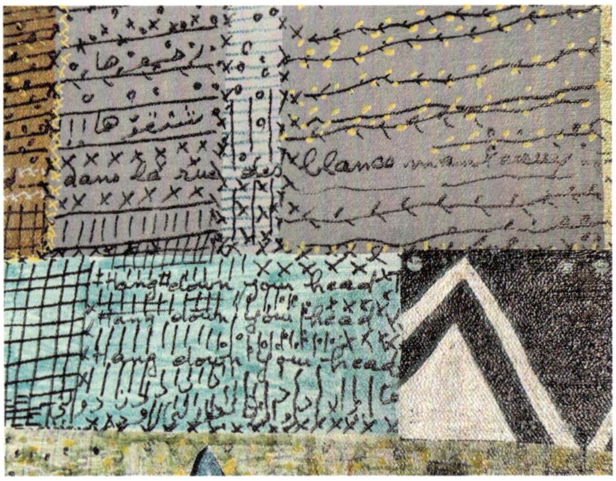
dans la rue
hang down your head
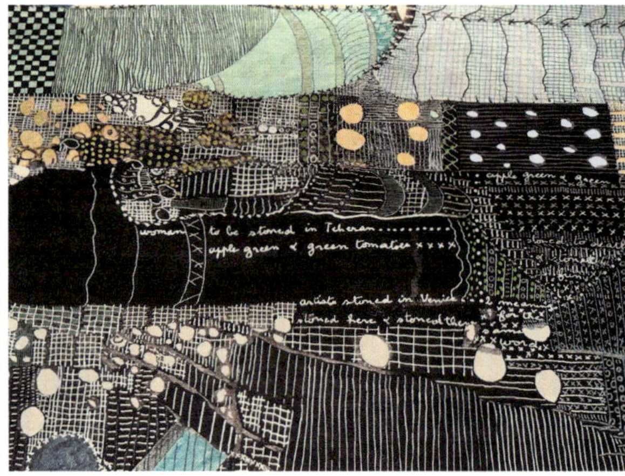
women to be stoned in Teheran
apple green & green tomatoes xxxx
stoned here & stoned there
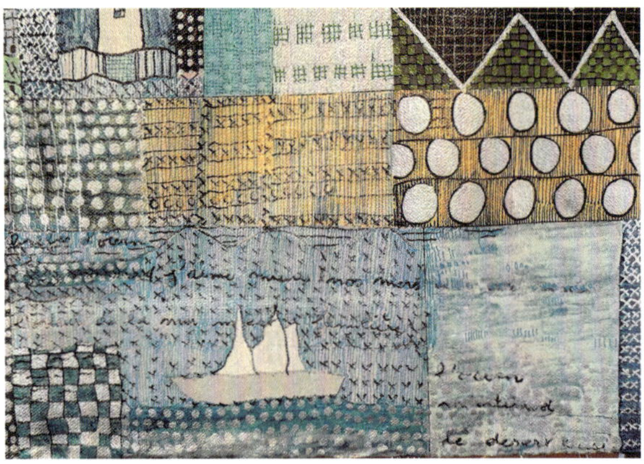
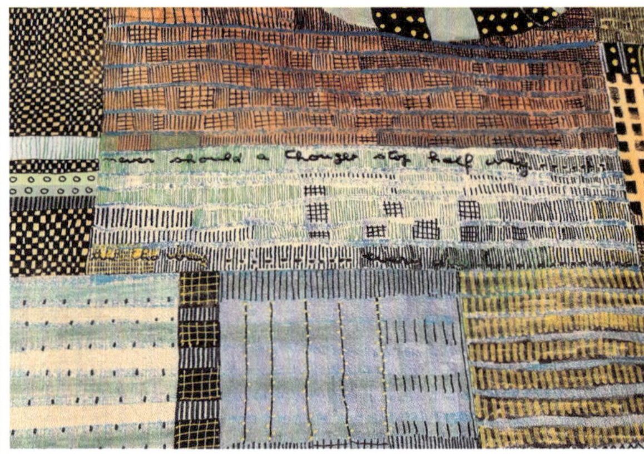
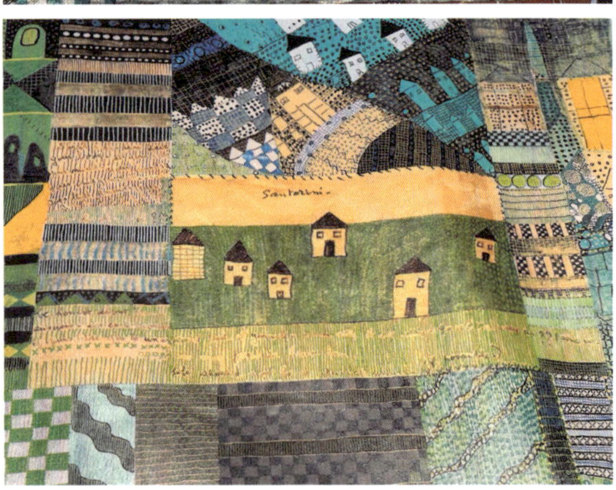
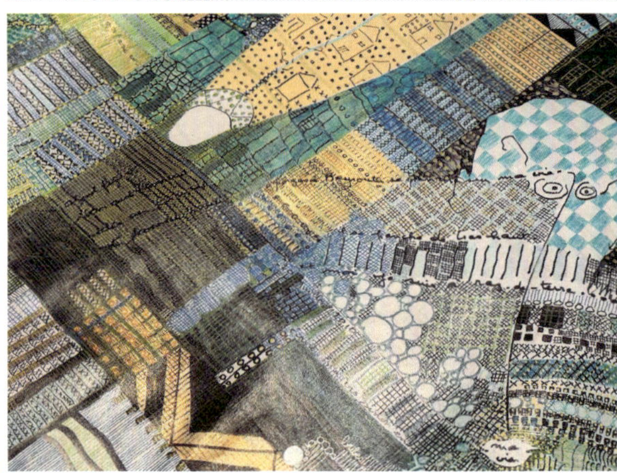

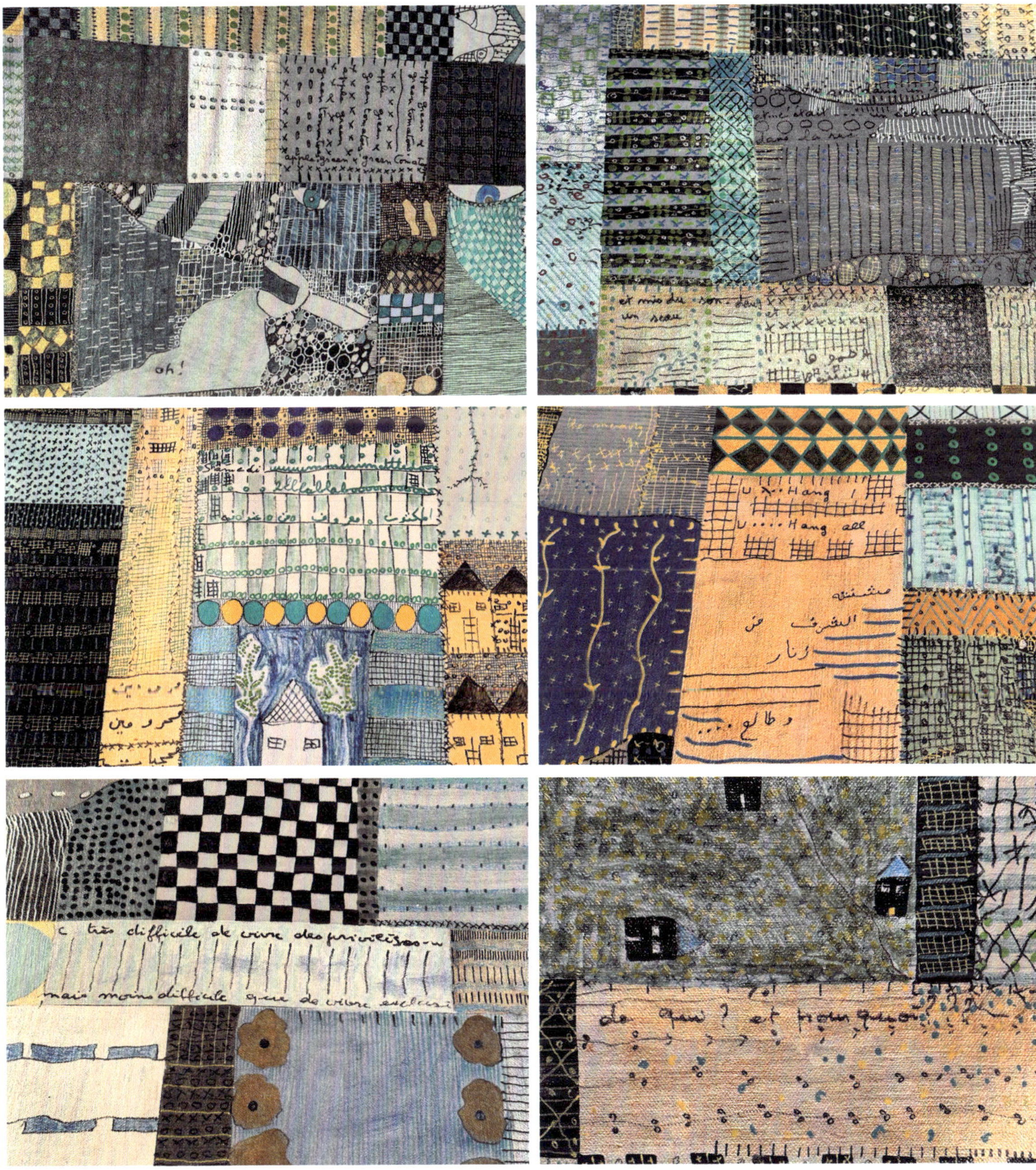

Apple Green and Green Tomato (details), 2010
Mixed media on canvas, 159 × 435 cm

Private collection, Los Angeles, California

This work explores the theme of death. In Iran, women are stoned and men are hanged. Through free association, two popular songs come to Caland's mind—one Anglo-American and the other French: "Hang Down Your Head Tom Dooley" (the title is also transcribed in Arabic a bit further on) and "Dans la rue des Blancs-Manteaux."[62] This chain of associations leads the mind to wander, and from it, the title and its wordplay are born: throwing stones (to stone women) or tomatoes—green tomatoes, green apples, Appleton (the name of her street), the green of her garden—ultimately leading to *Apple Green and Green Tomato.* The title reveals a dissonance between the repetition of a single word "verbal material"[63] and through condensation, associates with it colors, shapes, and substances (two fruits), while also evoking two locations (California and Iran) and the serious subject matter at the heart of the work. A few realistic figurative elements with recognizable forms appear: a boat, the tips of fingers and fingernails, the silhouette of a woman, bare-chested with exposed breasts, and a man hanging from the gallows. Across the canvas, two primary colors—blue and yellow—are accented with green, ochre, and black. There is no central focus; instead, the eye is first drawn to the dense composition on the left side. Defying physical logic, some houses have slanted walls, and the hulls of certain boats are too heavy for their sails. Yet the artist does not concern herself with this. In this infinite multitude of signs, motifs, colors, and lines, there is neither a beginning nor an end. Though it arises from an idea and a movement, the work becomes a territory where a fleeting emotional state is inscribed through the integration of countless visual elements. The canvas appears inert, suspended in time, but the bits of inserted text invite the viewer to take a stroll through its colors and symbols.

L'Indépendance du Liban racontée à L'Or Iman (see photos p. 116-119) is a commission from the Saradar Collection in Beirut, completed by the artist in November-December 2012. It was first exhibited during the artist's retrospective at the Beirut Exhibition Center[64] in January-February 2013. The choice of yellow-orange recalls the artist's words: "Sometimes it feels like you've lived so long. It's like a train rushing forward on rails. I love Venice. I love every minute of my life. I squeeze it like an orange and devour its peel because I don't want to miss anything." It was in Venice, at her California studio, that she created this painting before folding it into her suitcase and taking it to Beirut. The canvas, with burned edges and irregular contours, is slightly less dense than her previous works, and the orange background is almost evanescent in places, particularly on the right side. The left side, from bottom to top, is speckled with red, as is the opposite lower edge. The signs and motifs found on other canvases in the same series appear on this warm, tender canvas covered in earthy and fiery hues: flowers of various colors and sizes, houses with red roofs, checkered patterns, circles, palm trees, and flowering vines... In the square

62 Only song written by the philosopher Jean-Paul Sartre and sung by Juliette Gréco.

63 S. Freud, *Le Mot d'esprit et sa relation à l'inconscient,* (Gallimard, Paris, 1997), 83.

64 Beirut Exhibition Center was a temporary exhibition space, a warehouse with an interior space that could be adapted according to the exhibition. It was located on reclaimed land in the center of Beirut and was built by Solidere. It opened for a few years, hosting numerous themed exhibitions and retrospectives.

on the left edge, three orange flowers on a blue background are surrounded by a field of silver lines that cross and intertwine, rising toward four traditional houses, the red roofs of which are the only visible parts. These houses are concealed by a barrier made of white and brown checkered strips, some in orange, with three different patterns—two of which are bare. Moving upward, circular shapes and sketched outlines of flowers begin to emerge. Some surrounding lines seem hesitant, and a little further on, fields of color appear unfinished, almost empty. Among the checkered patterns and multitude of lines, circles, and dots, a path composed of small, irregular black dots winds its way from bottom to top across the canvas. At the center, toward the right, other shapes evoke the artist's work from the 1980s.[65] Toward the bottom left, a two-story house appears more realistic than in other works. Since the piece narrates the independence of Lebanon, one might assume it represents the presidency of Kantari, with six flower pots in front of the entrance. Those on the right are more prominent than the three nearly invisible ones on the left. Two long and slender palm trees flank the archway, leading to a balcony via a path. On one side of the gateway is a slightly unbalanced sentry box.

The text, which is more or less visible and legible, is scattered across the canvas. Childhood and adolescent memories, both visual and auditory, intertwine with reflections on the present and several monologues addressed to two of her close companions. On the right, a passage recounts her father's arrest on November 11, 1943. Time—nearly seventy years have passed—and the artist's neurological condition have affected her memory. Yet, the words convey the vivid impression of that moment: "chlikht chlakht," the sound of soldiers' boots. One can discern the mosquito net—its red and black edge, shaped like a circus tent, drawn with precision—torn by a French soldier's bayonet (this detail is later concealed as the work progresses). "Clic clac et vlan vlan," when the telephone wires are cut to prevent her mother, who is having her first heart attack, from calling the doctor. These sounds evoke a night of violence, a trauma that remains embedded in the artist's life. At times, the text gets lost amidst the patterns, from which small figures emerge. Elsewhere, only a face protrudes above a line, and among the motifs, one discovers a date and a place: "Villa Savoya, Rome, 1948"—alluding to the car accident she barely survived. A series of surgeries were required to reconstruct her face, jaw, and knee. She would carry the scars of nearly a hundred stitches across her body for the rest of her life. "Time is flatter than a desert," Caland writes in this work, as well as in a text for an exhibition in Beirut in 2006. Is it neurological damage from the accident, or simply a feeling? Is it a whispered confession from the unconscious, where chronological time does not exist?

65 These two paintings are Espace Blanc I and Espace Blanc II.

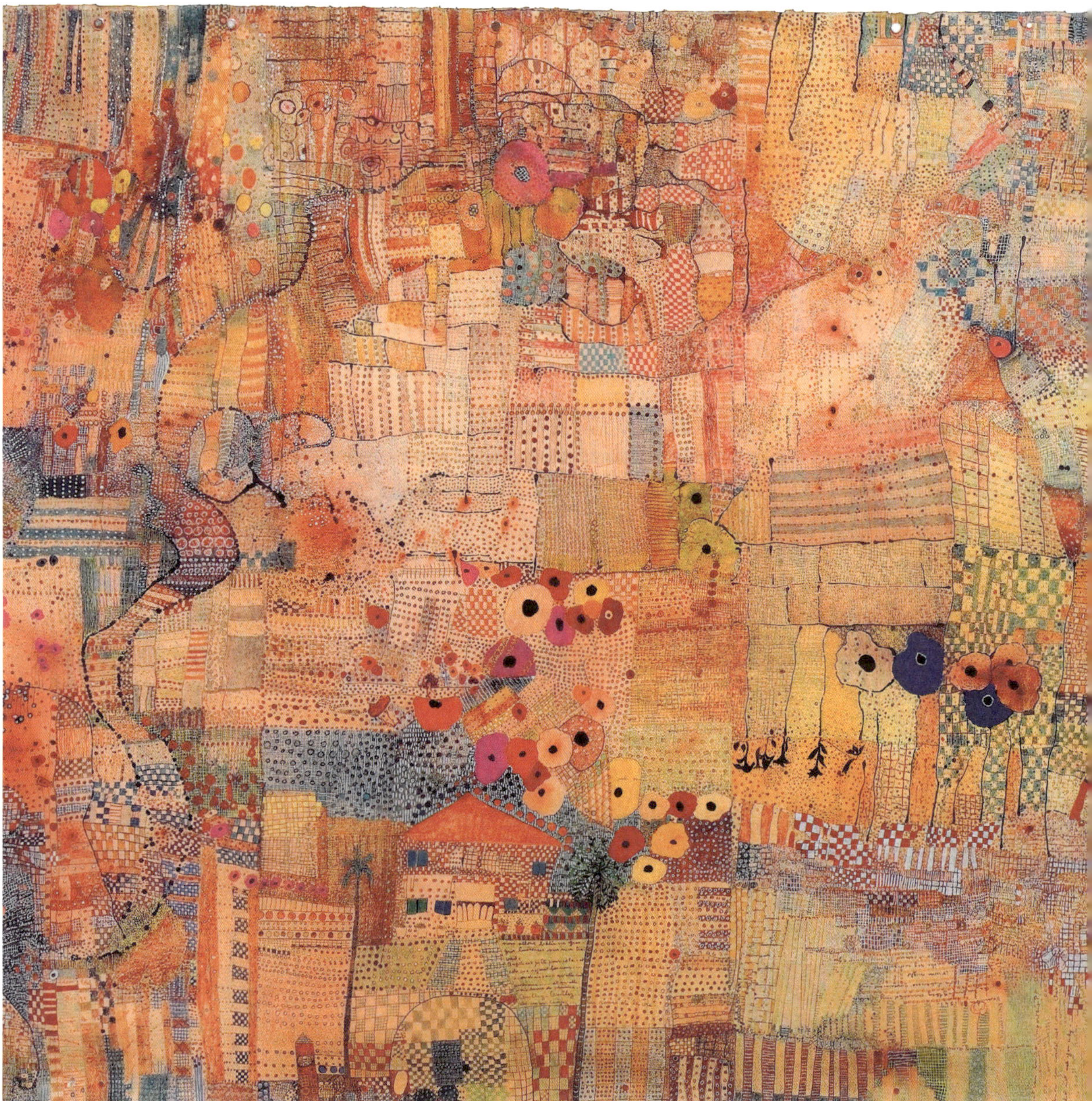

L'Indépendance du Liban racontée à L'Or Iman, 2012
Mixed media on canvas, 163.83 × 408.94 cm

Saradar Collection, Beirut, Lebanon

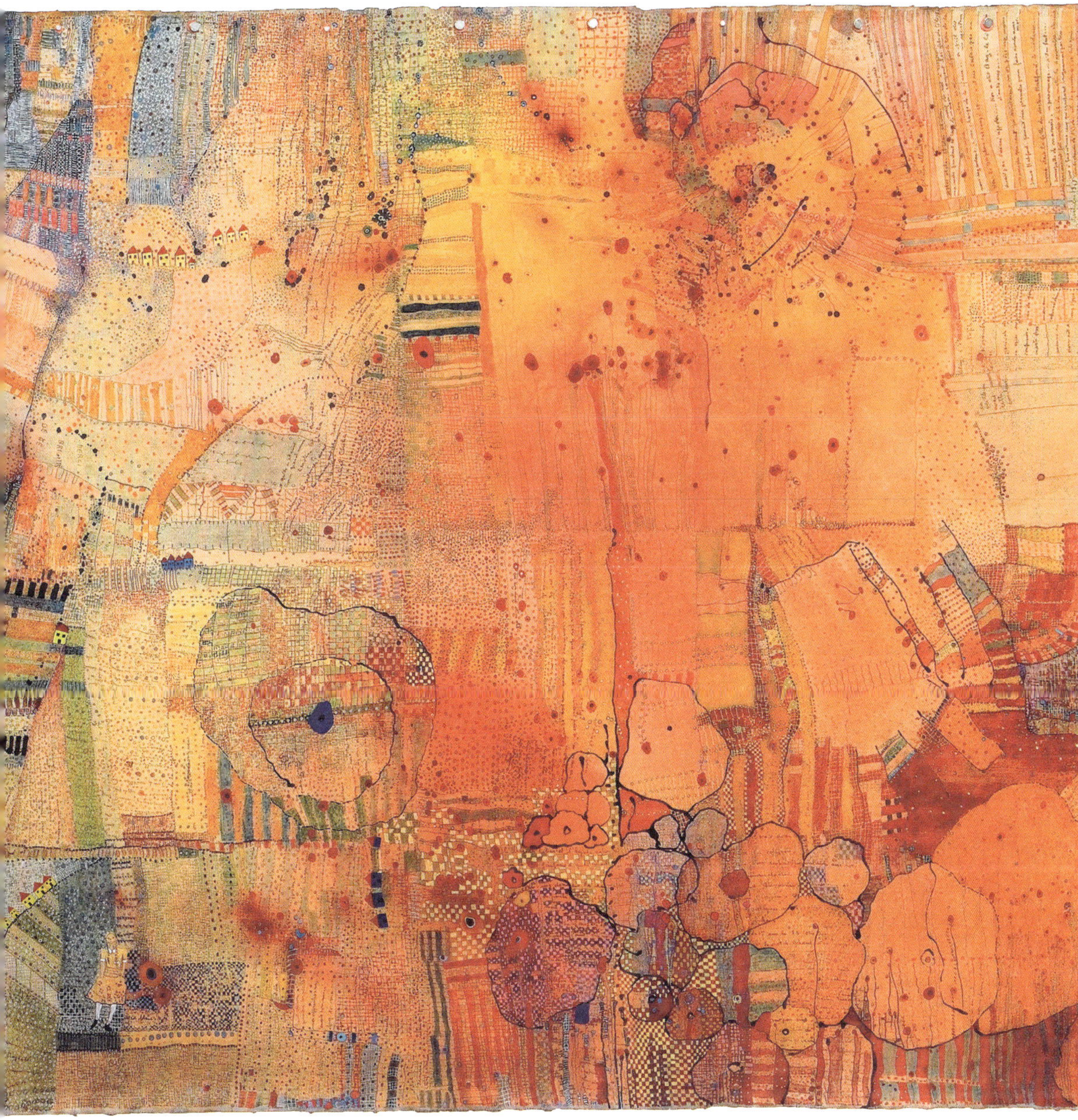

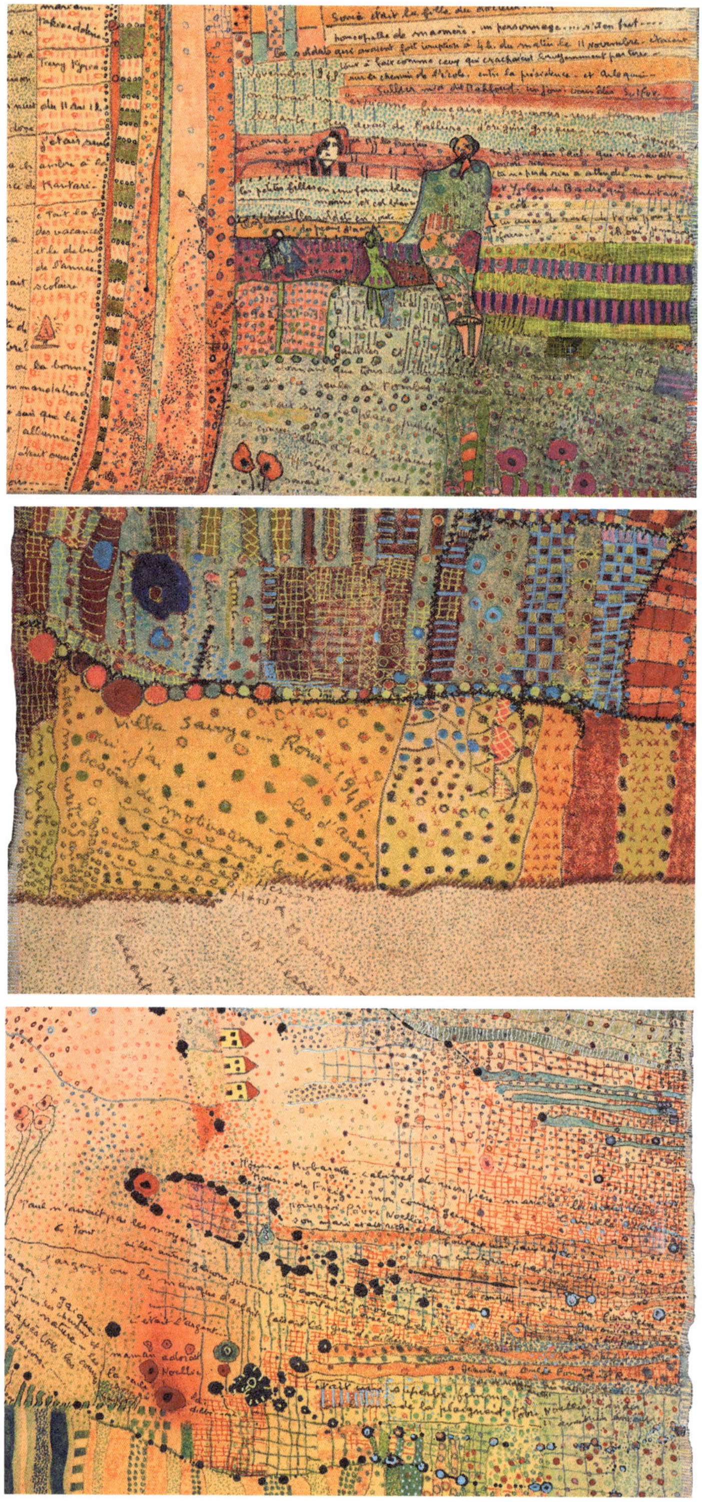

L'Indépendance du Liban racontée à L'Or Iman (details), 2012
Mixed media on canvas, 163.83 × 408.94 cm

Saradar Collection, Beirut, Lebanon

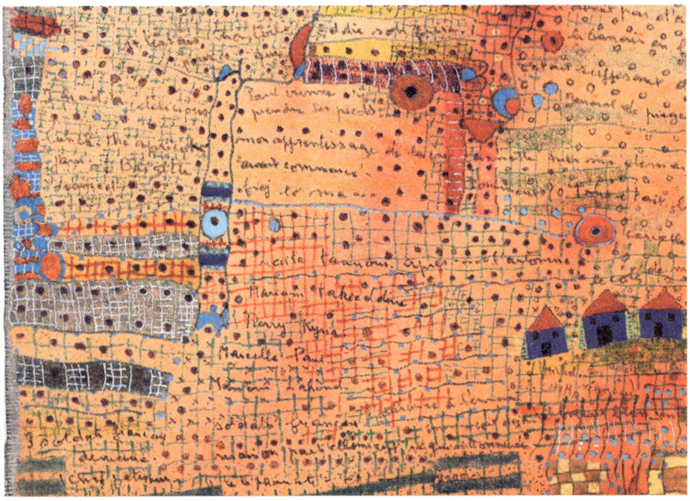

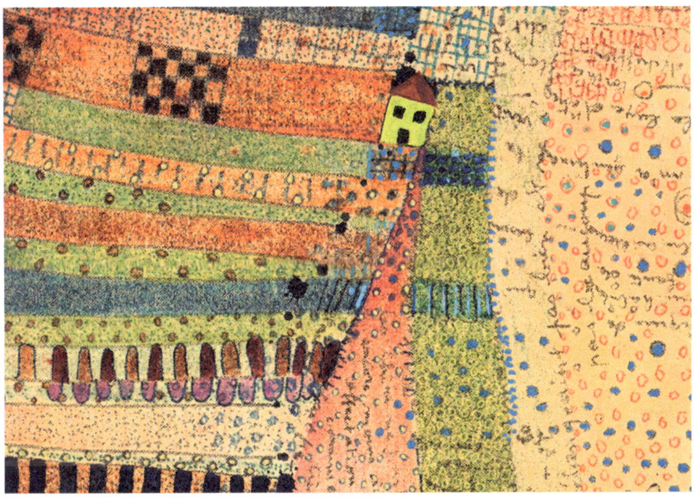

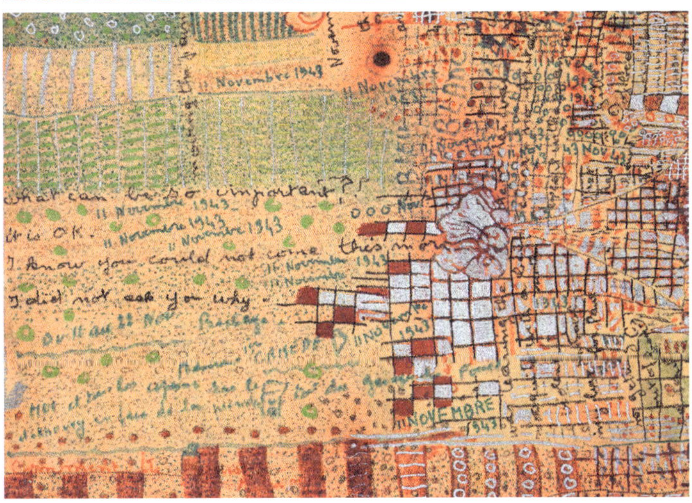

November 1943
What can be so important ?
It is O.K.
11 Novembre 1943
I know you could not come
I did not ask you why.
NOVEMBRE 1943

This is the final canvas completed by the artist. It is striking, yet the overlapping lines and motifs at times appear disordered, with less precision in the lines, flowers that seem only partially sketched, and writing that almost trembles—these are the first noticeable signs of a loss of motor skills. While the text remains largely legible, there are visible signs of cognitive decline: fragmented sentences, disjointed recollections of her childhood, a lack of continuity in thought, spelling mistakes (e.g., "présidente donneur," "مطايب" instead of "مصايب"—though the singular "مُصيبة" appears elsewhere in the text), the recurring date "11 novembre 1943," transposed letters in the word "tour" which becomes "toru," and unfinished sentences such as "... il fait le toru de sa"—all indicative of her cognitive decline. Despite these signs, Paul's presence is still felt. After the retrospective held at the Beirut Exhibition Center in January 2013, Caland returned to Los Angeles. In her California studio, a family member noticed her sitting at her worktable without any pencils, paper, brushes, or canvases (a highly unusual sight) and asked, "Don't you want to work?" Her simple reply was, "I feel empty." This emptiness is also reflected in two unfinished canvases containing writing (see photos p. 121). In the first of these unfinished works, against a blue background where the sky and sea seem to merge, the painting offers a journey from birth to death—linking water, an essential element of life, to a mythical celestial paradise. Slightly darker at the top left, a pale pink and translucent mauve wash runs down through the center to the bottom. The edges of the canvas are framed by small bright blue strokes made with a flat-tipped brush, resembling the rampart walkway and crenellations of a fortress.

The canvas is divided into two zones: the lower part, completed by the artist, features a face with two eyes, one of which is outlined, and a protrusion from which a line of small circles radiates toward the right edge of the painting. The upper part, however, appears to be drawn by a child, who clumsily writes "Happy birthday" vertically down the center.

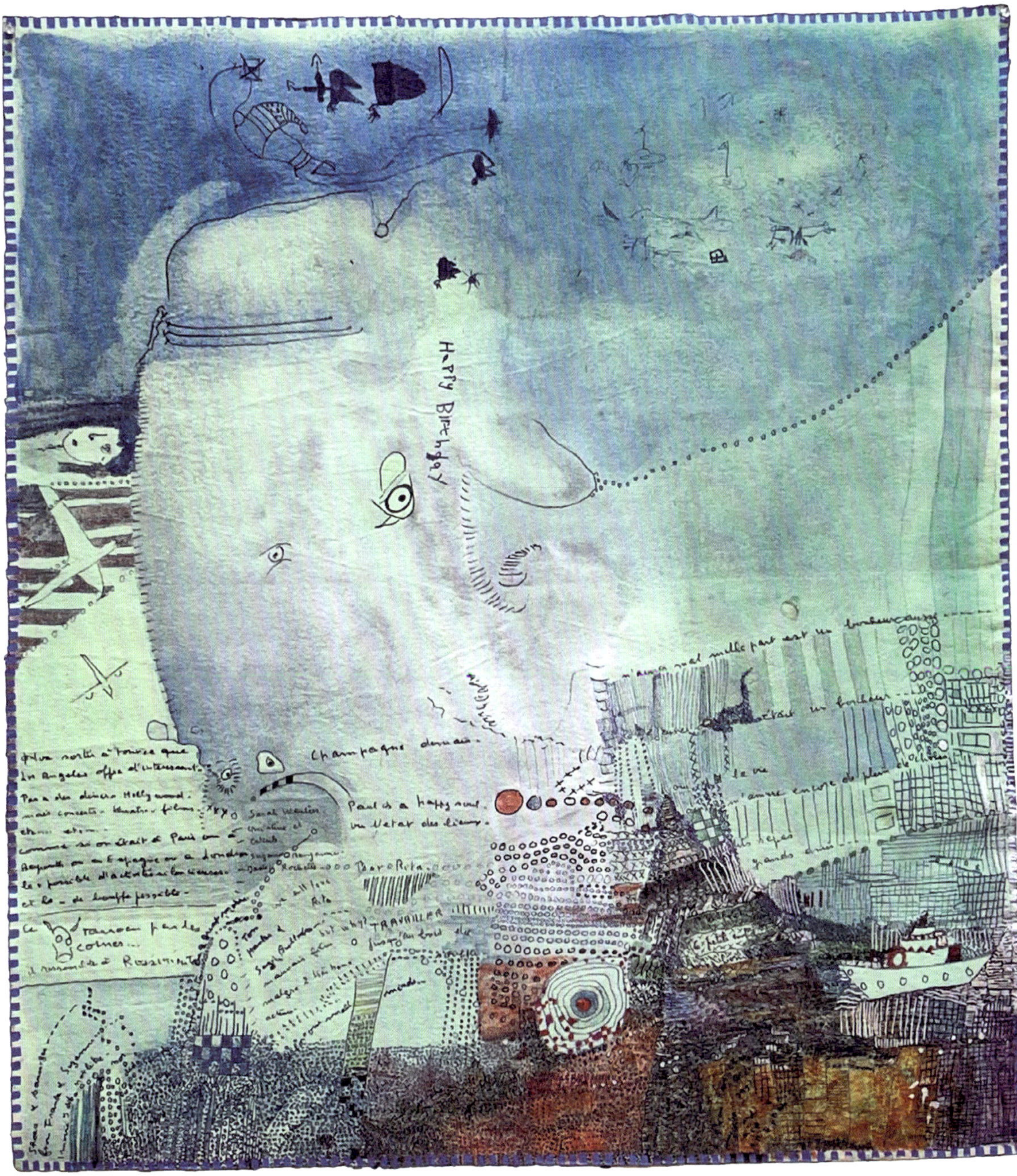

Untitled (Happy Birthday, unfinished*)*, 2012-2013
Mixed media on canvas, 102.6 × 92.5 cm

Private collection, Los Angeles, California

To the left, Caland depicts a child with a partially visible face; his left eye is open and looks straight ahead, while the other side of his face is obscured by a few lines of blue dots. Next to him are two airplanes—an unusual motif in the artist's work. One of the planes is distorted, while the other dives toward the text, most of which remains legible, with only a few phrases hidden beneath other signs. On the right side, a cruise ship floats. Near the ship's bow, concentric circles are drawn around a red dot encircled by navy blue, their widening diameters evoking the eye of a cyclone, indicating the direction in which the ship is heading. The canvas is enigmatic, partly because of the child-like drawings and clumsy handwriting, but also due to the sense of emptiness: the lines are less defined, the bands unfinished, and the shapes indistinct. In some areas, the signs and motifs resemble mere doodles[66]—scribbles made to pass the time. The work conveys both hesitation and compulsion. "WORK IIIII until my last breath," writes the artist, holding on to the act of creation, summoning her final reserves of strength to continue.

In the second work (see p. 124-125), the rounded top of a balding skull stretches out on either side, resembling an aerial or frontal topography. One eye is open, the other closed—does it represent a refusal to see? A wavering between life and death? On the left, the shimmer of silver and the lightness of flowers climb upward, surrounded by gray bubbles, soaring into the sky. On the right, the scene darkens with an aerial view in gray, where a phone number—9023286—appears. At the base of the skull, at the bottom of the canvas, a hill follows the skull's curve, filled with lines, bands, and motifs. The left side is greyer, with small squares reminiscent of aligned windows on buildings. The center is brighter, featuring the colors yellow, beige, and green, with bubble-like circles in matching colors that appear to float. In this painting, the lines—whether straight or wavy—are hesitant, sometimes left unfinished. The accumulation of signs and motifs gives the impression of uncontrolled doodling. Toward the bottom center, the text describing the figure is particularly striking because it is written bottom to top.[67] It returns to the important men in her life, starting with Paul. If the figure is not one of them, then who is this hybrid, unreal character, from whom a few bubbles escape, bridging the earth and the sky? Unable to complete the work—did the artist sense her neurological issues?[68] She writes in reverse. Across three lines on a uniform blue background, she expresses her fear of death and decay. Three pillars—some red, others blue—support the phrase *ma terreur* (my terror), with the last

66 R. Wilhite quoted in A. Moshayedi, H. Walker, "Sandy Lajer, Ed Moses and Robert Wilhite in conversation with Aram Moshayedi" in *Made in L.A.* 2016, A, The, Though, Only, catalog. On page 43: "I remember seeing some of her first works and thinking, 'These are doodles.' And yet they were doodles that became an aesthetic, a vocabulary, that enabled her to talk about a lot of different issues..."

67 Written in French: "Ce n'est pas Paul, Apostu M et ce n'est pas Pierre, [not legible] mon père aussi papa, Ou encore Apostu Occillo-coccinum Pas non + moustafa." [It is not Paul, Apostu, M and it is not Pierre [not legible] my father also dad, or even Apostu Occillo-coccinum. Nor is it Mustafa.]

68 "Huguette was affected by hydrocephalus, an excess of water in the brain's ventricles. This condition first impacted her motor functions, then her cognitive functions. It caused poor coordination of her movements, gradually preventing her from holding a paintbrush or pencil, and walking. It also affected her concentration, language, and memory. Her condition developed slowly over several years until it prevented her from communicating clearly." This is the diagnosis of the neurologist who followed and treated Caland during the last six years of her life.

two words of the sentence, *de mourir* (of dying), floating alone in the void.[69] A little higher on the canvas, written with a grey pen on a grey background, are the words: *peur de la mort* (fear of death) and *la mort après la vie* (death after life).[70] In this piece, she conveys her anguish—first in French, then later in English. Caland, whose writing was once fluid and concise, now struggles with French syntax, and the translation into English is less precise.

In July 2013, she returns to Lebanon to say goodbye to Paul, who dies a few days after her arrival. Two weeks later, she is admitted to the hospital to treat an infection. While sitting in her hospital bed, waiting for a young intern to succeed in performing a lumbar puncture, she—though unable to hold a pencil in her fingers for months—manages to write the name of her physician. And, as if in a cry she can no longer contain, she spells out the name in capital letters and, in a compulsive motion just below, scribbles a black mass made of doodles. This evocation of pubic hair, accompanied by the doctor's name, becomes her final "work." A drawing and a few uppercase letters—a desperate last attempt at dual communication (see photo p. 127). Throughout her life and career, Caland expressed what she felt with great profusion. Yet what she frequently practiced was the concealment of what she wrote—a process in which she drowned words in a vast ensemble of visual elements so they become lost, or covered elsewhere with signs, motifs, or paint. The following chapter addresses how this practice of concealment evolves into silence and abstraction.

69 Written in French: "Lettres à moi-même et ma terreur de mourir – Pas de mourir – mais de décrépir – ce que je suis en train de lutter contre." [Letters to myself and my terror of dying – Not dying – but decaying – what I am struggling against.]

70 "afraid of death" "death after life."

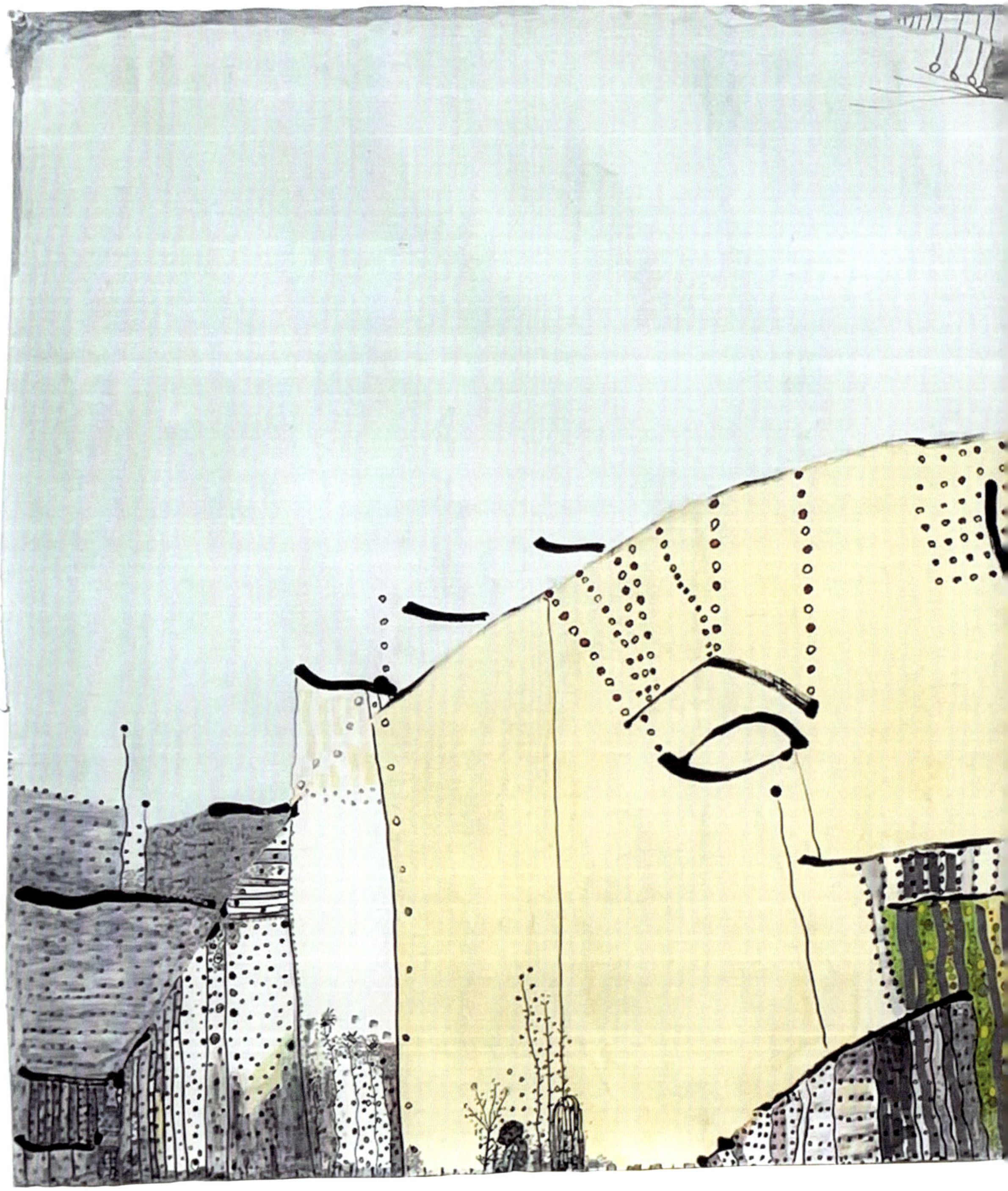

Untitled (unfinished), 2012-2013
Mixed media on canvas, 76.4 × 144.3 cm

Private collection, Los Angeles, California

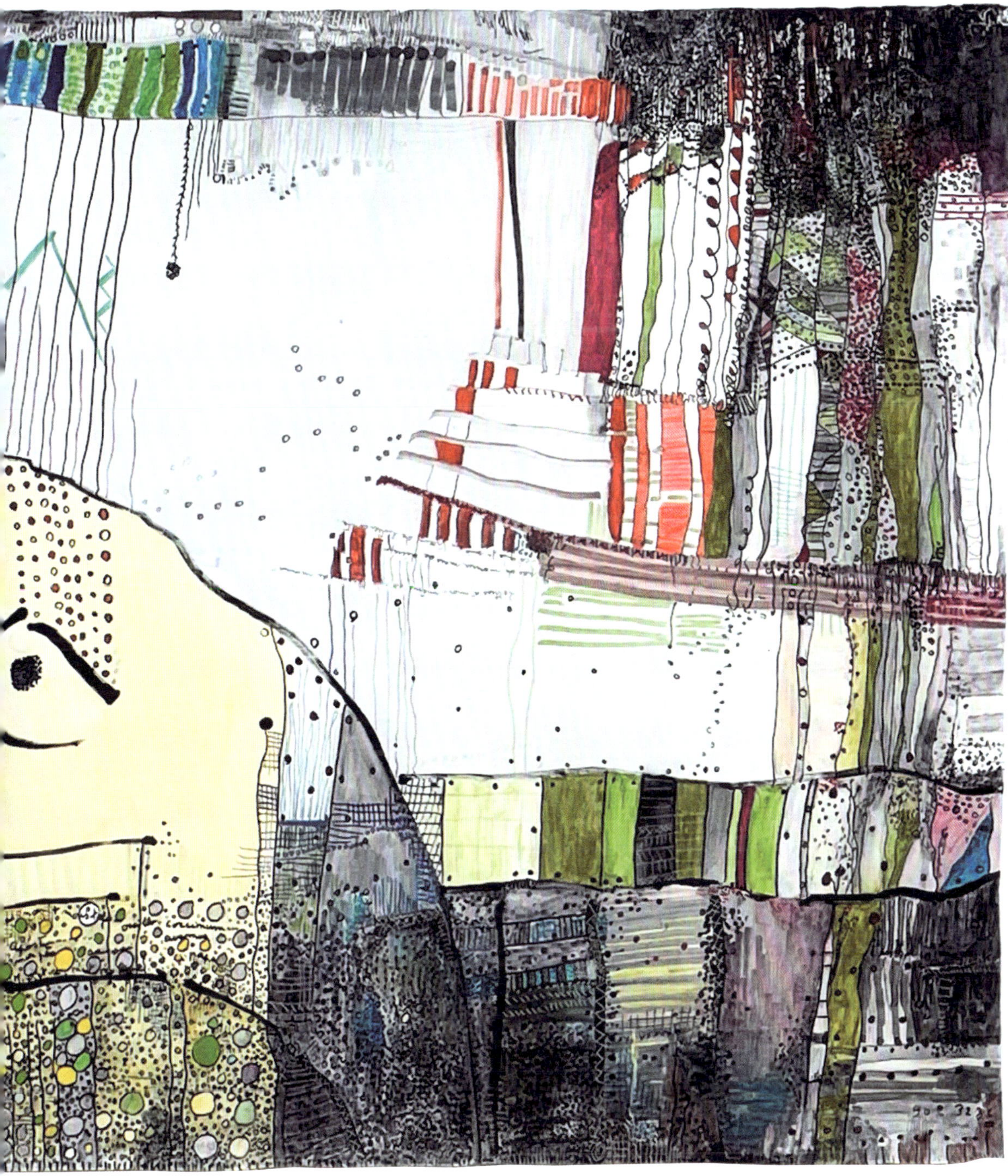

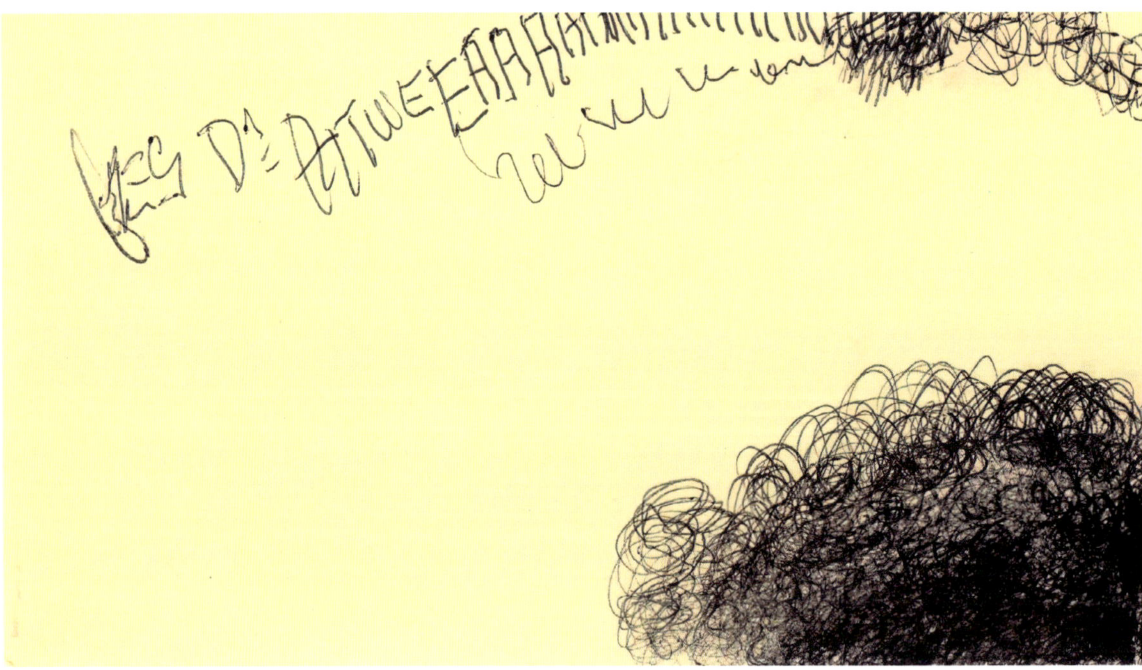

Dr Atweh, July 2013
Ink on paper, 10 × 13 cm

Private collection, Los Angeles, California

FROM CONCEALMENT TO THE UNSPOKEN

In the early 1990s, Caland, who had settled in California, began to regularly incorporate writing into her works—whether drawings, paintings, or smocks—and experimented with the opacity and transparency of text. This process of spoken and unspoken communication evolved alongside her collages, becoming more complex and abstract in the *Silent Letters* series.

The Collages

In art, the term "collage" refers to the process of cutting, pasting, and assembling various elements to create new compositions. It became "one of the dominant aesthetic processes of twentieth-century art,"[71] pioneered by artists such as Picasso and Braque, who incorporated different materials—like rope, newspaper, and wallpaper—into their works. The Dadaists and surrealists also embraced this technique. Art historian Kobena Mercer notes that "collage functions as a radical twentieth-century practice that upends traditional forms (painting, photography, sculpture, etc.) to create a distinct new form,"[72] a technique that artists like Robert Motherwell, Robert Rauschenberg, and others continued to use throughout their careers.

Caland's exploration of collage began with a personal chapter—an epistolary relationship with her lover Moustafa, which lasted nearly twenty years. In 1991, as the Lebanese Civil War was drawing to a close, a friend passing through Los Angeles delivered a package of letters. These letters, written by Caland to Moustafa in the 1960s and 1970s, had been entrusted to her during a visit Moustafa made to Paris after the war broke out in 1975. The letters, returned to Caland years later, symbolically reactivated and closed an important chapter in her life. Instead of succumbing to nostalgia, the artist chose to recycle them as part of her creative process. In a moment of vulnerability, she transformed these fragments of the past into works of art. In her Venice studio, she tore up the letters, integrating them into the series she created between 1991 and 1992—first in California, then in Paris, before returning to Venice.

71 H. Molesworth, *Leap Before you Look, Black Mountain College*, 1933-1957, (ICA/Boston and Yale University Press, 2015) 57.
72 Ibid.

An examination of the artist's archives reveals a significant collection of collages,[73] which can be categorized into four distinct series: the *Miscellaneous Collages* (1991–1992), where letters—either folded or laid flat—disappear entirely or almost entirely beneath the paint; *Self-Portraits*; *L'argent ne fait pas le bonheur mais il y contribue largement* [74] [Money (Doesn't Bring Happiness, but It Sure Helps)] (1994); and the *Nude Letters* series (2000), which includes five works in varying formats: *Lettres à Moustafa*, *Nude Letters*, and three untitled works (*Untitled I, II, III*), where the letters are cut and pasted in a more raw manner, with minimal added drawings or colors (apart from those already present on the letterhead paper itself).

These recycled letters are written on a range of substrates: fine paper in blue, white, and cream; organic brown paper; or Kaslik letterhead, which had a printed photograph of the property and its address on it. Over time, as the ink fades, some letters have become nearly illegible, leaving behind only traces of the text. In other cases, the text remains partially visible, revealing certain passages. The artist plays with the transparency and opacity of the text, depending on the treatment of each piece. In addition to the old letters, which are often camouflaged when glued onto paper or canvas, the works incorporate pictorial elements and "contemporary" writing, some of which are also partially obscured, transforming the entire composition into a kind of palimpsest. These intricate works, which tell a story within a story,[75] shift from concealment to the unspoken, allowing us to catch glimpses of the past, while also offering insight into the process behind their creation.

In *Ceci est un talisman* (see photo p.130), the Canson paper that forms the base of the piece has slight creases in places. Three—a magic number[76]—fragments of letters, cut into rectangles and glued together, create an abstract anthropomorphic shape—resembling a totem pole, and also evoking an aerial view of a tank. The angular shapes, lacking roundness, are softened by the blend of gold, bronze, gray, and pink hues, which give the work a radiant glow.

73 The data for the "catalogue raisonné" or index of artworks is being gathered, but the numbers of collages are not defined yet.

74 The self-portraits (1991–1992) in which letters are cut, pasted, rolled, and often enhanced with color, as well as the series on *Money (Doesn't Bring Happiness, but It Sure Helps)* (1994), are not addressed in this publication because they are so monumental that they will be published separately at a later date.

75 Y. Reuter, *L'Analyse du récit*, (Armand Colin, Paris, 2009), On page 59: "The term mise en abyme refers to the fact that a textual passage either reflects more or less faithfully the composition of the entire story or reveals, more or less explicitly, the techniques used to construct and tell the story." T. Todorov, *Poétique de la prose*, (Le Seuil, Paris, 1978), On page 37: "A secondary story is embedded within the primary one; this technique is called embedding."

76 R. Allendy, *Le Symbolisme des nombres, Essai d'arithmosophie*, (Charconarc, Paris, 1943), 65; Among the examples cited: "It is more interesting to seek the Ternary in the Mythology or Philosophy of peoples. Among the Indians, one can mention the three worlds: earth, atmosphere, and sky, the three sacred letters A.U.M, forming the sacred syllable, 'one and indivisible'"; "the three gunas or qualities of the active nature: Truth, Instinct, Darkness...". Among the Celts, "these are the three cycles of the soul: Anouf (material cycle), Abred (cycle of atonement), and Gwynfid (cycle of bliss)"; "There are references to the Ternary in many passages of the scriptures. The three times correspond to the trilogy of Creation, the Flood, and Redemption, showing the three traditional principles: creator, destroyer, and conserver, in action in nature."

The recycled letters, with only their edges glued, remain legible despite some fading of the ink. As the paper is reversed, a mirror is required to decipher a few words through the fine beige surface. However, following an idea or sentence is often a frustrating process, as the work must be turned in various directions—sometimes in vain.

In the text written during the creation of the artwork and then applied to the collage, the artist addresses unnamed friends—"my dear all"—to express how much they mean to her. She takes pleasure in filling the empty space of the paper, relishing the opportunity to *bêtiser* (a word she invents in French, which means "to act foolishly") "without drugs or acid, without mushrooms or alcohol, without amphetamines." She enjoys this playful verb and, through a series of associations and wordplay, drifts between past and present: "If dream interpretation is the royal road to the unconscious, it's the dreamer's free associations that allow the gradual discovery of its deepest springs."[77] She writes for her own pleasure, breaking the rules, liberating herself from her bourgeois background and American puritanism.[78] Among the words, we find lines from La Fontaine's fable *La Cigale et la Fourmi*: "The cicada, having sung all summer, found herself very deprived when the cold wind came," followed by her own comment: "si si"—like a confirmation; a return to childhood, a reflection on existential questions as an artist, and meaningful remarks on her current life. She mentions two artists' exhibitions as she struggles to gain visibility, as well as sharing news of a recent commission: "Moses is exhibiting at Louver NY, Seta is exhibiting at Sherry Fremkin's (sic)... Euva has returned from Mexico to New York, I'm religiously preparing to do Joan A. Quinn's portrait..."[79]

77 S. Tomasella, *Les Amours impossibles, accepter d'aimer et d'être aimé,* (Eyrolles, Paris, 2012), 32.

78 Huguette Caland, extract of the collage text for *Ceci est un talisman*: "lévitation, ambition, lévitation... famille, buanderie bien sûr parce qu'on lave son linge sale en famille" and "il faut conjuguer le verbe aimer – le verbe baiser – le verbe rire ou bien le verbe pleurer – le verbe s'est fait chair." [*This is a Talisman*: "Levitation, ambition, levitation... family, laundry room of course because one washes one's family's dirty laundry" and "One must conjugate the verb to love – the verb to fuck – the verb to laugh or the verb to cry – the verb has become flesh."]

79 Joan Quinn had her portrait done by major Southern California artists. Huguette Caland did two of them for her.

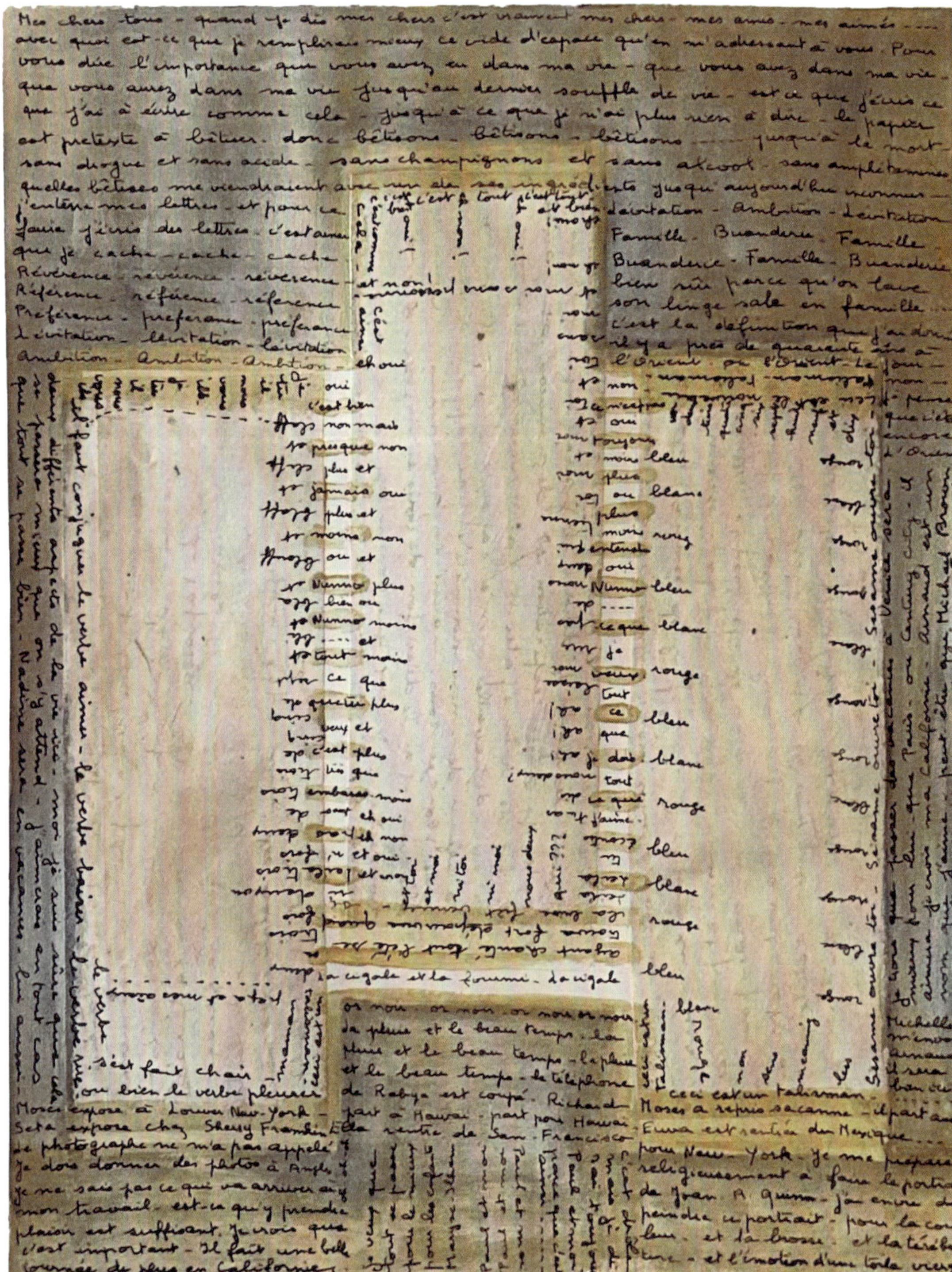

Ceci est un talisman, 1992
Mixed media on paper, 32.4 × 24.8 cm

Private collection, Los Angeles, California

We also encounter a magical phrase repeated three times, emphasizing its importance: "Open sesame, open sesame, open sesame, one two three four five six seven eight nine ten, this is the new talisman talisman." It evokes *One Thousand and One Nights*, granting access to a mysterious cavern that symbolizes the unconscious—a cryptic interplay between past and present, the conscious and the unconscious. At the bottom of the collage,[80] in a vertically written text, Paul is mentioned repeatedly.

The second collage, *Ma prison intérieure – My Interior Prison* (see photo p. 132), features a letter written in Paris twenty years earlier. The letter, which is largely illegible, is pasted onto Canson paper, which frames it, extending about 4 cm around the edges. The letter's thick paper appears to have been gently dampened in places, as though treated to alter its texture, to crease it, or slightly roll it; the right and bottom edges undulate slightly. Black bars contrast with the golden-pink hue of the underlying page, and the horizontal bar of this "inner prison" rests on a fold, running through the center of the work. A wash of black ink marks the upper edge, blending into the pink, which appears almost transparent. A more pronounced, centered black line marks the lower edge. A thin, curved line zigzags across much of the right side, narrowing at the bottom, where it floats above the black line. The writing is concentrated around the initial letter, with white text on black and black text on the rest of the work.

80 "Paul et moi Paul et moi [et en sens inverse le texte continue] Paul et moi c'est drôle mais je dirai toujours Paul et moi parce que c'est ainsi." [Paul and I, Paul and I [and in reverse, the text continues] Paul and I, it's funny but I will always say Paul and I because that's how it is.]

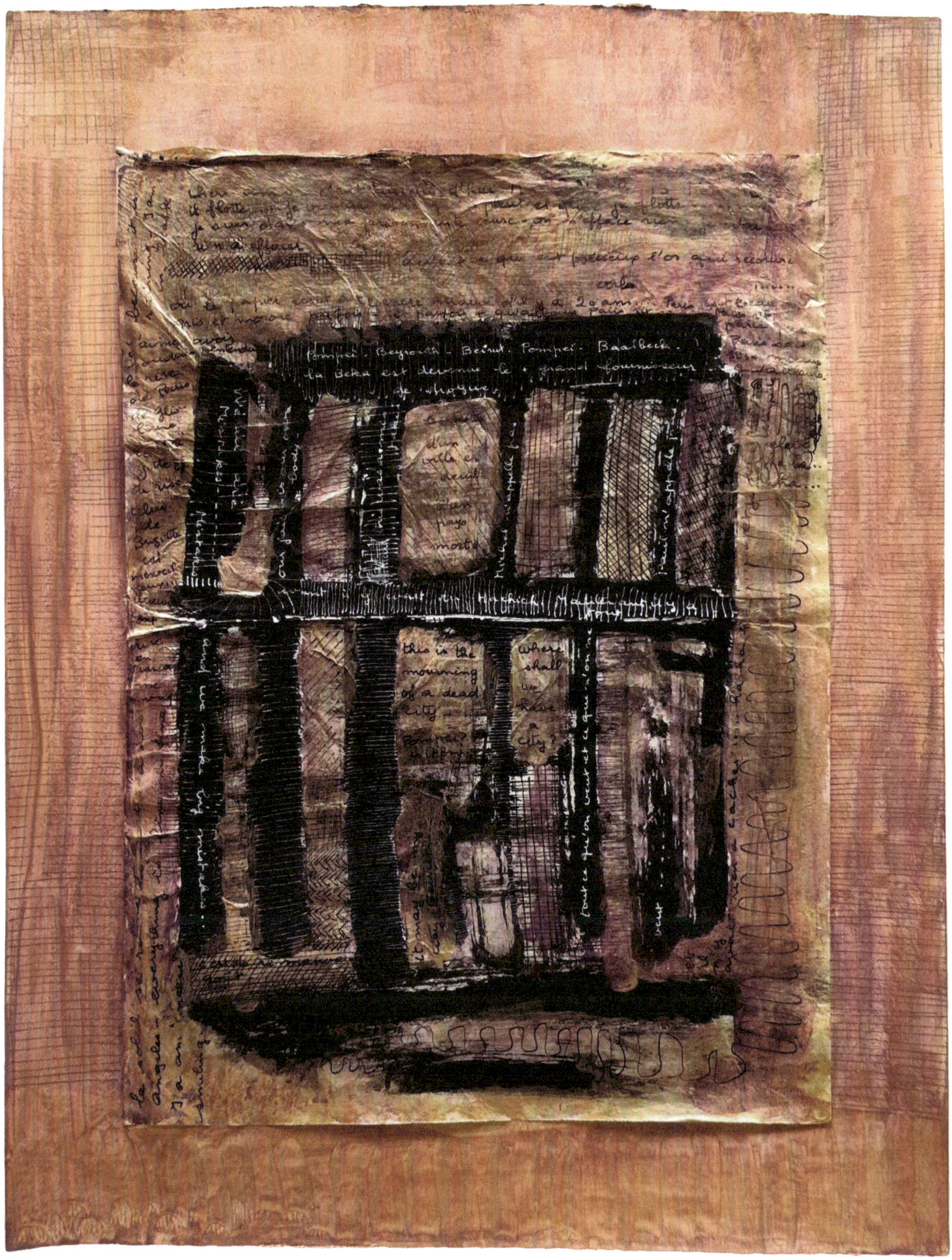

Ma prison, 1992
Mixed media on paper, 32.4 × 24.8 cm

Private collection, Los Angeles, California

The purple ink used in the original letter seems to justify the use of pink, deepened by black in the collage. The contrasting colors shift between matte and shiny, between clouds and sunlight. Behind the bars of her "inner prison"—her own body and the discomfort she's experiencing—she creates a bilingual piece, in French and English, on February 13, 1992 (the eve of Valentine's Day) in Los Angeles. The text is enigmatic, composed of a few sentences and juxtaposed words that function through associations: the rain falls, and from one situation to another, she "floats" to Paris to hear the "laughter of Paris, of Ghislaine, of Brigitte." Through the juxtaposition of names, destroyed Beirut evokes Pompeii (and possibly mirrors the artist's own state): "Pompeii - Beirut - Beirut - Pompeii - Baalbek." The last city mentioned has "become the biggest supplier of drugs," and a little further, she writes, "the remains of a city in mourning for a dead country," "it's the mourning of a city—Pompeii? Is it Pompeii? It could be my city, Beirut." Meanwhile, "Michel doesn't call," "Paul doesn't call." In a moment of nostalgia, she longs for the presence of the two stable men in her life: her brother and, especially, her husband, who has always been a pillar in her life. She confesses: "I'm afraid, afraid, afraid, as afraid as I can be—fear tranquilizes me—the very end of life—the last heartbeat—the last sex drive." Fear? Anguish? According to Freud, who distinguishes between anguish (*angst*) and fear (*furcht*),[81] "spontaneous attacks of anguish" are caused by events "that bring something new, unexpected, misunderstood, or disturbing."[82] Is it a declining libido? The inescapable approach of death? Unspeakable fear linked to childhood, to a home open to all, where politics is a constant threat (kidnappings and assassinations)? Has fear become part of her creative process? A fear she learns to tame. Years later, reflecting on these traumatic events, the artist writes: "The patience I've developed over the years has helped me ward off the terror of living and dying. The more time I spend on canvas or paper, the more I give myself the illusion of prolonging life."[83] Calming her fear by working is what she does until the very end of her possibilities and existence.

In these two collages, the recycled letters retain their mystery; the passage of time has caused the ink to nearly vanish in the first collage, and while words can be discerned through the thin paper, their meaning remains indecipherable. In both works, the artist speaks to her friends, who are, in theory, benevolent onlookers. Writing therapeutically, much like in a psychoanalysis session, she engages in free association with her unconscious. And yet, she writes "this is not to be read" (a negation that, according to Freud, often expresses its opposite), she offers glimpses of her intimate state of mind while complicating the reading of certain passages, which follow a drawing's outline and then shift direction. To decipher the content, the curious, determined, and patient reader must turn the work in all directions.

81 S. Tomasella, *Les Amours impossibles*, 19.

82 S. Freud, *Psychologie de la vie amoureuse*, 82.

83 A text Caland wrote for the exhibition invitation for Gallery Janine Rubeiz in 2006.

Lettres à Moustafa, Nude Letters, and Untitled (I, II, III)

In 2000, almost ten years later and in the space of a few days, the artist created five works composed of collages using the rest of the letters cut with scissors—a violent gesture, which also symbolically reduces the past into pieces. In a "chimney sweeping"[84] movement, this impulse once again allows the unconscious to express itself; thus, as the works are produced, they become lighter, as if, by recycling the letters, by giving them a new life, Caland was appeasing herself.[85]

The first canvas in this series, the most dense and textured (see photos p. 135), is titled *Lettres à Moustafa*. While the title references the material used in the artwork, it also blurs the lines between past and present: Are the recycled letters being addressed to him once again as the artwork is created? The canvas features fragments of letters—each written in French on white or beige paper, with no other colors—cut and pasted together, with a margin of 5–7 cm on all sides. The entire surface is then coated with glue, imparting a greyish tone to the painting, reminiscent of stormy days, and leaving a few fragments of the letters legible.

Once completed, *Nude Letters* (see photo p. 137)—the second piece in the series, measuring 202 × 203 cm—was hung for many months in the hallway leading from the front door to the main room of the artist's home. This was the space where she welcomed guests, in front of a large dining table that also served as her workspace. Situated at the heart of an open-plan layout, the room opened onto the kitchen on one side and a lush patio on the other, where the artist spent much of her time. Both powerful and discreet, the artwork quietly commanded attention. Mounted on a white canvas with a stretcher, *Nude Letters* echoes the spirit of *Lettres à Moustafa*. To better structure the space and contain her words and thoughts, the artist framed the central composition with a margin. Within this defined area, fragments of letters—written in French—are cut, folded, creased, layered, or glued individually in a seemingly chaotic arrangement, like a dismantled puzzle. These are then sealed with a thin layer of paint or glue. The work plays with the viewer's curiosity: a few isolated words emerge here and there, just enough to spark intrigue, yet not enough to reconstruct a coherent narrative—a playful contradiction between the canvas and its title. The letters, written over a span of twenty years on blue, green, light brown, and beige paper of varying textures, are largely illegible due to natural fading and glue. However, one long passage remains nearly intact and readable recounting when Caland meets an older painter, and just before the signature, the words "I love you" appear—faint but visible.

84 S. Freud, *Cinq leçons sur la psychanalyse*, (Payot, Paris, 2001), 14.

85 In a collage from the 1990s, Caland writes: "The author calms down, the reader reflects, enjoys, questions." "The author calms down / The author disturbs / The others..."

Lettres à Moustafa, 2000
Collage, mixed media on canvas, 203.2 × 101.6 cm

Private collection, Los Angeles, California

Toward the upper right corner, the artist has drawn an erect penis in green felt-tip pen. Its testicles form the upper half of a face, with an open eye drawn on each, and the foreskin is encircled by a belt resembling a belly dancer's hip accessory, just before stepping onto the dance floor. Upon closer inspection, three subtle drawings can be seen. Toward the bottom, on one of the glued paper fragments, a recent drawing in black pencil with a touch of yellow appears, evoking works from the 1970s—perhaps a nostalgic nod to the past and to Moustafa. In the center, another black pencil sketch shows the upper part of a face, cut off and inverted. Nearby, close to the bottom of the canvas, two fragments of red lettering—washed out like watercolor—stand out. The rest of this particular letter is scattered across the three additional canvases in the series: *Untitled I*, *Untitled II*, and *Untitled III* (see photos pp. 138-139). The canvas is raw and austere, its colors faded with time. While the scale and emotional weight of the fragmented letters lend the piece strength, it feels lighter than the first canvas. It's as if the artist, having "emptied her bag"[86] and released the weight of the past, can now approach the material with a sense of freedom, transforming it into something more aesthetically playful.

Indeed, the remaining three works—*Untitled I*, *II*, and *III*—are all nearly bare. In the largest of the three, letter fragments are arranged around the edges, forming a kind of empty frame (see photo p. 138-139), perhaps a visual metaphor for inner relief. The bottom and corners are slightly denser, while the other two canvases are even more minimal—each crossed only by a single vertical line running through the center.

"Foxing"—those traces of moisture, now stabilized—gives the work a patina that testifies to the passage of time: yellowed spots that evoke aged photographs, fading ink, and the people swept away by the cycles of life. The emptiness settles in and echoes their absence. In this interplay between conscious and unconscious, the artist finds release, transforming emotional residue into artistic substance. This process reaches the point of abstraction in the following series, titled *Silent Letters*.

86 Physically the bag containing the letters, and symbolically, her frustration at that time.

Nude Letters, 2000
Collage, paper, and glue on canvas, 201.9 × 203.8 cm

Private collection, Los Angeles, California

Untitled I (Nude Letters – Lettres à Moustafa), 2000
Collage, mixed media, paper, glue on canvas, 153 × 102.2 cm

Private collection, Los Angeles, California

Untitled II (Nude Letters – Lettres à Moustafa), 2000
Mixed media on canvas, 203.2 × 25.4 cm

Private collection, Los Angeles, California

Untitled III (Nude Letters – Lettres à Moustafa), 2000
Mixed media on canvas, 203.2 × 25.4 cm

Private collection, Los Angeles, California

Etymologically, the word *letter*—from the Latin *littera*, meaning a written character—refers to a symbol that represents a sound, a typographic sign, a message to a recipient, and, by extension, the literal or symbolic meaning of a word or text. It implies another person—the addressee—and by implication, an expectation of reply. In this sense, *Silent Letters* is an oxymoron. By titling the series in English, Caland directly addresses an English-speaking audience.[87]

Whether monumental, medium-sized, small, or minuscule, these works—marked by their intriguing minimalism—invite the viewer on a journey, offering a door into the artist's unconscious. Caland once admitted: "To silence myself, I draw lines... it seems like nothing, but drawing lines is a way to contain emotion, anger, anxiety—when you feel like insulting people, you draw a line."[88] While ink-covered lines first appeared in her notebooks in the early 1990s, and on some works from the same period, she developed this technique further toward the end of the decade—giving it new prominence on canvas and large-format paper. *Drawings #886 and #887* (see photos p. 142-143) demonstrate how this process evolved into textual abstraction. Both pieces are addressed to Moses. In the first, dated June 12, 1992—a rainy day in California—she plays with themes of absence and longing. She "edits" her letter by blacking out or removing sections she wants to hide, drawing lines that literally suppress the text, much as she had done in her 1990–1991 notebook. The words and phrases she left visible[89]—two sentences and three postscripts—hint at tension, disappointment, the urgent need to communicate, and a discomfort in expressing herself. They also subtly indicate what she might be concealing. If the motto "Never complain, never explain" was ingrained in her, the work also raises the question: Is she repressing guilt, caught in a relationship that brings her both dependency and distress? Does the ambivalence she feels feeds a kind of masochism? The second drawing, dated the same day, moves even further into abstraction. As she noted in the first piece, it's raining. By a chain of associations, water becomes a boat, sailing over waves of unsaid words. Instead of text, she draws soft, undulating lines. An "etc..." nestled between silent lines and a few others later obscured with ink, betrays her emotional state.

87 One might think that it's addressed to the artistic community that she sees regularly, yet ostracizes her.
88 Caland in Lettres à Francine, documentary by F. Elkoury, production/Maison européenne de la photographie, 2000.
89 "Dear Ed", "Love," "Huguette," "PS1," "PS2," "PS3," "I understand your absence yesterday," "you sure were there."

Ellipses between strokes or a fragment of a salvaged sentence at the end—just before the signature—reveal the emotions she's trying to suppress. These two drawings remained tucked away in a drawer for nearly twenty years before being rediscovered—a quiet testament to the private nature of her emotional processing.

#886, June 12, 1992
Ink on paper, 32.4 × 24.8 cm

Private collection, Los Angeles, California

#887, June 12, 1992
Ink on paper, 32.4 × 24.8 cm

Private collection, Los Angeles, California

In the *Made in L.A. 2016* exhibition catalog, Aram Moshayedi observes: "A fixation on the poetics of line is evident throughout her oeuvre, whether in the sinuous drawn lines used to demarcate fragmented parts of her own body and those of her lovers in early work on paper or in the almost obsessive repetition of standardized linear marks in her later works. Dedicated as she was, it would be remiss not to assume that there is something telling within this focus on the structural power of lines."[90] Describing one of the paintings in the *Silent Letters* series, Kaelen Wilson-Goldie notes that it is "composed of blocks of thick or thin lines and empty spaces, interlocked with each other with strokes... which, as they pass from density to evanescence, fade and thus resemble a Zen riddle."[91] The artist herself reflects: "My lines tell the story of my life, of people I've met along the way, loved and found and even lost..."

While the fluid lines recount the physical desires and eroticism of her arrival in Paris in the early 1970s, the lines—or strokes—that mature with age are capable of transforming discomfort into caresses drawn with a brush on various materials. These strokes reveal more or less important empty spaces; emptiness, "an eminently dynamic and active element,"[92] which happens to be the natural color of paper or canvas, in this body of work. Inside the brushstrokes appear shapes that transform, opening onto other worlds, and freeing the unconscious; invisible silent letters that allow each individual to make his or her own interpretation. Timeless, subtly nuanced, detached from all spatiotemporal reference points, the lines are horizontal or vertical, and are repetitive, like a prayer, an incantation. Sometimes the lines follow one another very closely, almost without gaps, with so much to confide. No matter what's going on outside: surrounded by brushes of all sizes, collected over the years and meticulously maintained, bottles of ink, pencils, and markers, she simultaneously concentrates and lets go. The repressed emerges, transformed. A line. She places the brush on a point on the edge of the canvas or chooses a precise spot on the Japanese paper. No room for error. With a slow movement, the line is drawn, sucked toward a final point that only she can see, then imposes, line after line, a rhythm on her composition. At first glance, their regularity suggests that these silent lines are identical, but on closer inspection, the eye detects subtle nuances. In places, interstices seem to define paragraphs, insertions, or a change of chapter. Precision of movement is accompanied by a focused slowness, and physical and mental stability. Regularity and mastery of the gesture and of herself determine both spirit and rendering. Drawing simultaneously involves letting go and controlling, the mind as much as the matter. Then, mastered to the extreme, the line becomes a condensation of a story, a part of life. An open book whose language, devoid of words and sounds, remains enigmatic.

90 A. Moshayedi, in *Made in L.A. 2016: A, The, Though, Only*,

91 K. Wilson Goldie in *4 Colunms.org*, June 25, 2021, accessed online March 18, 2023.

92 F. Cheng, *Vide et plein, Le langage pictural chinois*, (Le Seuil, Paris, 1991), 45.

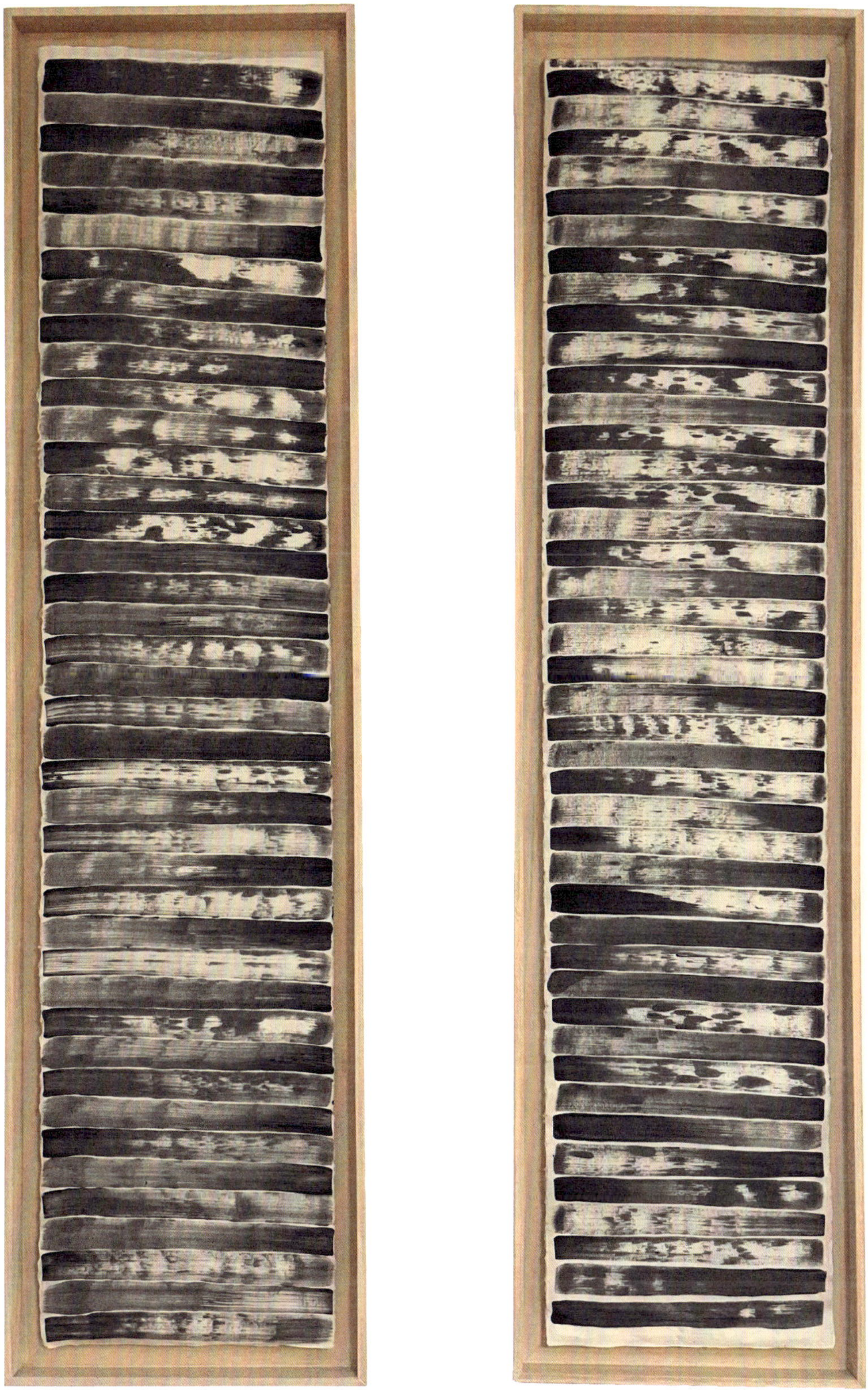

Silent Letters, 2000
Ink on handmade Japanese paper, 142.5 × 32 cm

Private collection, Paris, France

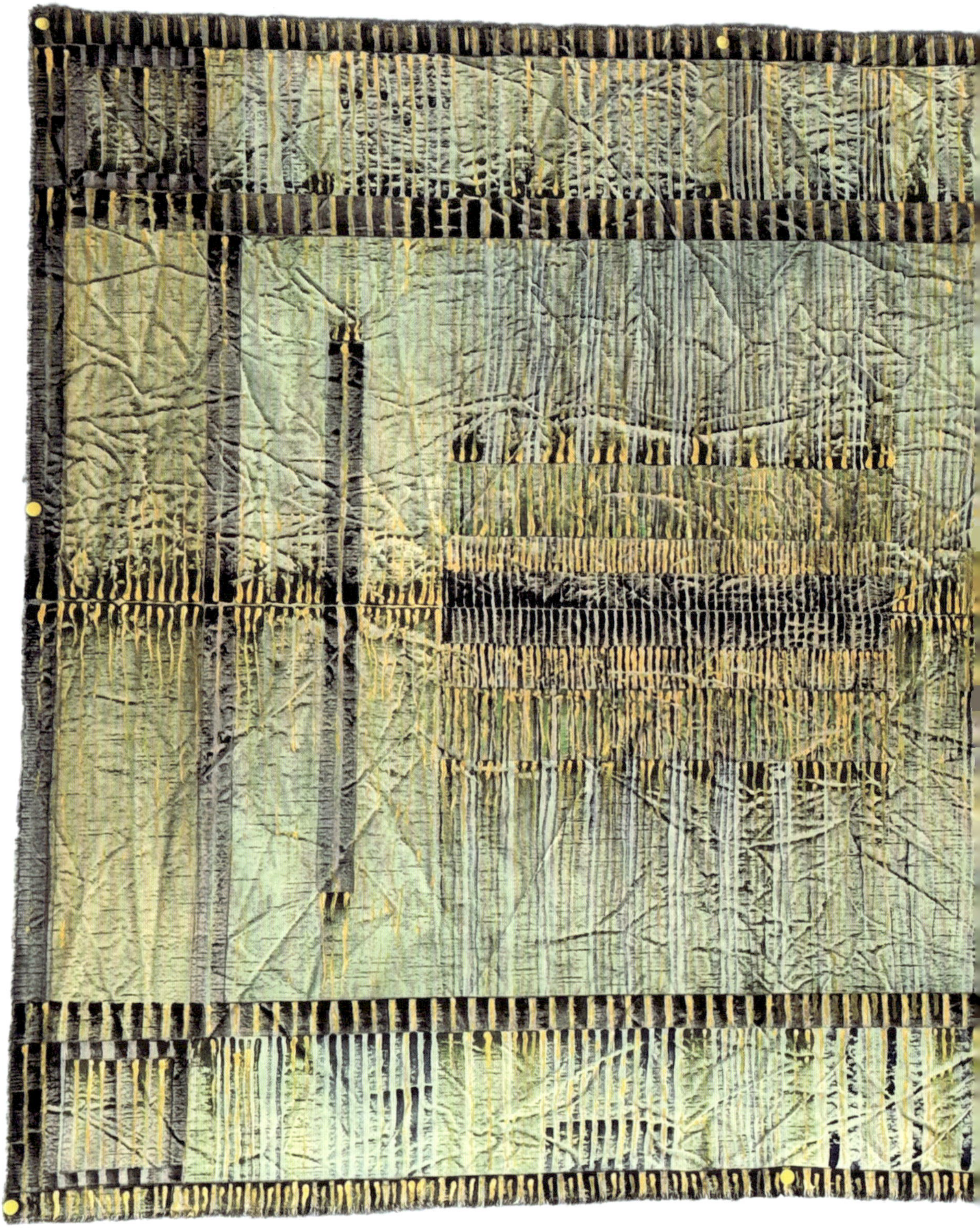

Silent Letters, c. 2000
Mixed media on canvas, 140 × 90 cm

Private collection, Baltimore, Maryland

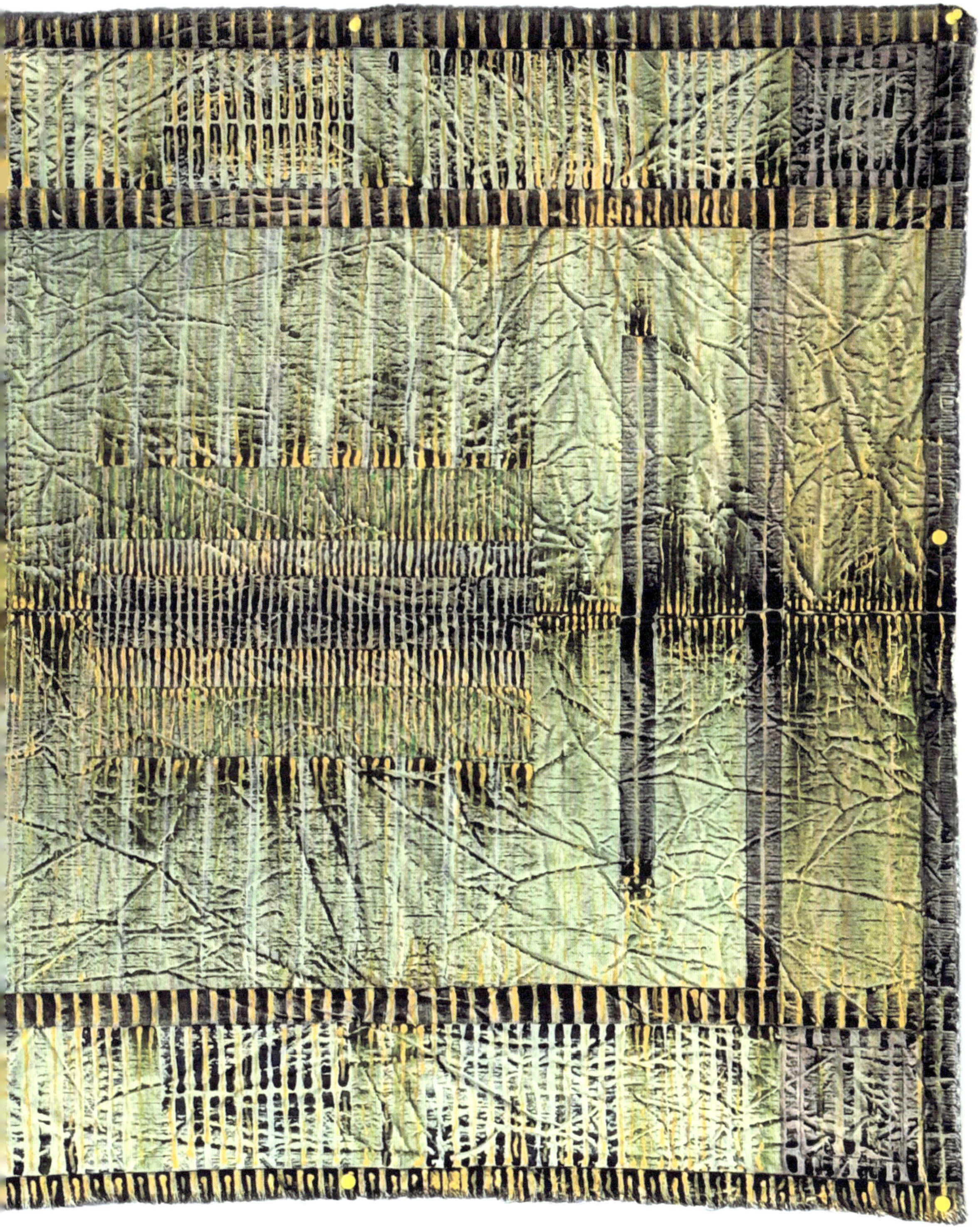

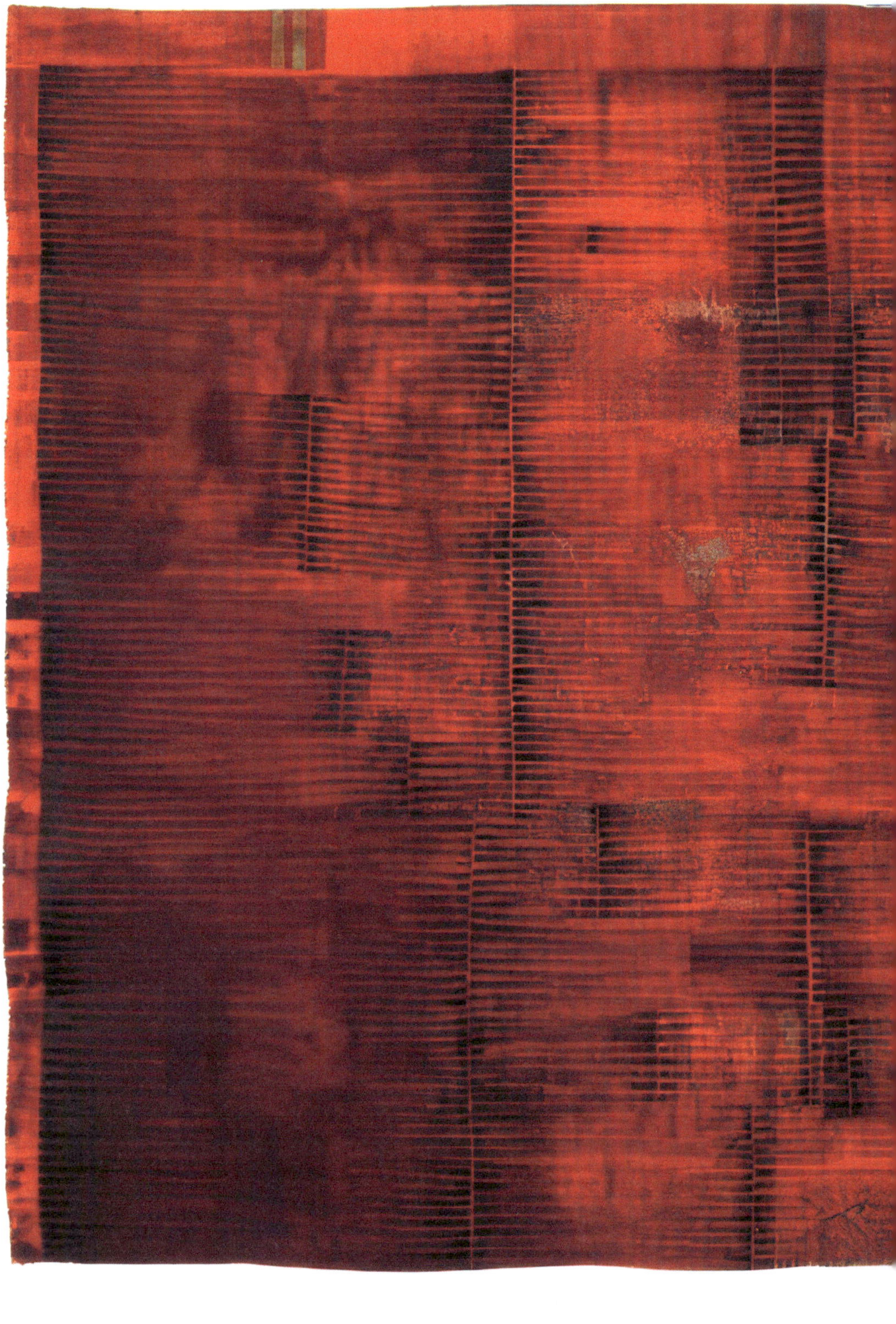

Silent Letters, 2006
Mixed media on linen, 190 × 290 cm

Private collection, Beirut, Lebanon

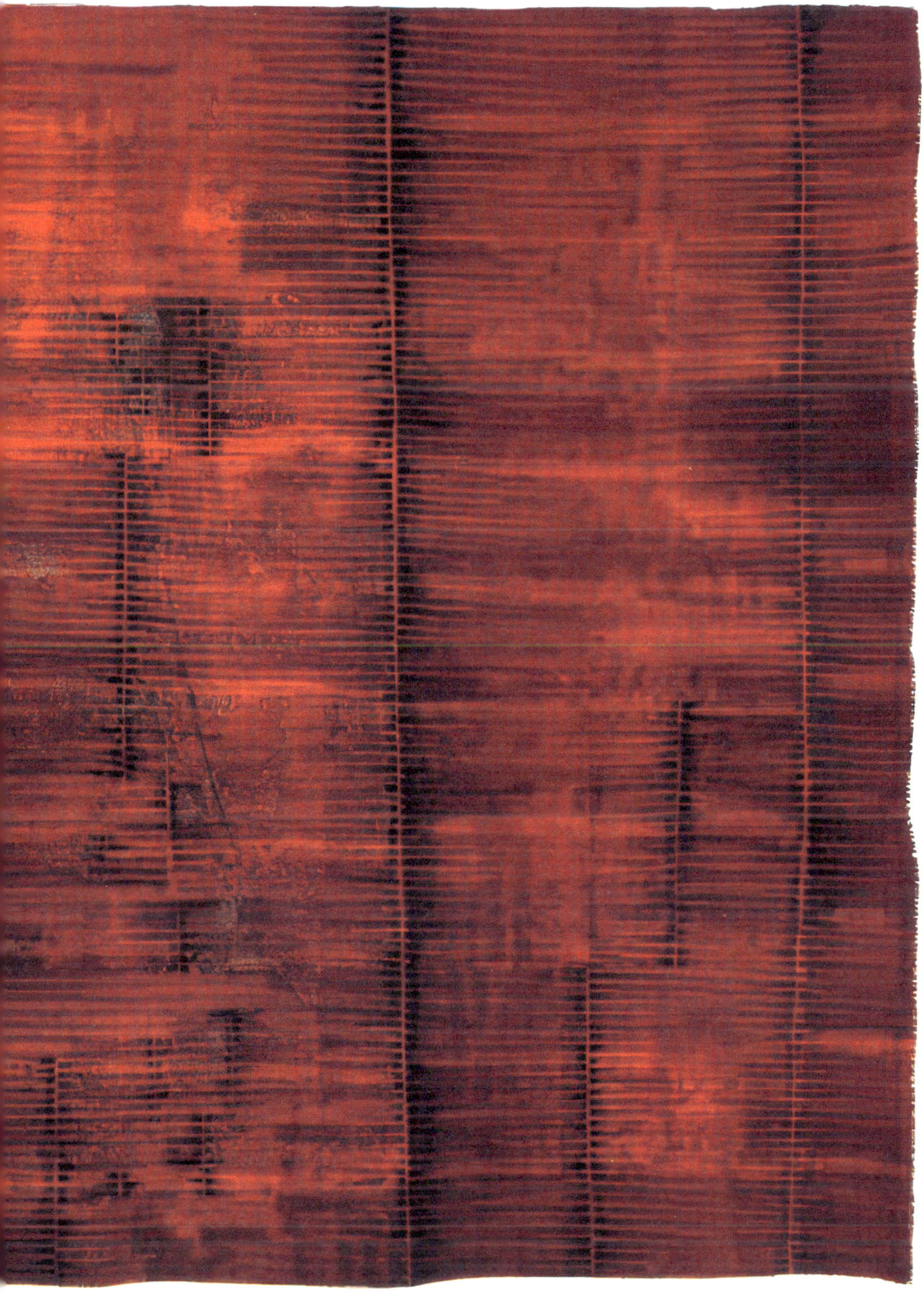

Some of these works evoke a Talmud[93] page in which various commentaries on the text are inserted: in the center is a passage from the Mishna and the Gemara, surrounded by other commentaries (Rashi of Troyes, his disciples the Tosaphists, or others). So, whatever the primary reason for these brushstrokes, they evoke the "hyphen between human and the supernatural... [which] embodies the process by which the man's drawing joins the gestures of Creation (The act of drawing the Line corresponds to the very act that draws the One from Chaos, that separates Heaven and Earth)..."[94] These flat paintings invite viewers to immerse themselves. The only visible background is the emptiness of the material (canvas or paper), in which the eye can lose itself. There's no need for staging: as if imbued with *Li,*[95] the vital breaths, the line whispers the essential. Sometimes the brush is dipped in ink, sometimes in paint, and some works are done with various pencils on canvas, jute, or paper, most often imported from Japan—handmade, fragile, or thicker, and either with a visible grain or almost smooth.

As in traditional Chinese painting, this series conveys a sense of breath and rhythm—echoing the chiaroscuro of yin and yang. Blurred boundaries between the East and West are seen as lines begin alternately from the right (as in Arabic and other Semitic languages) and from the left (as in European languages). The restraint and minimalism of some works contrast sharply with the vivid bursts of color in others. These therapeutic lines—produced through long hours of focused, meditative labor—allow the repressed to surface and liberate the artist. In the series that follows, her line recovers its spontaneity and exuberance, and once again, Paul returns.

93 The word "talmud" comes from the Semitic root l-m-d (in Arabic تلميذ *) and means "study"; it is "the body of Jewish civil and ceremonial law and legend comprising the Mishna and the Gemara."

94 Cheng, *Vide et plein*, 73.

95 Ibid., 109, "[Principle or internal structure]: The primacy given to vital breaths allows the artist to transcend his tendency toward overly realistic illusionism. For him, it is less about describing the outward aspects of the world than about grasping the internal principles that structure all things and connect them to one another."

PAUL, OR THE NARCISSISTIC WOUND

Throughout this body of work, the repeated appearance of the name Paul is striking. It appears in nearly every piece that includes writing: tucked among motifs in a large painting on wood, where the barely visible words "Bye bye Paul" (see photo p. 88 [detail] and 153) are carefully hidden beneath embroidered cross-stitches; inscribed repeatedly on a wooden stick hanging in a refined Beirut salon, like a quiet invocation repeated over fifteen lines (see photo p.152); written in the corner of a drawing, along the lines of a collage, or across a vast stretched canvas. Paul is everywhere. Who is he—and why does he appear this way?

Caland falls in love with Paul—"the pure object of eros"[96]—with the intensity of a twelve-year-old's first infatuation: completely and irrationally. As sociologist Francesco Alberoni describes it, falling in love is "the nascent state of a collective movement for two"[97] that "shakes institutions to their foundations."[98] But for the teenager, it's a one-sided emotion, a solitary plunge in which the verb "to fall" takes on its full, weighted meaning. She meets Paul when she is twelve and he is sixteen. Half-French through his father and half-Lebanese through his mother,[99] he is handsome, a gambler (horse races, poker...), a smoker, and a rebellious figure who frequents Beirut's red-light districts. He is quiet, reserved, and only drawn to tall, slender, statuesque women—everything Huguette is not. And yet, she is infatuated. Perhaps, he is moved by her feelings. After all, she is the daughter of a president, which adds intrigue. But the imbalance causes a series of rejections that wound this unconventional, spirited, round-faced girl, with her explosive laugh and boundless imagination. These early narcissistic wounds leave lasting scars. Throughout her life, her self-portraits—whether painted, drawn, or collaged—are never flattering. Her blind love toward Paul, and the fantasy she constructs around him, echo in many of her self-portraits: often featuring only one eye—or none at all (see photos p. 156-159). A symbolic erasure, a refusal to see, or perhaps a reflection of the way she felt unseen.

96 F. Alberoni, *Le Choc amoureux*, (Éditions Ramsey, Paris, 1981), 31.

97 Ibid., 9.

98 Ibid., 23.

99 Huguette's father-in-law, Pierre Caland, was the director of a tobacco company in Lebanon and Syria. He was assassinated in 1940 before she met Paul. Paul's mother was the sister of Georges Naccache, a virulent political opponent of Huguette's father.

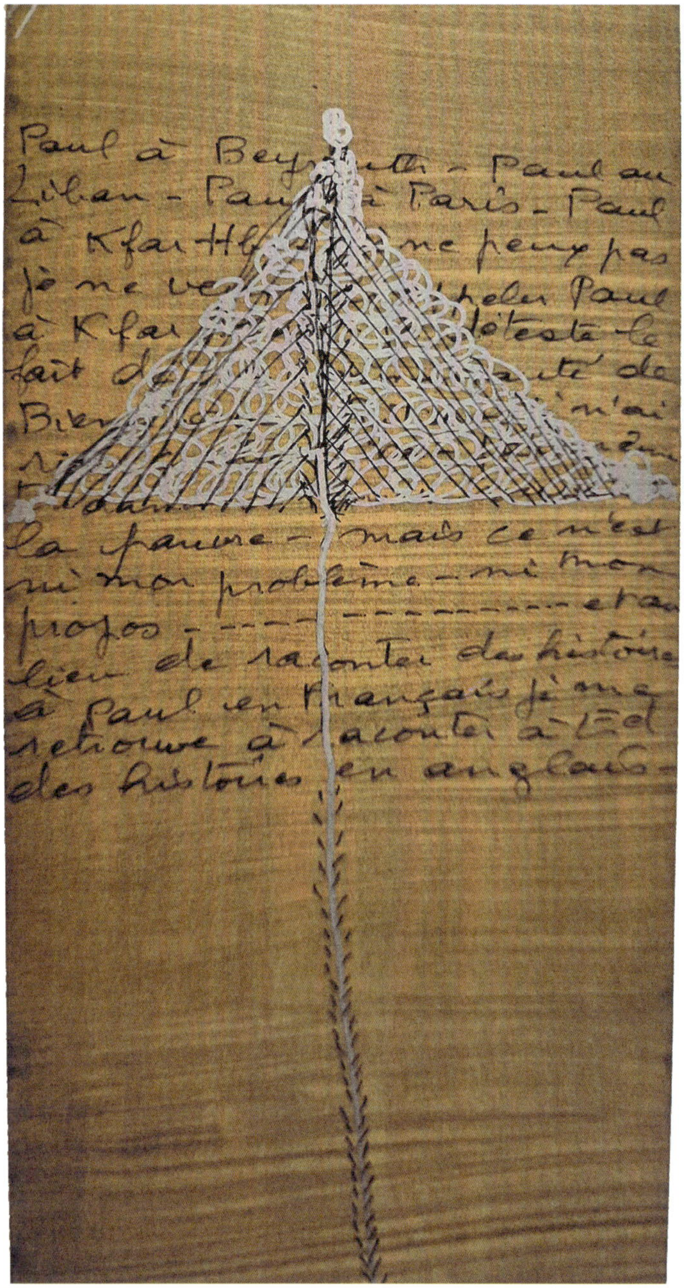

Untitled (detail), c. 1998
Mixed media on wood, 200 × 25 cm

Private collection, Beirut, Lebanon

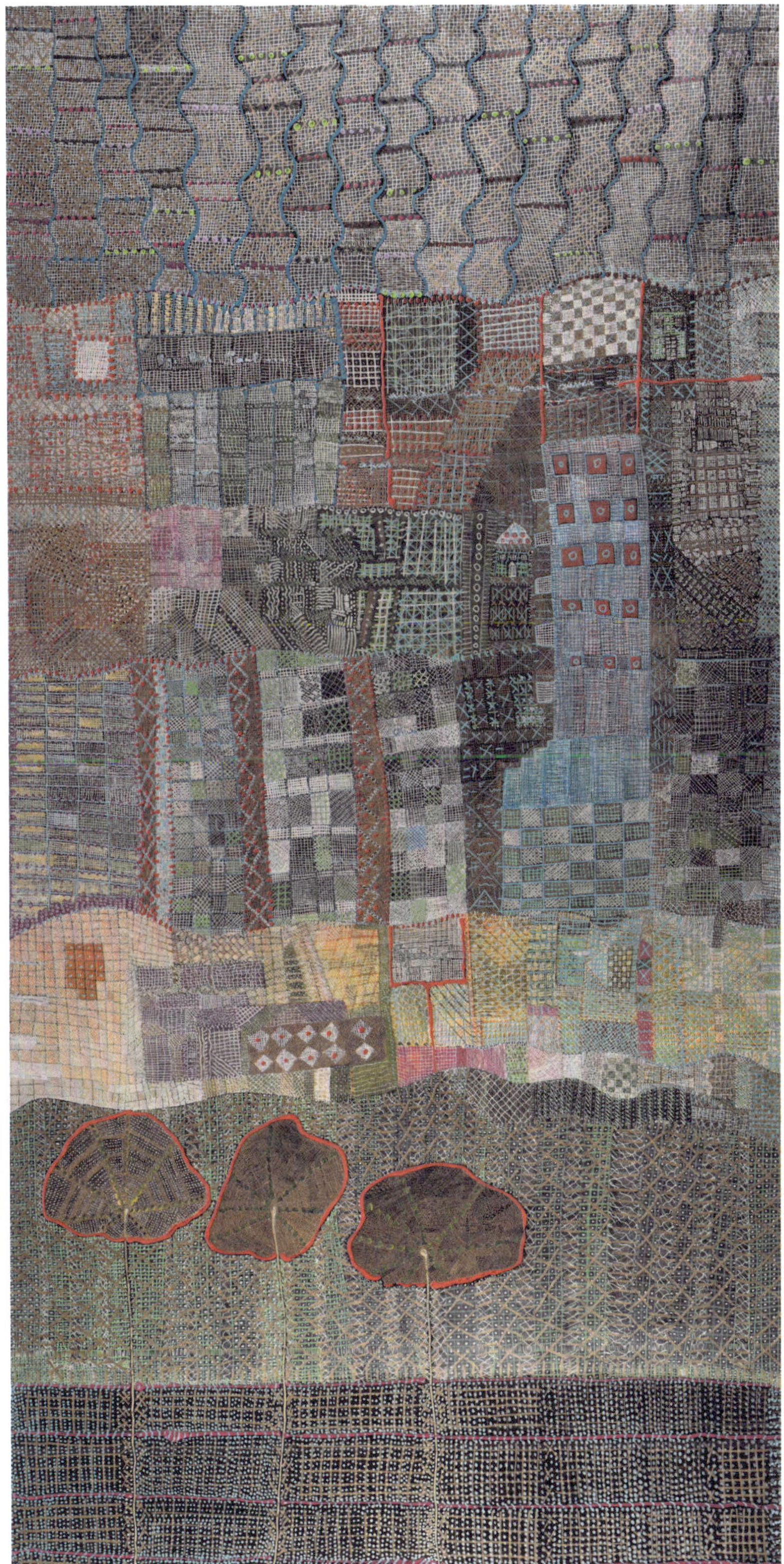

Zikrayat toufoulati fi loubnan, 1998
Acrylic on panel, 244 × 122 cm

Private collection, Beirut, Lebanon

For years, as a teenager, Caland defied every social norm and prohibition out of sheer passion—all while her father held the highest office in the country. For more than eight years, she and Paul saw each other in secret. Her parents had no idea, even though Paul was part of a group of boys who were friends with her brother and often visited the presidential residence to play cards or simply hang out. It wasn't until eight years later, that by coincidence, her parents met Paul in their hallway for the first time. The introduction took place in front of the astonished eyes of the other young men, all of whom—thanks to their families—already knew the president and his wife personally.

When Caland married Paul in 1952, she already knew her love would never be returned, and that "loving for two" wouldn't change anything. In fact, she later admitted that by the time of their wedding, her feelings had faded. But under the pressure of family expectations and social conventions, the marriage went ahead.[100] There was no dramatic rupture, but a slow, inward unraveling over the course of ten years—similar to the process described by Catherine Marin in her book on breakups: "A rupture is not always visible or dramatic; sometimes it happens without obvious change, through quiet inner decisions, new directions, the abandonment of certain aspects of life that simply cease to be alive."[101] And so, on April 29, 1952, at the Kantari Palace—also the official presidential residence—the young woman married the man she had once loved madly, and, for some time, loved out of sheer stubbornness. By marrying him, Caland broke every rule of her social class, leaving behind a lasting imprint. Perhaps she found herself trapped by her former desire, and "a prisoner of others' expectations."[102] In this space, grief for the past became a private, intimate, and enigmatic process.[103] Still, to "please Paul," they had three children, and Caland believed she was fulfilling her duty as a wife. More than a decade later, when her father died, and she was confronted with the painful truth of a loveless marriage and the dead end it had become, she seized control of her life. As soon as she became the author of her own destiny, she claimed her freedom—and the adventures that came with it—reclaiming a self that had long been devalued by her husband. Despite her naturally joyful character, she carried deep disappointment. But rather than succumbing to the shadow of the "lost object," the life force within her triumphed over melancholy. She chose to become herself, to invent herself. Paul, in the end, was an impossible love story—but one that, in a strange way, came full circle. That was a kind of victory. His best friend, Moustafa, would become her lover and the emotional glue that held the family together. By taking control of her own life, she created a "transitional space"[104] and enrolled at the American University of Beirut to become an artist.

100 Michel, Caland's youngest brother, was sent by her parents to inquire if Paul intended to marry his sister. Paul's answer was: "If this is her wish."

101 Marin, *Ruptures*, 14.

102 Ibid., 23-24.

103 S. Freud, *Deuil et mélancolie*, (Payot & Rivages, Paris, 2011), 27.

104 D. Winnicott, *Les Objets transitionnels*, (Petite Bibliothèque Payot, Paris, 2010), 14.

This decision gave her the space to mourn her father—to whom she was very close—while simultaneously no longer leaving room for Paul or the weight of an unhappy marriage. To decide is also to resist being pulled back into a world of compromise and sorrow. She followed the uncontrollable impulse to live, an energy that ultimately saved her. The tools of her artistic practice—canvases, tubes of paint, pigments, turpentine, brushes, drawing paper, and pencils of every kind—became her "transitional objects." They not only helped her survive the emotional fallout of her marriage but also allowed the couple to continue coexisting peacefully. In the end, they would never divorce. Despite life's turbulence, her journey was marked by grace, helped by her joyful, mischievous spirit. Later, from the 1990s onward, feeling more vulnerable, the artist carried these "transitional objects" with her—in her pockets, and her tote bags— allowing her to be in a constant creative mode.

By leaving Lebanon for Paris and changing the terms of her marriage, Caland elegantly signaled the unease within the couple. Once she settled in the French capital in 1970, the artist began to fully live life on her own terms. While she may have lost the object of her youthful love, she reclaimed the narrative. Over time, she adjusted her "emotional investment," giving herself permission to explore new desires—sublimating her relationship with Paul and transforming it into creative material. In the erotic drawings of the 1970s, he appears as a recurring figure. During the years she was involved with the Romanian sculptor Apostu, his presence seemed to recede. But in the 1990s—especially around 1991–1992—he re-emerges prominently in her work, particularly in collages and drawings. This renewed presence may have been sparked by her return to past letters and memories, or perhaps by the challenges she faced integrating into the Los Angeles art scene. In the final decade of her career, as she reflected on her childhood, Paul once again became a central figure—this time in both written texts and visual art. From this rich and emotionally charged body of work, two pieces stand out: *Une vie en quelques lignes*, a collage in which the text itself becomes a form of visual expression, and *La mariée, Kantari, avril 1952* a painting that recounts her marriage to Paul.

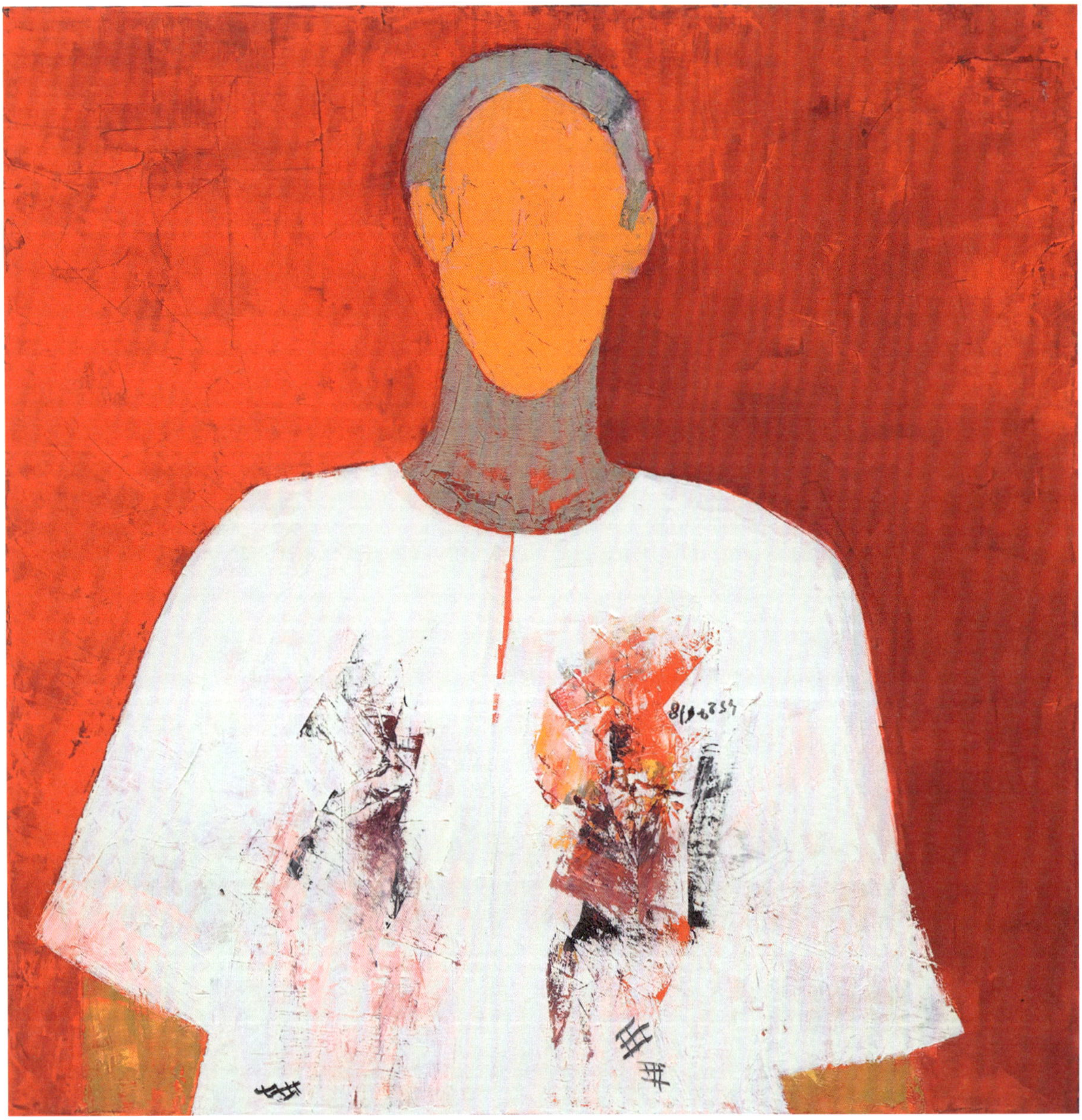

Selfportrait in Smock, 1992
Oil on linen, 76.2 × 76.2 cm

Private collection, Los Angeles, California

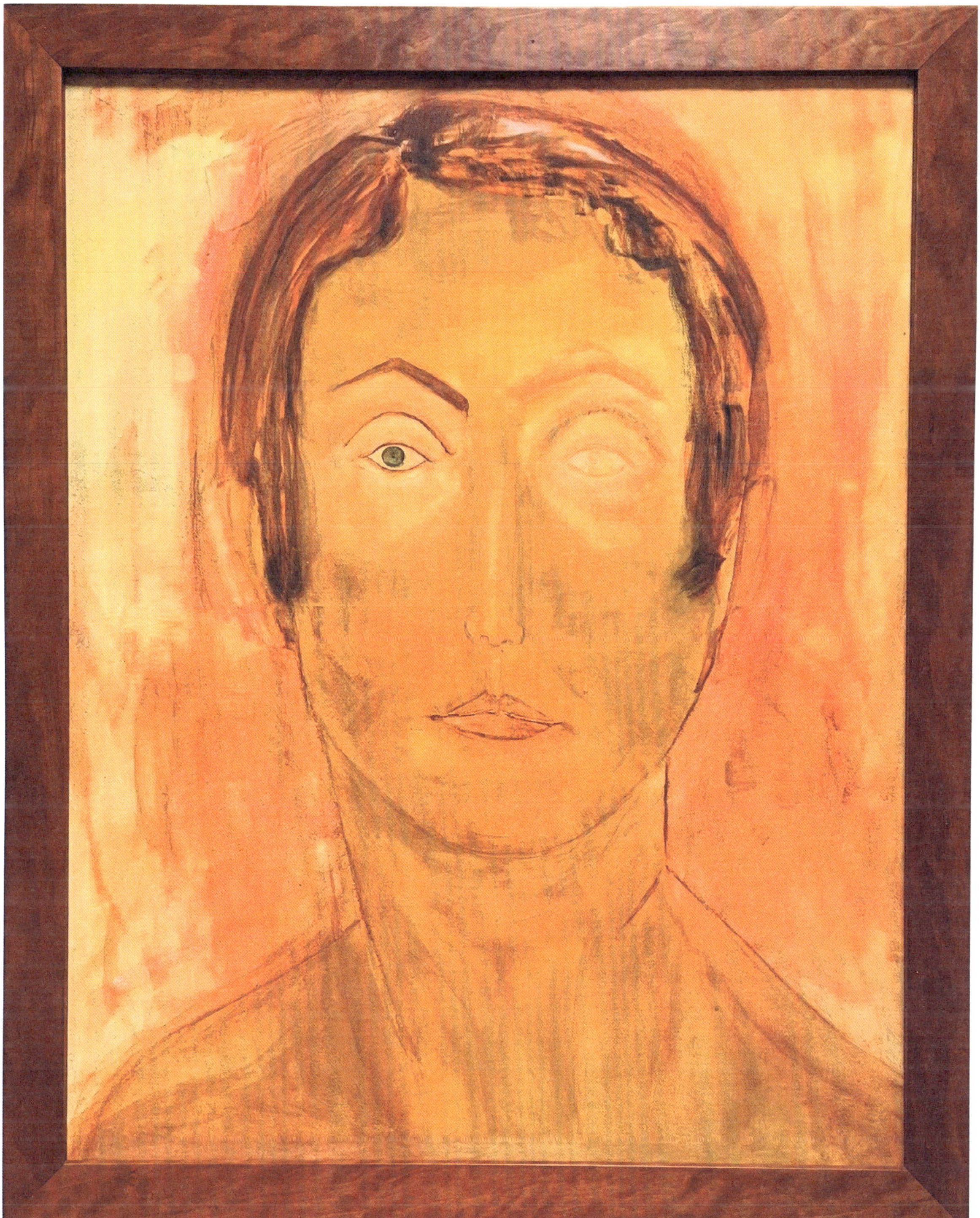

Autoportrait, 1967
Oil on linen, 109.2 × 88.9 cm

Private collection, Los Angeles, California

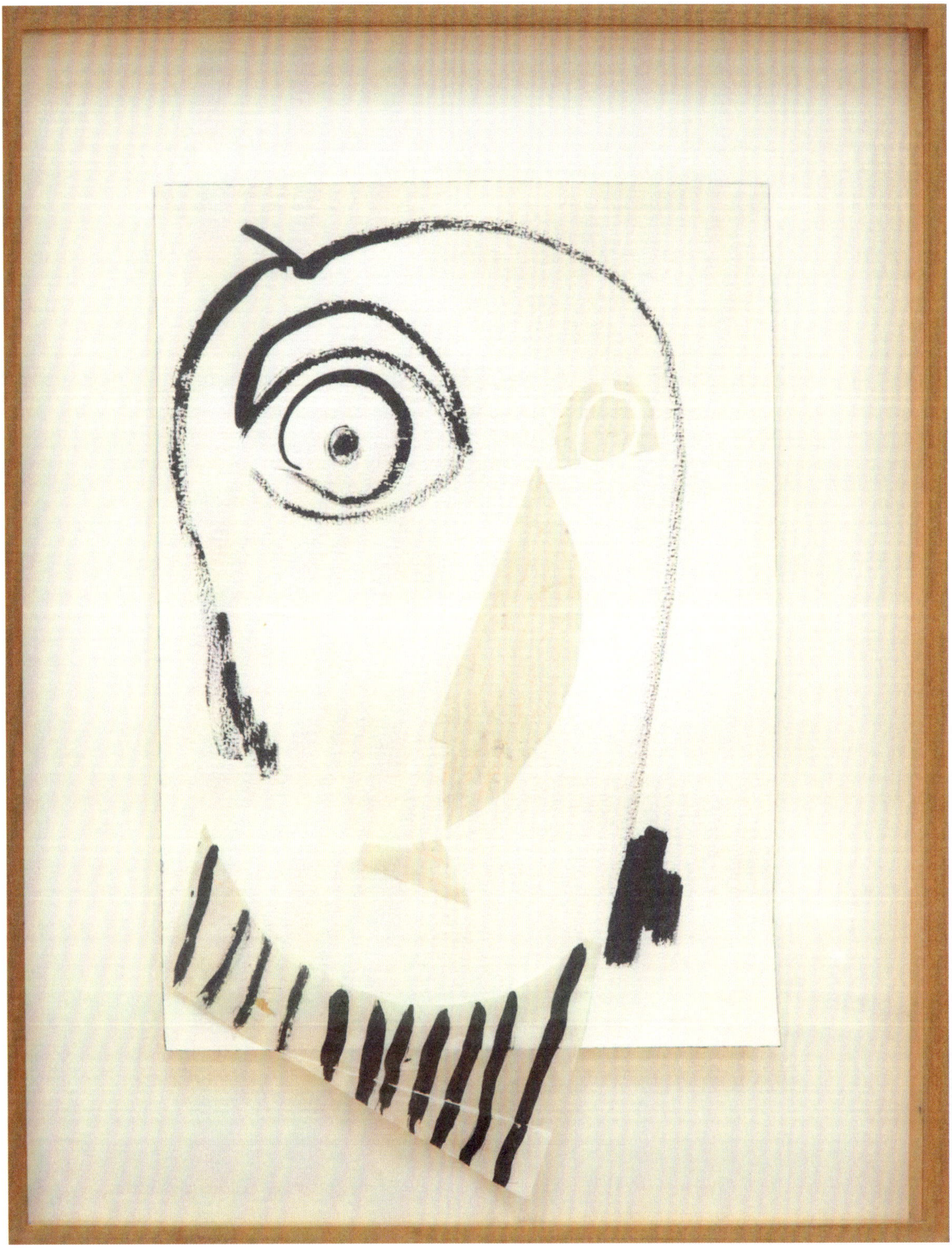

Selfportrait in Letters, 1991
Mixed media on paper, 23.25 × 19 cm

Private collection, Los Angeles, California

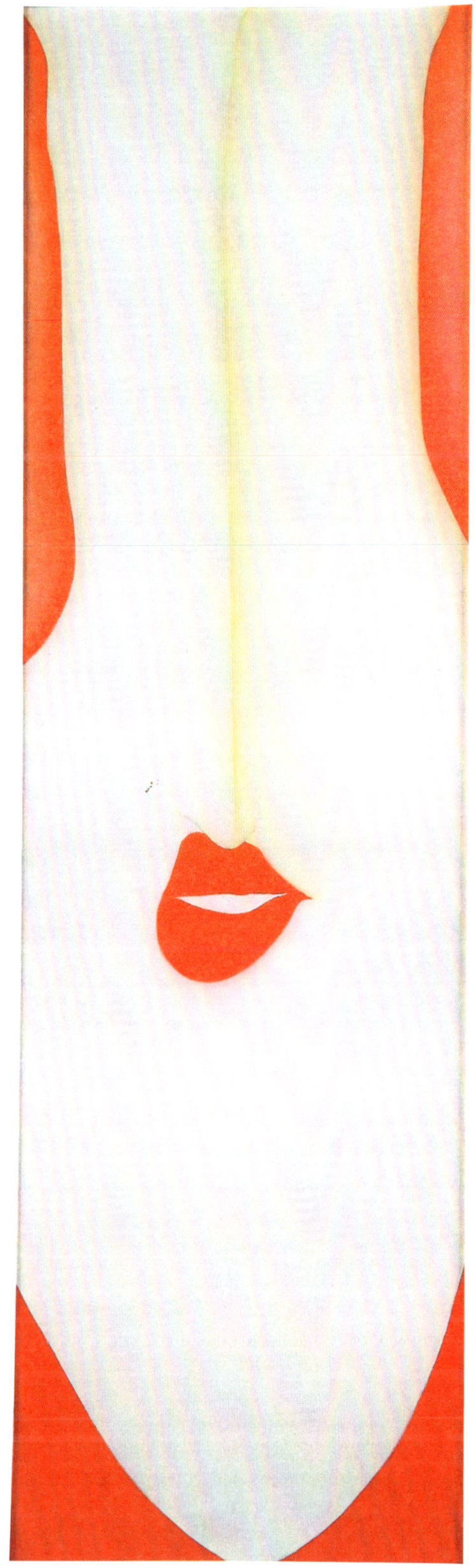

Autoportrait, 1972
Oil on canvas, 150 × 45 cm

Private collection, Paris, France

The collage, described as a "talisman" and dated June 27, 1992 (see photo, p. 163-166), is composed of three sheets of drawing paper of varying sizes, layered and glued together. The first thing that draws attention is the elegant, consistent handwriting, which traces lines of various lengths across the piece—horizontally, vertically, and diagonally. On the right side, below the center, an eye is positioned on a hand within a triangle, a symbolic figure evoking the Holy Trinity, "harmony and wisdom,"[105] serving as protection against the evil eye. The shape of the index fingernail, which crosses the eye in the drawing, resembles a pupil; the work recalls the talismanic shirts of the Ottoman tradition. Only the background of the central sheet is painted. Two black stripes run across it and split into four toward the right, partially revealing the pink background. These stripes emphasize the upper edge and hover above the writing, transitioning into pearl grey and then into a delicate blend of iridescent pinks and whites. The alternating colors occasionally reveal the paper's grain. The numbers "66 - 22 = 44" commemorate Paul's sixty-sixth birthday. The text on this central sheet is written mostly horizontally and narrates her love for Paul, the reasons behind her departure, and the significance of the family that Caland forms against all odds.[106] A few diagonal lines intersect the page, connecting at certain points along the edge with other lines of text from the adjacent pages, forming geometric patterns. Although the text begins with "Dear, dear, dearest June...", the ellipsis quickly shifts into a reflective monologue that blends past and present. Despite the affectionate opening, this is not a letter—June cannot reply. A sense of refinement and tenderness permeates both the visual composition and the writing itself. The use of iridescent pink and white adds to the work's delicate beauty, but also makes the text difficult to read in places, especially where the artist writes in soft pink pencil or nearly transparent light grey.

The second page, slightly larger than the first, contains various types of inscriptions and acts as a frame for the central sheet. More playful in tone, the artist expresses herself freely in both English and French, without censorship, using a simple and direct style. Her words flow horizontally, vertically, and diagonally across the page, emphasizing the importance of sexual pleasure:

105 Allendy, *Le Symbolisme des nombres*, 48, 9-70.

106 "...I left Lebanon 44 years ago, Paul was 44 (written in pale pink ink on white) (black ink on white paper) "When I left him to the women who fought over him with force and pettiness, I didn't like them – I couldn't measure myself against them... Paul and I were married for life; we have three children. I didn't want to, nor could I, be part of the struggle. For me, the struggle for everyone was over. I had had my share – the best... Our children and our adolescence, I let [missing words] fight for what had ceased to be my primary concern. From 43 to 52, it was Paul; from 52 to today, it has been life... Paul is still a part of it – how and why exclude him? It was never conceivable for [missing word]... him. The children and I were always meant to form this kind of unit, where each of us can always turn to recharge. We exist in space, and the essential thing is to remain in orbit to avoid free fall. I cannot give a logical explanation of how all this holds together, but it does, and maybe it holds by miracle – what are miracles, if not the intangible and the inexplicable... other than through a capacity to love and feel... each addition. To each [missing word], we also run with space... [almost illegible]. A few years and an addition that becomes part of us all, that enriches us. In this, space and time are abolished. I catalyze emotions, I store them to nourish my [missing word] long after my life... Long after my death, a red rose climbs on my terrace, a pink rose in a vase at my window fades away, and the Californian sun struggles to overcome the mist – it will succeed shortly..."

"Sex is a search for my inner life – my intimate self – sex is pure – sex is lovable."[107] This reflects a subtle interplay between pleasure and experimentation that feeds into her creative process. Now in her sixties, Caland—who, at the start of her marriage to Paul, allowed her family life to suppress her sexuality[108]—continues to challenge the norms of a patriarchal society, the bourgeois expectations of her social milieu, religious taboos, and the puritanism of American culture.

The third page, significantly larger—roughly four times the size of the centerfold—contains much of the text and serves to frame the entire composition. The writing here is partially legible, and in some areas barely decipherable, layered in two or three overlapping levels and oriented in opposing directions. Caland alternates between narrative and directly addressing Paul,[109] blending memories of the past with present experiences, including an account of an earthquake so powerful it prompted concerned calls from family members abroad. Referring to the event, she remarks, "you'd have thought the earth was orgasming."[110] The layout of the lines across the three sheets complicates the reading experience. Some sentences intersect at right angles, others veer off suddenly, spinning across the page in a way that can induce dizziness. Anyone attempting to follow the text must physically rotate the work to trace a thought or complete a sentence. One particular area—where horizontal, vertical, and diagonal lines converge—remains enigmatic. While its message can partly be inferred ("even then, Kantari organized itself into a club"), it ultimately resists full clarity.

107 Written in English: "Sex is research for my inner life – my inner self – sex is pure – sex is lovable,– I love sex...Feel, feel, feel, feel, Feel, feel, feel, feel, Feel, feel, feel, feel, Feel, feel, feel, feel. Then elsewhere?" And those who are no longer young and have flesh that is no longer smooth (continuation on the right side) and firm. And the sex of the old and the old? The painful and problematic erection. Sex is research for my inner life – my inner self – sex is pure – sex is lovable."; "The exploration of tenderness that makes one accept failures – and the miseries. Loud and clear – sex suits him well – poor human beings, dependent on a body that often lets them down."
"I love sex, says she with a radiant smile, sex is a purification – I love sex, says she innocently – I love sex."

108 M. Foucault, *La Volonté de savoir*, (Gallimard, Paris, 1976), 9.

109 "And so many other things, it's really me who taught you how to drive, yes it was in my car that you passed your driving test – I didn't like staying at home without the [...] at the beginning of our marriage... so that you could go to the stable – my mother suffered from it – I covered for you by saying I had nothing to do outside the house."
"My God, how I wanted you – your black hair [...] and the visible ribs – hollow cheeks and the triangle of your face..."; "The other men in my life – I'll talk to you about them one day – you'll have to listen – years, as they add up, turned us into friends."

110 During a phone conversation a few hours after the earthquake.

Through a text filled with tenderness and mischief, the work revisits fragments of the past and of another world—one that remains deeply present in the artist's life. The narrative unfolds according to the structure of the composition. On the central sheet, Paul is ever-present as Caland recounts both the joys and disappointments they shared. On the second sheet, which extends outward from the center, she explores themes of pleasure and sexual awakening. And on the third and largest sheet, the text turns to her current life—where Paul still plays a part—intertwining fears and hopes. The empty spaces between the crisscrossing lines seem to invite future adventures, watched over by the protective symbols of the eye and the hand.

Eighteen years later, in 2010, Caland created a painting on canvas (see photo, p. 169) that she hung without a frame, as a tapestry. In the foreground stands a woman with a featureless face and no hands. Both unsettling and captivating, she appears to be gently tilting—or perhaps levitating. The title's spatiotemporal markers, *La Mariée — Kantari, avril 1952 (2010)*, locate the scene in springtime, in Kantari, a district of Beirut. This was the artist's childhood home, which later became the presidential residence, bringing with it a formal and official atmosphere as well as constant unrest. In this composition, large matte-black flowers with a central white dot stand out against a checkerboard background and bands of color that give the piece a subtle sense of depth. These black flowers contrast sharply with others—white, gray, sky blue, blue-gray, green, ochre, and mauve—each marked by a central black dot. They surround the bride and also appear, more discreetly, near her feet at the bottom of the canvas. The bride wears a black veil adorned with intricate motifs; its base resembles a Sufi hat resting atop her head. The veil—imagined as black tulle pierced by pinpricks of light or a sheer fabric scattered with thousands of white flecks—is also decorated with golden flowers and seems to billow upward, as if lifted by the wind. Similar golden flowers are scattered across her moiré white dress, itself speckled with tiny circular forms.

This bride is a fantasy—an expression of the desire to become another woman, so light she could float. Her featureless, absent, and elusive face also reflects the absence of a gaze—the gaze her husband does not offer her. Her head rests on a neck encircled by black lines. Is it a high collar with delicate bars, meant to be decorative? Or does it evoke the feeling of being behind the bars of a prison window? Or perhaps both?

The upper part of her bodice is fastened with small black buttons that lead to a sculpted black ruff, reminiscent of a thick, bushy mustache. Two horizontal rows of dots, with others floating in alignment between them, outline the chest, flattened beneath fabric that shapes the upper torso. This area is framed by a black-and-white checkerboard line. The skirt, cut in a V-shape from the hips, reveals another checkerboard line positioned at the pubic level. The shimmering white dress emphasizes a wasp waist—the idealized figure the artist imagines will captivate the young man she is marrying—and flares at the hips. Though beautiful and feminine at first glance, the stiffness of the dress suggests a kind of protective armor, concealing the lower body, the seat of desire and pleasure. Her small, delicate right foot,

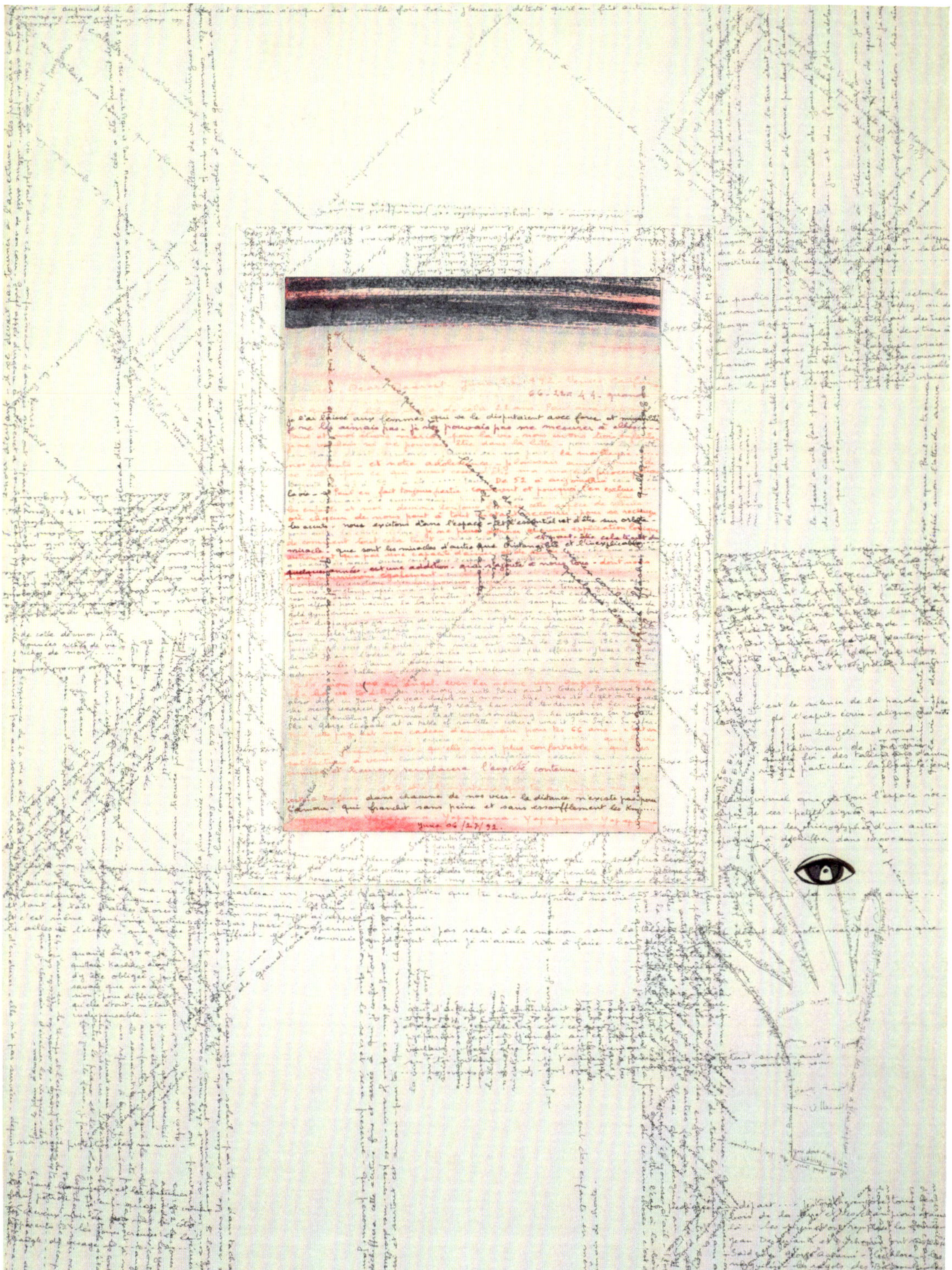

Une vie en quelques lignes, June 27, 1992
Mixed media on paper, 69 × 80 cm

Private collection, Beirut, Lebanon

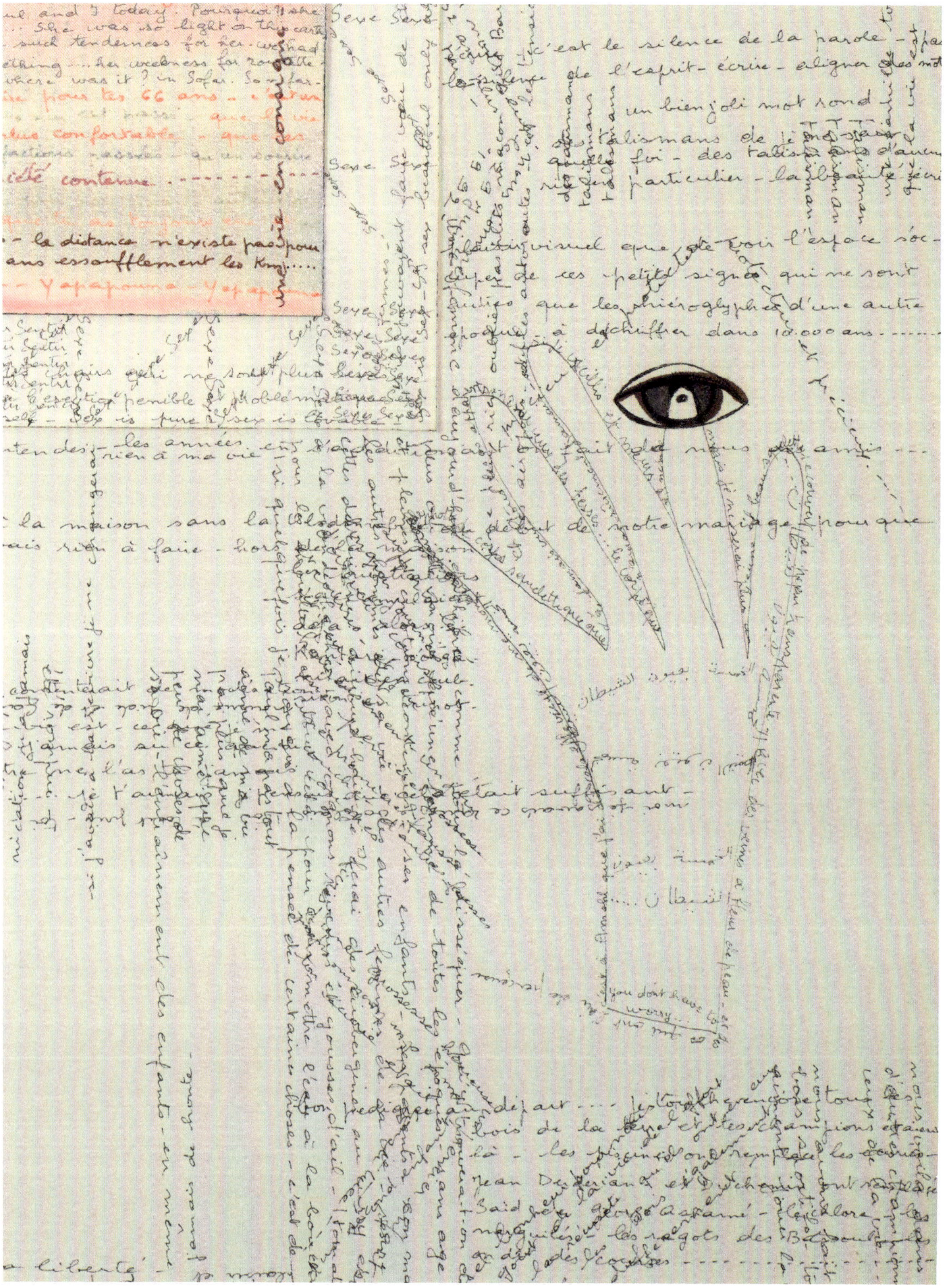

Une vie en quelques lignes (detail), June 27, 1992
Mixed media on paper, 69 × 80 cm

Private collection, Beirut, Lebanon

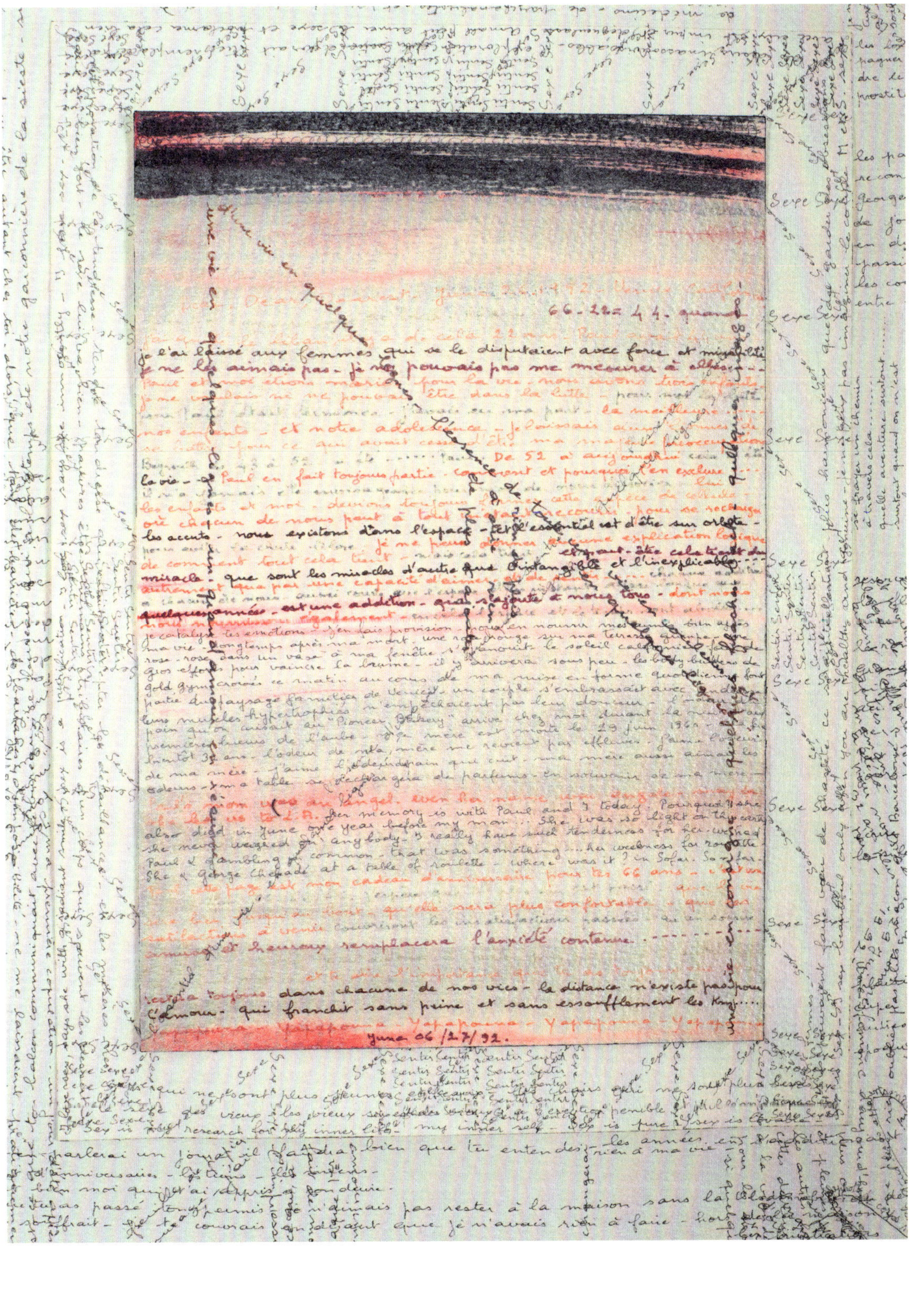

Une vie en quelques lignes (detail), June 27, 1992
Mixed media on paper, 69 × 80 cm

Private collection, Beirut, Lebanon

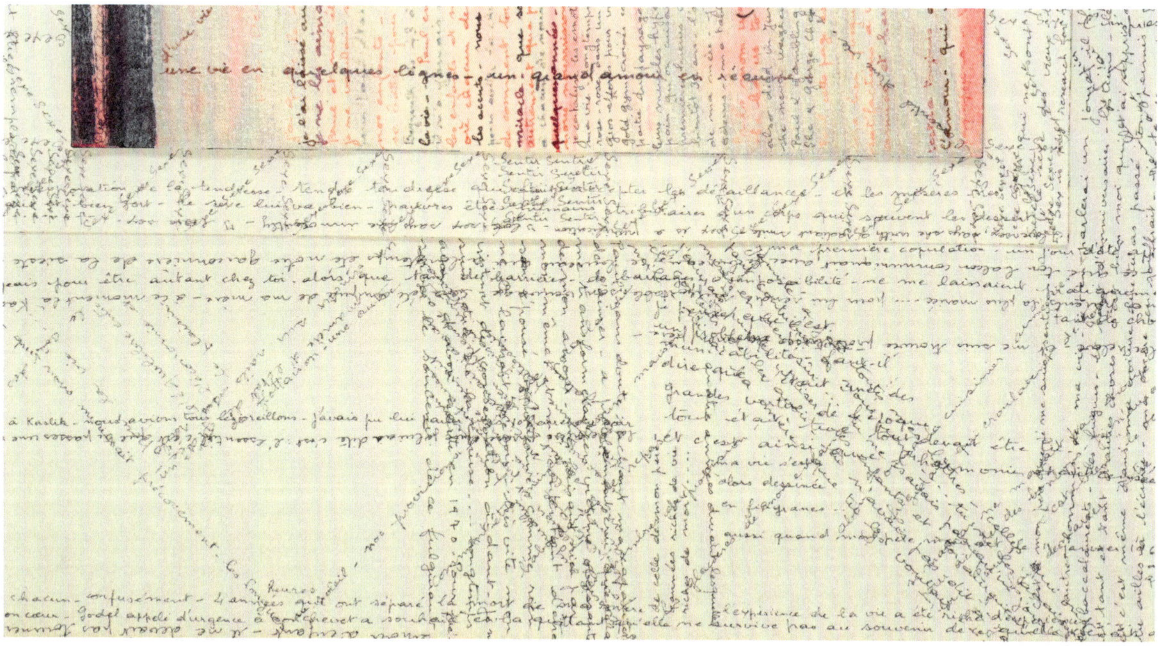

Une vie en quelques lignes (detail), June 27, 1992
Mixed media on paper, 69 × 80 cm

Private collection, Beirut, Lebanon

emerging from beneath the gold-and-white moiré skirt and pointed toward the left edge of the canvas, appears to lead her toward an exit—even as her body faces forward, toward the viewer.

In this painting, Caland makes extensive use of black and white—colors regarded as "non-colors" for centuries, yet reclaimed by artists as early as 1910 and now embraced as "authentic colors."[111] Black, like "dark matter," evokes the void before the Big Bang—a primal explosion that is at once terrifying and life-inducing. White suggests purity, mourning, and loss; two very symbolic hues. The hands—those essential tools for making, shaping, and expressing—are conspicuously absent. Instead, her oversized arms resemble wings: "My energy comes from the earth and gives me wings to fly..." A necessary, redemptive flight. The bride lifts her fabric-covered arms, releasing secrets she entrusts to the canvas. Her body forms a divide between two realms of the text: to the left, the expression of intimate emotions; to the right, a recounting of the wedding's organization and the unwavering support of her parents.

The sentences are short, almost telegraphic, and stripped of emotion—as if, between the ages of twelve and eighteen, all the emotional energy of her life had been consumed by this passionate love. The realization of its impossibility seems to have forged a kind of emotional armor, allowing her to mentally escape the situation. Without giving any name, Caland writes: "I loved him as one loves at 12... I stopped loving him at 18." Four words—*aimé*, *aime*, *aimer*, and *amour* [loved, loves, to love, and love]—punctuate these two brief sentences, capturing the intensity of her feelings and underscoring the depth of a narcissistic wound. It was, after all, with the artist's own money that the wedding rings were purchased. Marriage was neither her desire nor his. Moreover, the cross-stitch patterns that trace the contours of the dress and its various components seem to hold everything together—both the garment and the woman wearing it. As in the earlier collage, fifty-eight years after the wedding, black still looms over the bride's head, encapsulating space. Yet it is a blackness from which light emerges—in this case, the luminous white and gold dress that occupies a significant portion of the canvas... and of the artist's inner world, representing the process of sublimation. Then, in a moment of reverie, the latent emotional content is released—and once again, a painful experience is transformed into artistic creation.

111 M. Pastoureau, *Noir, Histoire d'une couleur*, (Le Seuil, Paris, 2008) 8.

La Mariée, Kantari, avril 1952, 2010
Mixed media on canvas, 252 × 98 cm

Private collection, Beirut, Lebanon

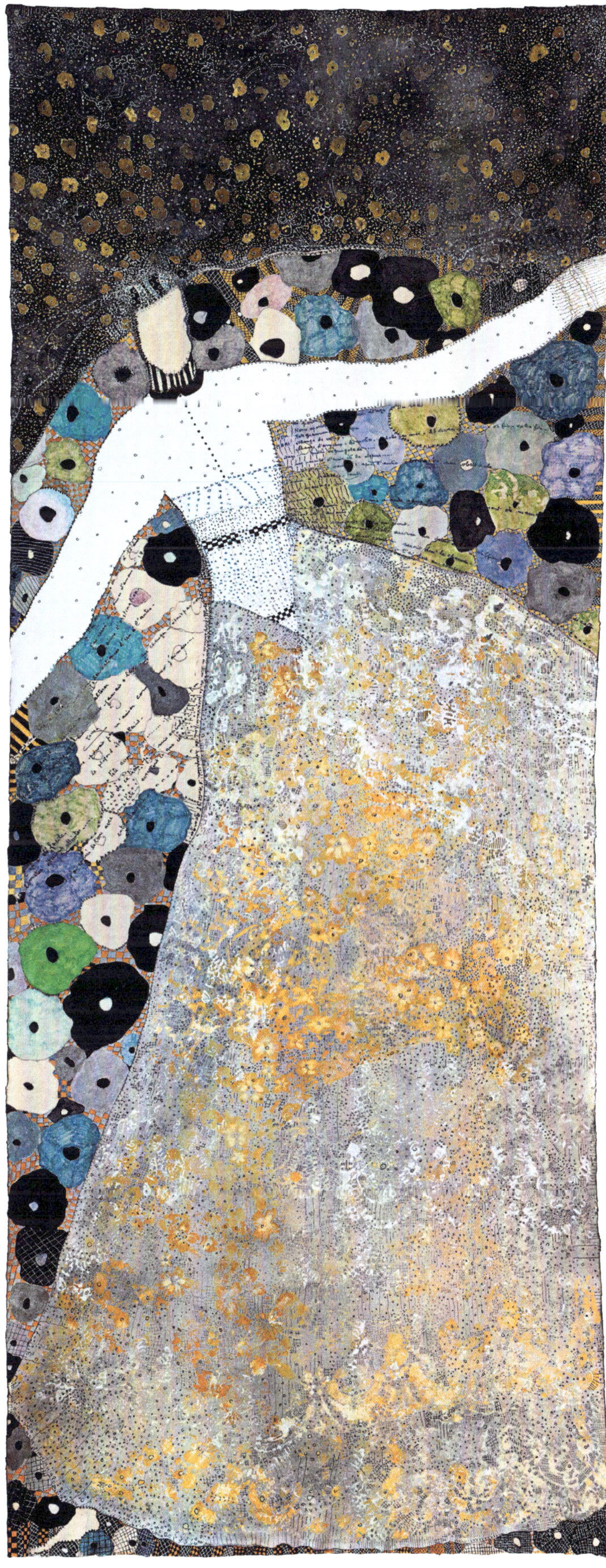

CONCLUSION

Throughout Caland's career, the integration of writing into her visual art served different purposes at different stages. Initially, in the late 1960s, she used the Arabic alphabet playfully across her paintings as a subtle form of social and cultural dissociation. This marked a gesture of independence—not only from her husband but also from the French-speaking milieu to which she belonged. By incorporating Arabic script, she asserted an alternative identity, embracing a sense of *Arabité* or Arabness that sets her apart. Then, beginning in June 1970, when she moved to Paris, French—her primary language—allowed her to infuse her work titles with the lightness and spontaneity that she was experiencing in her new life and adventures; even as the Lebanese Civil War was raging back home, which felt distant in her Parisian life. During her years with the sculptor Georges Apostu, her notebooks—filled with tender observations and her fine, rounded, fluid handwriting—documented shared moments of daily life. After his death, writing took on a new role: the diary she kept, often accompanied by drawings, became a tool for mourning and healing.

Later, after relocating to California—where she struggled to integrate into the local art community—the writing in her paintings, drawings, collages, and notebooks of the 1990s became primarily therapeutic. Like a form of "chimney sweeping," it allowed her to release her unconscious and ambivalent emotions, transforming resurfaced narcissistic wounds into creative expression. In a process akin to daydreaming—often shared with the viewer—Caland worked through chains of free association, drawing the viewer into her inner world.

Yet, shaped by an upbringing grounded in the ethos of "never complain, never explain," and perhaps driven by guilt over having been deceived (notably by Ed Moses), she frequently concealed or partially obscured the very texts that allowed her to voice latent anxieties. This oscillation between disclosure and concealment blurs the line between the conscious and unconscious, and introduces an element of play: with irony and whimsy, she invites the viewer into a game where meaning is elusive: words may disappear under ink, symbols, or washes of color; lines of text twist and turn, making them difficult to follow. This interplay of the spoken and unspoken intensifies when expression becomes impossible. In moments when words fail—or when she deliberately refuses to use them, "reduced to silence"—Caland retreats into the abstraction of the *Silent Letters* series. Here, the repressed still emerges, but shorn of language, remaining enigmatic. In this same spirit, she invents a silent, symbolic, and aesthetic language made up of signs—fragmented lines, checkerboards, cross-stitches, small and large circles—and recurring motifs such as a red-roofed house, flower, palm tree, or sailboat. Though these elements appear familiar, their deeper meaning ultimately escapes us.

When Caland returned to Beirut in 1994, she was deeply moved by the sight of a city ravaged by civil war—but equally touched by the beauty and resilience of the women of her homeland. Through poetic texts in French—serving also as a form of emotional and sensory archiving—her words, written in black ink over soft grey washes, amplify the expressive power of the text, where content takes precedence over form. She pays tribute to women and conveys her complex emotions toward a city she reclaims spiritually, even as she chooses to live elsewhere. During that same decade, everyday scribbles—notes, phone numbers, appointment times and dates—recorded in Arabic, French, and English, become documentation of lived moments across continents. These traces appear on her work dresses (*Smocks #31* and *#30*), garments that shift function when, during an exhibition opening, they are transformed into a spontaneous happening: guests are invited to sign and inscribe them with words, turning the smocks into communal canvases.

Having freed herself from the emotional weight of the past by creating, in 2000, her final collages based on Moustafa's letters, and having found a way to articulate the unspeakable through the *Silent Letters* series, Caland reaches a point of catharsis. Soothed by this process of sublimation—an immersive engagement with art that allows her to "play seriously"[112]—she is finally able to turn the page. Having processed life's upheavals, she continues to draw from her fears and narcissistic wounds as vital sources of artistic inspiration. She subtly confides her physical pain in her works (*Rossinante*), revisits her childhood and family memories, expresses enduring love for Paul, and invents a "*déliaison sur mesure*"—a "customized unbinding"—that allows her to detach while still remaining loyal to her emotional truth. In "reclaiming power over her experiences,"[113] she seems to declare, with both strength and subtlety: "I have digested life. I have not forgotten. I have made it my creative material. I have lived as I saw fit—and above all, I have preserved your place."[114] It is her way of remaining faithful both to her first love and to the adolescent that she once was, embodying what could be called a "prodigious force of symbolic resistance... and also an art of living."[115] Philosopher and psychoanalyst Anne Dufourmantelle once observed, "Gentleness can turn evil around and undo it better than any other response."[116] The enduring presence of Paul in Caland's life invites deeper reflection on her original choice of a partner—someone who, in every way (physically, culturally, intellectually, emotionally), was her opposite. Was this an unconscious decision that would one day provide her with the creative fuel she needed—to ultimately leave him, forge her own path, and invent her own life? Had she lived a happy, conventional marriage, would she have become an artist at all?

112 D. Arasse, *On n'y voit rien*, (Denoël, Paris, 2000) 13.
113 A. Dufourmantelle, Puissance de la douceur, (Payot Rivages Poches) 15.
114 Ibid., 15.
115 Ibid., 23.
116 Ibid., 20.

However, digesting one's life and transforming it into art is not the same as engaging in psychoanalysis—even when the words incorporated into the artworks allow repressed emotions to surface. In fact, Caland frequently represses this latent content once it begins to emerge in moments of reverie, covering it with marks, strokes of ink, or layers of paint. This act of repression is sometimes taken to the extreme, resulting in total abstraction. A refusal to see the words... they vanish the moment they are formed, or better yet, they never appear at all—replaced instead by precise, controlled gestures. But psychoanalysis cannot exist without language, and here, silence becomes a form of resistance. Was avoiding analytical introspection, for Caland, one of the very conditions that allowed her to remain an artist?[117] Moreover, this publication does not attempt to analyze her—that could only have been her own choice—but rather seeks to better understand her creative process.

From her early use of the Arabic alphabet to the silent or fragmented lines that evolve into a personal language designed to "remain incomprehensible," Caland constructs a world of her own. She positions herself outside of artistic trends and movements, transcending borders and cultures, while subtly referencing societal events. Rather than "disturb[ing] the silence and stillness of the pictorial work,"[118] her delicate inscriptions—imbued with humor and lightness, even in times of deep hardship—enrich the work. They invite the viewer to follow the unfolding story of a life and a career that spanned nearly fifty years.

117 Lou Andréas Salomé dissuades Rainer Maria Rilke from undergoing psychoanalysis.
118 J. Berger, *Ways of Seeing*, (BBC/ Penguin Books, London, 1972), 32.

ARTIST BIOGRAPHY

Huguette Caland grew up in an aristocratic, urban, and primarily French-speaking environment on her mother's side, and a mountain-rooted, perfectly bilingual background on her father's side. Her father, Bechara El-Khoury, came from Rechmaya in the Chouf region. A lawyer by training, he was fluent in Arabic and French, as well as Latin and Greek, which he learned during his Jesuit education. From a young age, Bechara was immersed in political life and listened to the adult conversations around him,[119] familiarizing himself with the political landscape of the time. After practicing law, he was appointed secretary-general of the Lebanese government in 1920. He went on to become the president of the Court of Criminal Appeals, head of the Ministry of the Interior in Lebanon's first government under the French Mandate, president of the council, head of the Public Education Ministry, founder of the Destour Party in 1932, and a staunch opponent of French domination in Lebanon. In 1943, he became the first president of the Republic of Lebanon. In 1922, he married Laure Chiha, sister of Michel Chiha—a banker, politician, and writer.

It was into this complex political landscape that Huguette was born in 1931. At sixteen, she studied for a year with Fernando Manetti, an Italian painter residing in Lebanon. She began studying law at Université Saint-Joseph but had to stop after a serious car accident. In 1952, she married Paul Caland, whom she had met at the age of twelve (ten years earlier) and had fallen in love with. Paul was the nephew of Georges Naccache, a fierce political opponent of her father, then president of Lebanon—and to complicate matters, Paul was also French. Together, they had three children. Later, Moustafa, her husband's best friend, became her lover: "The trio scandalized society not only through their presence but also through their recurring depiction in Huguette's art."[120] Upon her father's death in 1964, she discarded her entire wardrobe, symbolically freeing herself from the past by choosing to wear abayas—loose-fitting garments in which she finally felt comfortable. She then enrolled at the American University of Beirut, studying fine arts from 1964 to 1968. Her first painting, Red Sun/Cancer (1964), was a monochrome red canvas symbolizing both the illness that claimed her father's life and the dawn of a new era. In 1968, she co-founded Inaash, an organization helping Palestinian women in refugee camps support their families through embroidery work.

119 B. El Khoury, *Lebanese Realities*, (Éditions L'Orient-Le Jour, Beirut, 2007), 17–21.
In the mid-nineteenth century, Bechara's paternal great-grandfather served as a judge representing the Christian community under the Druze *kaimakam* (district governor), before becoming a member of the Court of Appeals. His father held high-ranking administrative posts toward the end of the century, initially as the head of the Arab Bureau within the *Mutasarrifate*, and subsequently as the director of the Civil Appeals Department.

120 K. Wilson-Goldie, *Huguette Caland, Body Works*, May 24, 2019, https://www.tate.org.uk/tate-etc/issue-46-summer-2019/huguette-caland-body-works-kaelen-wilson-goldie.

In 1970, she left Lebanon for Paris. "I wanted to have my own identity," she told *The Los Angeles Times*[121] and *The New York Times*. "In Lebanon, I was the daughter of, the wife of, the mother of, the sister of. It was such a feeling of freedom to wake up alone in Paris. I needed to stretch... I thought I was strong enough to face the world with my work. I thought I had wings to fly and I said goodbye to everyone."[122] In Paris, she mingled with many artists, including André Masson, Louis Féraud, Adalberto Mecarelli, Pierre Schaeffer, and Andrée Chédid. In 1978–1979, she created *Nour*, a collection of haute couture abayas for Pierre Cardin. When her partner, Romanian sculptor George Apostu,[123] died in late 1986, Caland left Paris. Throughout those years, she produced an impressive body of erotic works—drawings and paintings—particularly the *Bribes de corps*, *Limousin*, and *Granite* series.

In 1987, Caland settled in California, first renting a room at a friend's place, then two small houses, before building her dream studio in 1997. "California is a blessed place. I feel at home in Venice. I have many friends, I know many artists. There's an interesting diversity. I love the way things move. I was told it was a cultural desert, but it's not. [...] It's a blessing for me."[124] She built the studio like "a cathedral," as she spent most of her time there. The space was designed for her work, with no doors except for the guest bathroom. She joked: "I never want to feel claustrophobic in my house."[125] There, she produced many works, including the series *Silent Letters* (1997–2004), *Christine* (1992 and 1997), *Hommage to Pubic Hair* (1992), *Autumn* (2009), and *Childhood Memories* (2010–2012). In addition, she hosted her neighbors, friends, and the local art community—Ed Moses, Tony Berlant, Billy Al Bengston, Chris Burden, Nancy Rubins, Larry Bell, Frank Gehry, etc.—as well as numerous visitors. She regularly made the space available for cultural events and charitable causes. Yet, "though she built a community of artists in the U.S., the Los Angeles art scene was, quite surprisingly, harsh toward Caland.[126]" She lived there until July 2013, when she returned to Lebanon to say goodbye to her husband. There, she discovered she was suffering from a neurological condition and remained until her death in September 2019.

Her professional recognition began in Lebanon in the mid-1990s, spread across the Middle East in the 2000s, and reached international acclaim starting in 2012. She participated in group exhibitions in the U.S., Europe, and the Middle East,[127] including *Le Corps découvert* at

121 A. M. O'Connor, "*Her Magical World*," *Los Angeles Times*, June 2003, accessed online on February 18, 2023.

122 K. Q. Seelye, "*Huguette Caland, 88, Dies: Celebrated Freedom in Art and Life*," *New York Times*, September 30, 2019, accessed online in May 2023.

123 Georges Apostu was a Romanian artist, who became a political refugee in France in 1983. He was officially married to Bogdana, a Romanian violon-cellist, who still lived in Bucharest. He had two official mistresses whom Caland was aware of. Caland and Apostu, who were lovers (1983–1986), never shared an apartment but traveled together mainly in France where he used to work in quarries in the Limousin or elsewhere. The two would live with local families, who would host them. During this period, Caland created a series of terra-cotta sculptures that were produced into bronze in 2014.

124 O'Connor, "Her Magical World."

125 Ibid.

126 K. Wilson-Goldie, "'Liberated, Rebellious and Historically Consequential': Remembering Huguette Caland" (1931-2019)," New Books Network, consulted online February 2023.

127 See resume page p. 200-202.

the Institut du Monde Arabe, *Modernités Plurielles (*2014) at the Centre Pompidou, *Prospect 3 (*2015) in New Orleans, *Made in L.A.* (2016), the Sharjah Biennial (2019), *Women in Abstraction* (2021) at both the Centre Pompidou and the Guggenheim Museum in Bilbao. Her solo exhibitions included those at Tate St Ives (2019), Mathaf: Arab Museum of Modern Art, Doha (2020), the Drawing Center, New York (2021), and Wiels, Brussels (2022), Reina Sofia, Madrid (2025), Deichtorhallen, Hamburg (2025). Her works are in the institutional collections of the Tate National and the British Museum in London; the Centre Pompidou in Paris; the Metropolitan Museum and MoMA in New York; the Toledo Museum of Art; LACMA and the Hammer Museum in Los Angeles; Ministry of Culture, Saudi Arabia; the Guggenheim Foundation in Abu Dhabi; Mathaf in Qatar; and both the Sharjah Art Foundation and Barjeel Art Foundation, along with numerous private collections worldwide.

ANNEXES

1. Illustrations and texts in the artwork

2. The Evolution of Writing and its presence in Art

3. Huguette Caland

4. Bibliography

ILLUSTRATIONS AND TEXTS IN THE ARTWORKS

Tout est possible dans une ville démolie, (Everything is Possible in a Demolished City), 1993

Ink on Canson paper, 21 × 29.7 cm

Private collection, Beirut, Lebanon

(view page 104)

Everything is possible in a demolished city
Ruins can only allow us to dream
Of hope – an exhausted region calls
For transfusions – for fusions – blood is
Dangerous nowadays – it also carries
Death like rockets – we take
all the chances – but maybe from us
guinea pigs – will emerge human beings
healed by the war – by suffering that will wish
peace and tolerance for a few
generations … and then one
day other wars – will have other peace
and will encounter the soul enriched by even more
history – heavier with more sensuality
How I love this country …. How much I love it… more
so than I imagined – I love it abstract
And concrete and starved to death – mutilated
With as many cancers as grains
Of polluted sand – a country more lively than
Soft countries with mowed lawns of which oozes
boredom – the worst kind of death.

Les Femmes de ma ville, (The Women of My City) *1993*

Ink on Canson paper, 21 × 29.7 cm

Private collection, Paris, France

Translation of *Huguette Caland, A Life in a Few Lines,* from the catalog published by Reina Sofia

(view page 105)

The eyes of the women of my city are
messengers of love– survival that recounts
experiences with acceptation – simplicity
without emphasis – murmuring rather
more than the opposite – a nod of the head
a tear that appears at the corner of the
eye – moving women
bearers if tragedies and hope. Rounded
by love and tenderness – perfidious women
of Beirut – reservoirs of sensuality
neither occupations nor preoccupations
have made you lose that vision
that unforgettable vision of life
of death – of childhood – women
of Beirut how I love you – all of you
toothless old women – young women full of breasts
and buttocks – of grace or of problems

Une vie en quelques lignes, (A Life in a Few Lines), June 27, 1992

Mixed media on paper, 69 × 80 cm

Private collection, Beirut, Lebanon

Translation of *Huguette Caland, A Life in a Few Lines,* from the catalog published by Reina Sofia

(view page 163-166)

A life in a few lines – the absence of a whole lifetime in color and in

a few lines

a life in a few lines – the summary of a great love

A life on record – a few flashbacks – a few images

Nothing more

to say – nothing

more to add

On the central page darkened by two black bands of different sizes, placed on a pink background; just at the bottom, an iridescent band

Dear, dear, dearest June, Venice California

(Pale pink on light grey background)

A sentence *(written in very pale gray)* of which one can guess some letters but cannot decipher the word entirely; it ends with an ellipsis and a colon:

To the right of the paper in violet/mauve:

66—22= 44 when

I left Lebanon 44 years ago Paul was 44 years old

(Pale pink on white background)
(Black ink on white background)

When I left him to the women who fought over him forcefully and

miserably I did not like them – I could not stand up to them...

Paul and I were married for life we have three children and I neither

wanted nor was able to fight for me the fighting

for all of us was over [?] I had had my share [?] the best...

our children and our adolescence I was leaving... [?]

(Two missing words)

to fight for what had ceased to be my main preoccupation

from 43 to 52 had been Paul from 52 to today that had been

my life ... Paul is still a part of it – how and why exclude you from it...

it has never been conceivable for [?] to of... him

the children... and I would always have to form this sort of cell

where each of us can at every ... return to recharge....

the batteries... we exist in space and the most important thing is to

Be in orbit

to avoid plummeting I cannot give a logical explanation

of how all this holds up, but it holds up and maybe this is a

miracle – what are miracles if not the intangible and the inexplicable...

Other than by an ability to love and to feel... each addition

(Almost illegible)

a few years and an addition which adds itself to us all and from which

we also feed ourselves in that way space and time are abolished

I catalyze emotions and store them up to my [] long after

my life... a long time after my death a red rose on my terrace climbs a

Pink rose in a vase at my window fades in the Californian sun making

great efforts to overcome the mist – it will succeed soon – the body builders at

Gold gym that I ran into this morning during my daily fitness session are

part of the familiar landscape of Venice – a couple kissed tenderly

their abnormally enlarged muscles were no obstacle to gentleness the

aroma of the bread

that was baked at the "pioneer bakery" reaches my home during the

night and in

the early hours of dawn my mother died on the 29th of June 1960 that was nearly 35 years ago the perfume of my mother comes back to me as a

whiff – I like the smell

Of my mother I like the smell of bread baking – my mother also liked

smells – my table will be empty of its perfumes – in my memories of my mother

Paul's mother was an angel even her name was Angel...

(Two illegible words)

also died in June one year before my mom.

She was so light on this earth

She never weighed on anybody . I really have such tenderness for her we had

Paul & gambling in common – that was something – her weakness for roulette

She & Georges Chehadé at a table of roulette – where was it? In Sofar ... So far.

Paul this page is my birthday present for your 66th birthday – it's a

I hope that more .... After.... That life

Will be good until the end that it will be more comfortable that our

future satisfactions will cover up the past dissatisfactions that smiles

(or trouble ???)

[?] [or troubles] will funny and happy will replace the contained anxiety.......

And to tell you the importance that you have always had

will remain in both of our lives – there is no such thing as distance for

love – which crosses without difficulty and without shortness of breath the kms.....

Yapapouna yapapouna yapapouna yapapouna yapapouna

June 06/27/1992

Smell smeel smell smell

Smell smeel smell smell

Smell smeel smell smell

Smell smeel smell smell

Sex sex sex

Sex sex sex

Sex sex sex

Sex sex sex

Over the initial text
In a diagonal line:

A life in a few lines – the absence of a whole
lifetime in color

(Just below the last part of this line)

and in a few lines

A line across the entire letter creating a left margin:

a life in a few lines – the summary of a great love

Two diagonal lines in the opposite direction, from bottom to top:

The essence in colors

The essential in a few lines

The essence of a life in a few lines

The essence of a life in a few lines

A line on the right, read from bottom to top, creates a smaller margin::

A life on record – a few flashbacks –
a few images

In the center vertically, three small lines written from top to bottom.

Nothing more

To say – nothing

More to add

Second page underneath this one (onto which the initial letter is glued)
On four central lines on all four sides: feel =

To feel to feel to feel to feel

To feel to feel to feel to feel

To feel to feel to feel to feel

To feel to feel to feel to feel

Diagonally: "sex sex" all around the surface between the first drawing/"letter to
Paul" and the edges of the second sheet of paper = 2.5 cm

On the second sheet of paper, on the lower side of the work:

[?] and those who are no longer young and have
flesh that is no

Longer smooth

(Continued on the right side)

and firm

And the older people's sex and the old people? The difficult and problematic erection

Sex is research for my inner life – my inner self – sex is pure – sex is lovable

On the right side of the work, second page:
(Continuation of the first line at the bottom)

They could have taken a vow of chastity it would be so much more harmonious than to hold on to obsessions

Sex is sex – sex is beautiful only when you are healthy and genuine – I cannot imagine the couple M and S

(Moustafa andSalma?)

sex

Second page, at the top of the work:

Unfulfilled desires – exploration {] should be replaced by

With them is impure and disgusting – amahl might like sex and proclaim it's good

Second page, to the left of the work:

Exploration of the tenderness that makes one accept failures – and miseries

Loud and clear – sex suits them – poor human beings dependent upon a body that often serves them poorly;

(Last line on the edge to be read upside down):

I love sex, says she with a radiant smile, sex is a purification – I love sex says she innocently – I love sex

On the largest sheet:
Lower part of the page, with the hand on the right side
Left side:

It is my father that I felt I was

The other men in my life – I will talk about them one day – you should hear eventually – the years as they add up have made us friends

In the center, on one line:

Nothing to my life

The baccalaureates – the escapes – yours – mine [] of theirs

and so many other things it is me that has [taught] you to drive

it was even in my car that you passed your driving test – I did

not like to stay at home without the [] at the beginning of our marriage so that

you could got to the stable – my mother suffered because of it – I covered

up for you by saying that I had nothing to do outside of the house

When in 1970 I left Kaslik – before

I was forced to – I knew that my decision – as difficult ss it was – was essential for me...

Lower in the same direction:

My real protector was my mother –

The languorous eyes and the

petrol blue suits – God how I wanted you

You [] black hair and the visible

ribs – hollow cheeks and the

triangle of the face....

Lower center:

Who, moreover, would be satisfied with moderation

..... and...... I

was preparing myself I never knew what you wanted maybe you never

knew yourself ... - I loved you I thought it was enough –

On the lower part of the page, to the right:

Good pedigree to begin with .... I still touch all the

wood on earth and your champions were

there – swimming pools have replaced the stables

Jean Derdérian and Duchemin have replaced

Said Georges Ashamé – the chlorine

The hookahs – the gossip of the Bassouls

The rumors of the races...........

Just above the hand on the tip of the index an eye
As a bracelet:

The five in the eyes of the devil

The devil in the eyes of the fine

Then the same sentence written upside down
On the wrist:

The five in the eyes of the devil

A bit lower:

You don't need to Worry

Pivoting the piece, in a paragraph to the right:

Paul no doubt [] my ability to love him – probably believed that it would transform me into an obedient victim of my love – never doing anything by myself and being content as his wife []
(two words) just as

(Two words)

he could not anticipate that very soon spurred by my instinct of self-preservation – I withdrew from the race... a long time before I left in 1970. To preserve the memory of this dazzling

(At the edge of the page, the writing going toward the top of the artwork)

childish love- it should not turn into bitterness at the first confronta-

(At the top edge)

tions --- - I would have today the memory of that love blessed a thousand times – I would have hated it to be otherwise ....

On the right side of the artwork a paragraph almost symmetrical to the one on the other side:

Reserve of water reserve of oxygen – reserve –

Flowers grow on my terrace and

tomatoes too – parsley and mint

rosemary and basil – I am waiting for some

big sunflowers which will dominate the

situation and go looking for their sun

above the balustrade – Paul

never looked after plants....

maybe in his old age he will

like – plants and his grandchildren....

Writing is the silence of words – not

the silence of the mind – to write – to line up words

A pretty round word

talismans from an unknown

faith – talismans from no

particular rite – the beauty written

The visual pleasure of seeing the space busy with

these little signs that are

nothing by hieroglyphs of another

time -to be deciphered in 10,000 years' time....

On the lower part of the piece, on the larger piece of paper:

Immoderate love...

(Written upside down)

And also and especially this love for you which is like each 1st

had made me today – what I am – my sorrows – my disappointments –

the impression that the secret will be preserved – that nobody will ever

(Upside down)

Decipher this fine and compact writing in which I confide all that which has

Tight writing against the second page, in the quarter bottom part of the page:

My first copulation – a summer day after sunbathing for a long time on the floor in your bedroom

(Upside down)

I remember the red of the sunset – did your balcony communicate with the office that office that for a long time was our bachelor flat for the siesta – siesta snatched behind the back of my governess – of my

(Upside down)

family – how did I find ways to be at your house so often –when there were so many obstacles – barricades of impossibility – left me with practically no freedom – and how also for many years did you manage to come so often to my house

– without ever running into my parents the most married .... To make it supportable without [...] sage was amputated from my mother – at that time, Kaslik swarmed with life – with amorous intrigues the 29th of June 1960 – feast of Saints Peter and Paul – my mother was dying in Kaslik – we all had the mumps – I had been able to speak to her around 10 in the evening the last sentence I said to her was: the most important thing is that you have a good night – it was the worst night of her life

Top of the piece *(upside down)*

The wildest desires were

in the air – but life throbbed in everyone – confusedly – 4 years hours

(On the top alone: heures - hours)

that separated the death of my mother from that of my father

Years filled with life

filled with death-----

A little higher

Four years during which

Further towards the edge of the page

the experience of life was rich in experiences.....

Under "in the air":

Acute pulmonary edema – the final stopping of her heart – Godel who was called urgently to her bedside upon leaving her expressed the wish that she should not survive the memory of what she [had to] endure – she did not survive – I have been an orphan ever since ----

A paragraph at the bottom left of the piece: read while pivoting:

In 1952, his cheeks had

filled out – the

languorous eyes now controlled

their languor

Faced with my

presence – the petrol blue

suits had become

more subdued –

The black hair still

took up a lot of

time ----

Bodybuilding too

Bravo Yapapouna

Next paragraph:

I felt that the most important things

had been transmitted

to the children that until death

they would know what

my answers to their questions would have been

Love also should cross

distances – it was strong

(One line different text)

Enough to do so – I

(Lower on the page upside down)

stocked up on love

set my priorities – to know the difficult paths

that I was choosing – to evaluate the risks

Next paragraph

I think that it is

a problem [...] [of]

communicability – need we

say that it was one of the

great virtues of the era –

everything was too much everything had to be [read?] –

and it is in this way that harmony was supposed to be established

between the piano and the violin

Thus my live was drawn

between the lines –

Also, when my father died on the 11th of January 1964 – I had interior

time and space....

At the top right corner of the piece, paragraph:

I no longer – remember te make of

make of Michel Haddad's car – the one in which we

shared so much – the first kiss on

a stormy night after being cleaned out at the races

Lower:

Today the earth trembled in Venice – the
movement was peculiar –as if the earth were

pleasuring her lover – it was the movement of a
woman making love

The past soon made way for the present – and the
normal concerns of earthquakes

in California – took priority over the love of
gambling and of the women of an adole

cent that I evoked yesterday

Today for me – it remains to be seen whether I will
have a green card and I am destined to have
just enough

to ensure my material independence – yes of course
– if I am going

to find myself in a much more comfortable
situation – of course

not

to make one's way

through this

what an adventure especially

especially when one is

not yet a woman

and never a gambler

At the bottom of the page:

a ready-made family – made to measure – that is
what Paul found –

how funny life is the hoped-for otherwise the
expected happens

Before:

never forget anything again neither mâcon nor
Barcelona

and the airports – and the motorways – and the
tensions

Below:

talismans

talismans

talismans

Lower, written upside down:

talisman
talisman
talisman

In diagonal in the center right:

Michel
and Paul called
me because
the earth trembled yesterday
by the bedside of my mother
who died 32 years ago
I felt
closest to Michel – as close as
possible – that day Nina
Helou rescued us
from a multitude of intruders –
and provided us with a short
respite ---
before confronting the
others
My mother was there only for us
32 year later .... it is the 29th of June 1992

On three lines,
in diagonal:

To speak about you to a sheet of paper
To trust life is an act of great courage I have
To my instinct –

In diagonal on the other side next to the hand:

For you the
For your bed
Calculations in installments of life and in economy
It is important that pleasure be calculated
In relation to the economy of
Medications
Of doctors – of psychoanalysts – and in relation to
the cost

Of a nervous breakdown

On the right of the page:

The long walks in the Bekaa accompanying you
to Joseph Skaf's house and rather than learning
civil law you got to know Hilmet – the beautiful

prostitute on someone else expenses

The words studied carefully according to the

recommendations of said the jockey – or of

Georges Ashamé -------
this justified passing one third

of the day in the stables – and two thirds

talking passionately about the races – the only true

passion that I witnessed – the races –

races and more races the rivalry

between gambling and women is the only true one

In a square on top of the page:

Khalil called me – the advantage of earthquakes

is that people that you have get in touch with you
to say –

(Right angle)

Look we're thinking of you –

(Right angle)

Aïda called – Vicky too – and Maryse without

(Right angle)

knowing that the earth had trembled

(Right angle)

Ghislaine not yet nor Marie-Claire –
Helen from Washington

(Right angle)

yesterday – who else is there in Lebanon?

(Right angle)

Paul and Michel and Milad

(Right angle)

trapped in the blue?

(Right angle)

[...] because I think about him

(Below)

His eyes-----

The economy between

(Right angle)

the price of things and the appetite for life

(Right angle)

often always [on?]

Sun that burned our skin – which ignited our

(Right angle)

desires – which made us precociously mature
mature – the long hours

(Heures (hours) one word on a line in between the two lines of the right angle)

in the sun – our provisions [?] for life

How to be [] but []

The abundance of meals

The rooms full of provisions –

Les glacières de mon enfance -----

Abou the beloved cook

The refrigerators overflowing with

If my mother had not sent me with the chauffeur

to buy sweets – I would probably never have

had Paul – it's good – green is hope

I [became disillusioned?] to cut a long story short

Around the hand:

It was to Amahl that I said I [have just] of me []

Skeletal that I had never seen all the

apparent bones even the bones of the buttocks ---
the body that

I would surely never have

If I grow old and die of anemia

But I would never be again

I would have [been a] beautiful skeleton

Covered in transparent skin with veins close to the
surface

And bones like drills

(Right angle below the hand)

Precious and protective

Protective and precious

La mariée, Kantari, avril 1952, 2010
Mixed media on canvas, 252 × 98 cm
Private collection, Beirut, Lebanon

(voir page 168-169)

Text under the right arm on several lines:

I have loved him as one loves at 12 year old

I have stopped being in love with him at 18

I lived my life in parallel (black stain) loved by determination

We were hermetic towards one another

He was unable to alter me

When I understood that he will not go further and changing was not for him...

That he couldn't love me like I loved

The ceiling was reached

My head had bumped into...

It was easy, the limits were reached ... and of this hole I flew away...

I dug the hole with my head... with everything that was necessary...

One line that follows the contour of the dress starting at the waist:

For the [?] programs instead of the presidential house for the party the Saint Georges Hotel

At the top like a suspension lost in the veil just above the left hand:

"here goes the bride"

A little lower, along the edge of the veil, like a staggered continuation just above the left arm:

"here flies the bride"

On the other side under the left arm:

... at my father's arm

Apostolic nonce

Telegram from the pope

Husband... vow exchange

RING exchange, ours bought by me 23 pounds of extra fine gold

livres [] d'or fin extra fin

Floors... what a quick deterioration

La mes parents d'avoir été là depuis ....

[?] one obstacle after another

The hardest to get over – Paul –

Big wedding yes –

Why –

To pretend not getting married without the [?] of my mother

They were perfect

[One illegible word : defais, delais]

... giving to the end –

[] for being there at the beginning [] difficult

Had I known how hard the road would be –

I learned while understanding [plusieurs mots]of this

[sous fleur grise]....

THE EVOLUTION OF WRITING AND ITS PRESENCE IN ART

Since the end of the Middle Ages, many artists have integrated writing into their artworks. This inclusion takes various forms: signatures or initials, dedications that transform the piece into a message, sentences[1] or words imagined as spoken by the characters depicted,[2] inscriptions like street names[3] or geographic markers,[4] or even textual identifiers added to noble figures within the work to make them more easily recognizable to viewers. In some cases, text becomes a key narrative or symbolic element within the composition. For instance, in his portrait of the Arnolfini couple, Jan van Eyck inscribed "*Johannes van Eyck fuit hic*" (Johannes van Eyck was here), affirming his presence at the scene, and thus his elevated status, which allowed him to attend this wedding. Similarly, the portraitist Hans Holbein the Younger (1497–1543) often included the sitter's age or sometimes only a date, with or without a name,[5] adding a documentary quality to his portraits. In Albrecht Dürer's portrait of Emperor Maximilian, completed after the emperor's death, the artist includes the Habsburg coat of arms in the upper left corner and, on the right, a text that praises the monarch and records his birth and death dates—serving as both a commemoration and documentation. In Enguerrand Quarton's *Pietà* of Villeneuve-lès-Avignon (1455), a faint inscription appears in the halos, more or less visible depending on the lighting. Rather than identifying the figures, the text encourages the viewer "to pronounce their names with respect as often as possible."[6] As Michel Butor notes, this echoes the tradition of Egyptian tombs, where hieroglyphic inscriptions were intended to ensure the continual utterance of the deceased's name.[7] Each of the twelve medallions painted by Pieter Bruegel the Elder contains a proverb from the period that corresponds with the depicted character.[8] In his other works, Bruegel places at the bottom of a medallion a poignant phrase attributed to the figure: "As the world is so misleading, I will go in pain."[9] In paintings of urban settings,[10] billboards often appear, contributing to the narrative or atmosphere. Even in historical works such as Jacques-Louis David's *The Death of Marat*[11] (1793) and *The Distribution of the Eagles at the Champ-de-Mars*[12] (1810), textual elements are incorporated as part of the composition.

In the early 20th century, artists began including titles directly within the artwork[13] or adding handwritten notes along pencil-drawn lines.[14] Some works depict open books[15]—ranging from clearly legible to completely abstract[16]—while others feature newspapers[17] or clippings.[18] Many artists began to imitate writing,[19] invent scripts[20], or use letters[21] as visual elements. In the United States, Robert Rauschenberg and other artists from the Black Mountain College[22] were notable for incorporating text into their visual practice. Ed Ruscha, in particular, based much of his work on typography and lettering.

In the Middle East, since the early Islamic period, Arabic calligraphy has been an integral part of architecture and its elements adorned across tiles, fountains, sculptures, reliefs, and more. In modern and contemporary art, many artists have continued this tradition by incorporating writing into their visual work. The *Hurufiyya* movement—sometimes referred to as "Arab abstraction"—emerged in Iraq in the early

1970s. Rooted in modernist principles, it sought to explore the aesthetic and spiritual potential of Arabic script. Key figures such as Shakir Hassan Al-Said (influenced by Sufism), Jamil Hamoudi (1924–2004), Madiha Omar (1909–2005), and Dia Al-Azzawi(b. 1939), among others, signed the manifesto *Al-Buʿd al-Wahid* (Only One Dimension), which drew on Sufi vocabulary and introduced new theoretical frameworks for the use of Arabic letters—frameworks they envisioned as applicable across the Arab-Islamic[23] world. Numerous artists from across the region have integrated text into their work for a wide range of purposes—religious, political, and social, or as talismans, poetic verses, or visual elements enriched with drawings and paintings. including artists from Lebanon: Aref el Rayess, Lutfi Ghorayeb, Etel Adnan, Jamil Molaeb, Shafic Sayegh, Walid Raad, Mohamad Khatat Katanani, Marwan Rechmaoui; from Iraq: Abdul Rauf Rafei, Shaikha Al Kaabi, Issam Khayat, Madiha Umar, Shakir Hassan Al-Said, Jamil Hamoudi, Hassan Massoudy, Dia Al-Azzawi (notably in his *Muʿallaqat* series); from the United Arab Emirates: Mohammed Mandi, Abdul Qadir Al-Raes; from Algeria: Rachid Koraichi, Mohammed Khadda; Ali Hassan (Qatar); Fatima Behbehani (Kuwait); Mohammed Mandi, Abdul Qadir Al-Raes (UAE); Mahmoud Hamad (Syria); Kamal Boullata (Palestine); Rachid Koraichi, Mohammed Khadda (Algeria); Omar El-Nagdi (Egypt); Ahmed Mater (Saudi Arabia); and Lalla Essaydi (Morocco), among others. Special mention should be made of Carla Salem, who creatively blends Arabic and Japanese calligraphy, and Adlita Stephan, who invents glyph-like forms that resemble letters but are not linguistically readable.

When discussing this topic Huguette Caland is never mentioned perhaps because this is the first study to address it. Yet the significant number of her works that feature writing clearly indicates an intentional practice, one that invites deeper inquiry. Recent research uncovered a painting of hers from 1968 containing a few Arabic letters and signs, which—pending further discoveries—may mark the genesis of her incorporating writing into her artwork. However, for approximately the next fifteen years, Caland's work—predominantly erotic—did not contain writing. It was only in 1983 that text began to reappear, first in her notebooks, and then, starting in the early 1990s, as a recurring expressive element within her pictorial work and across various media.

1 M. Butor, *Les Mots dans la peinture*, op. cit., p. 104-110 – as in the work of Juan de Valdès Leal, *Postrimerias* (1672)

2 *Portrait de vieille femme de Giorgione* (1508-1510).

3 *Rue des Francs-Bourgeois de Barthold* (1868)

4 *Inondation à Port-Marly de Sisley* (1876).

5 M. Butor, *Les Mots dans la peinture*, op. cit., p. 36.

6 Ibid., p. 49.

7 Ibid., p. 49.

8 Ibid., p. 59 Museum Mayer van den Bergh in Antwerp

9 Ibid., p. 62 which is located in the Naples Museum and which is titled *Le Misanthrope* (1568)

10 Léonard Defrance, *À l'égide de Minerve*, XVIIIe siècle, Dijon, musée des Beaux-Arts

11 M. Butor, *Les Mots dans la peinture*, op. cit., p. 130-134, where one can see the letter from Charlotte Corday that Marat is holding in his hand, two other written sheets, the dedication "To Marat" and below the signature "David."

12 Ibid., p. 152-153 the painter inserts historical inscriptions.

13 Ibid. p. 65 image p. 66 In certain works by Picabia, Duchamp, or Juan Miró (e.g., VOILA LA FEMME, 1915, in capital letters centered at the top of the work), 70-74 *Le passage de la vierge à la mariée* (1912) inscription at the bottom left of the work; *In La clef des songes* (1930), a compartmentalization or a title—shifted in meaning—is inscribed in each box below the object. In the work entitled *Escargot Femme Fleur Etoile* (1934), the title is written with fluid calligraphy, without any stops or breaks; everything is attached and arranged in the upper part of the canvas.

14 Paul Klee wrote above the watercolor with the title: *Einst dem Grau der Nacht enttaucht… (Jadis surgi du gris de la nuit*, 1918)

15 As in the work of Holbein the Younger, *Les Ambassadeurs français Jean de Dinteville et Georges de Selve* (1533)where we see the text.

16 M. Butor, *Les Mots dans la peinture*, op. cit., p. 122-128, Van Gogh *Nature morte aux livres* (1887) it is barely visible, whereas in *Romans parisiens* (1887), only a few lines are drawn on an open page whose content is illegible, or *Still Life: Board with Three Onions* (1889) where there is a stamped envelope with an address which cannot be read, and a book with a few legible words in the title. A… *de la santé* and the name of the author, F. V. Raspail, in Édouard Manet's painting *Portrait of Émile Zola* (1868), the author has an open book resting on his knees.

17 *Portrait de Louis Auguste Cézanne père de l'artiste* (1866), painted by Paul Cézanne, or in *Portrait d'un inconnu lisant un journal dit aussi Le Chevalier X*, 1911-1914 d'André Derain

18 Ibid., p. 135-141, in a collage of Picasso's called *Bouteille, verre et violon* (1912-1913)

19 Ibid., p. 144, Van Gogh, *Arbre selon Hiroshige* (1887)

20 Ibid., p. 145-146, De Chirico in *Le Printemps* (1914) and Kandinsky in *Succession* (1935).

21 Ibid., p. 149, like the "R" in *La Villa R* (1919) by Paul Klee or even *As de pique* (early 1918?) a drawing-poem by Juan Gris.

22 H. Molesworth, *Leap Before you Look, Black Mountain College*, op. cit., op. cit., exhibition catalog with the same title. Ruth Asawa, who often composed works with repetitive motifs used the Black Mountain College stamp to create one of her works in 1976 entitled BMC, or Secrets (1949), a work by Susan Weil, Rebus *Letter to Her Parents* (1947) by Lorna Blaine Halper, *Letter to Ruth* (1952) by Ray Johnson, p. 24.

23 S. Naef, Online course as part of the master's program in art criticism and curatorship, Université Saint-Joseph in Beirut, January 13, 2023.

HUGUETTE CALAND

Solo exhibitions

2025 (upcoming): Deichtorhallen, Hamburg, Germany
2025 Museo Nacional Centro de Arte Reina Sofia, Madrid, Spain
2024 *Huguette Caland, Les années parisiennes*, Mennour Gallery, Paris
2024 *Huguette Caland: Outside the Line*, ICA Miami, Florida
2023 *Huguette and Nadine, The Story of a Friendship*, Janine Rubeiz Gallery, Beirut
2022 *Huguette Caland: Tête-à-Tête*, Wiels Museum, Brussels, Belgium
2021 *Tête-à-Tête*, The Drawing Center, New York
2021 *Kissing Life*, The Arts Club, Dubai, UAE
2021 *Bronzes*, Kayne Griffin Gallery, Los Angeles
2020 *Faces and Places*, Mathaf: Arab Museum of Modern Art, Doha, Qatar
2019 *Huguette Caland*, Tate St Ives, Cornwall, UK
2018 *Early Work: 1964*, Janine Rubeiz Gallery, Beirut
2018 *Exhibition 2: Huguette Caland*, IAIA, New York
2016 *Silent Letters*, Nathalie Karg Gallery, New York
2015 *Bronzes*, Janine Rubeiz Gallery, Beirut
2014 *Early Works: 1970–85*, Lombard Freid Gallery, New York
2013 *Retrospective 1964–2012*, Beirut Exhibition Center
2011 *Undercover*, Peter Findlay Gallery, New York
2011 *Mes jeunes années*, Janine Rubeiz Gallery, Beirut
2010 *Caché, Caché*, Venice
2009 *Silent Memories*, Janine Rubeiz Gallery, Beirut and Peter Findlay Gallery, NY
2009 *Autumn*, LA Contemporary, Los Angeles
2006 *Rossinantes*, Janine Rubeiz Gallery, Beirut
2006 Samy Kinge Gallery, Paris
2005 Michael's, Santa Monica, CA
2003 *Introspective*, Janine Rubeiz Gallery, Beirut
2001 *Bleus de Nuit*, Hiromi Paper International, Santa Monica
2001 *Silent Letters*, Sami Kinge Gallery, Paris
2000 *Silver*, Janine Rubeiz Gallery, Beirut
2000 *Where Do You Draw the Line*, Elena Zass Gallery, Laguna Beach
1999 *Silent Letters and Touchables*, Off Main Gallery, Santa Monica
1998 *Scapes & Escapes*, Elena Zass Gallery, Laguna Beach
1997 *Faces and Places II*, Janine Rubeiz Gallery, Beirut
1994 *Faces and Places I*, Janine Rubeiz Gallery, Beirut
1992 Gallery 5, Santa Monica, California
1992 Toepel Gallery, Kirkland, Washington
1992 Bella Interiors Gallery, Santa Monica, California
1988 *Body Parts*, MAG Gallery, Santa Monica, California
1984 *Grande soirée libanaise*, Monaco Art Center
1980 Faris Gallery, Paris
1973 Contact Gallery, Beirut
1972 Delta Gallery, Beirut
1970 Dar El Fan, Beirut

Group exhibitions

2025 (upcoming) Museum of Recent Art, Bucarest, Romania
2025 (upcoming) Jane Lombard, New York
2025 (upcoming) Salon 94, NYC
2025 Lisson Gallery, Paris
2024 Esther Schipper, Berlin, Germany
2024 *Présences arabes, Art moderne et décolonisation*, Museum of Modern Art, Paris
2023 Taipei Biennale, Taipei Fine Arts Museum, Taipei, Taiwan
2023 *Partisans of the Nude*, Wallach Art Gallery, Columbia University
2023 *In the Heart of Another Country: The Diasporic Imagination Rises*, Sharjah Art Foundation, Sharjah, United Arab Emirates
2023 *Beirut and the Golden Sixties: A Manifesto of Fragility*, Mathaf, Arab Museum of Modern Art, Doha, Qatar
2022-2023 *In the Heart of Another Country*, Deichtorhallen, Hamburg, Germany
2022 *Crossed Perspectives*, Tanit Gallery, Beirut
2022 *Manifesto of Fragility*, La Biennale de Lyon, France
2022 *Beirut and the Golden Sixties*, Gropius Bau, Berlin, Germany
2022 *Vessels*, David Zwirner, London, United Kingdom
2022 *On the Edge: Los Angeles Art 1970s-1990s from the Joan and Jack Quinn Family Collection*, Bakersfield Museum of Art
2021 *Women in Abstraction*, Guggenheim, Bilbao, Spain
2021 *FIGURE/S: Drawing after Bellmer, The Drawing Room*, London, United Kingdom
2021 MEI: Middle East Institute of Arts & Culture, Washington D. C.
2021 *Elles font l'abstraction*, Centre Pompidou, Paris
2021 *Boundless Drop to a Boundless Ocean*, Orlando Museum of Art
2021 *Threadbare*, Stephen Friedman Gallery, London, United Kingdom
2020 *Glimpse into the Past*, Tanit Gallery, Beirut, Lebanon
2020 *Painting*, Kayne Griffin Gallery, Los Angeles
2019 *Surrogates*, Kayne Griffin Gallery, Los Angeles
2018 *The Fabric of Felicity*, Garage Museum, Moscow
2018 *Polarities*, David Totah Gallery, New York
2018 *Summer Nocturne*, Santa Barbara Museum of Art
2018 *Arab Print Volume IV*, Meem Gallery, Dubai, United Arab Emirates
2018 *A Century in Flux: Highlights from the Barjeel Art Foundation*, Sharjah, United Arab Emirates
2018 *10*, Anton Kern Gallery, New York
2017 *Künstlerinnen aus dem Morgenland*, Galerie Tanit, Munich
2016 *Made in LA*, Hammer Museum, Los Angeles
2015 *Metropolis*, Edward Tyler Nahem Gallery, New York
2014 Lombard Freid Gallery, New York
2013 *Modernités plurielles*, Centre Pompidou, Paris
2012 *Le Corps découvert*, Institut du monde arabe, Paris
2012 Espace Claude Lemand, Paris
2012 Carnegie Art Museum, Oxnard, California
2011 Selections de la Frederick R. Weisman Art Foundation, Los Angeles
2010 *APEAL*, American University, Washington D.C.
2010 National Museum of Women in the Arts, Washington D.C.

2010 Pacific Design Center, Weissman Foundation, Los Angeles
2009 Lucy Topalian Gallery, Kuwait
2005 Inauguration of the National Public Library, Beirut
2005 Gallery St. Germain, Beverly Hills
2004 *Free Style*, Pacific Design Center, Los Angeles
2001 Salon international d'art contemporain, Artuel, Galerie Janine Rubeiz, Beirut
2001 St' Art, Galerie Janine Rubeiz, Foire d'Art contemporain de Strasbourg, Paris
2000 *Night Skies & Skyscrapers* with Bob Wilhite, Boulder Public Library, Colorado
2000 *Signs of the Zodiac*, Elena Zass Gallery, Laguna Beach, California
1999 *Europ'Art*, Galerie Janine Rubeiz, Foire internationale d'art
1997 *Special Janvier*, Galerie Janine Rubeiz, Beirut
1997 *Europ'Art 97*, Geneva
1996 *Blessings and Beginnings*, Skirball Cultural Center, Artist's Invitational, Los Angeles
1996 *Facing the Dragon*, Artopia, Los Angeles
1996 UCLA Art Rental and Sales Gallery of the Hammer Museum
1996 *The Female Perspective*, Museum of Art and Cultural Center, Los Angeles
1995 *Forces of Change*, Women Artists of the Arab World, Regional Center for the Arts, Walnut Creek, California
1995 *Art Preview*, Artopia Art Gallery, Los Angeles
1993 *Forces of Changes*, Artists of the Arab World, National Museum of Women in Arts, Washington D.C.
1986 *The Arab World Today*, Delegation of the Arab States to UNESCO, and Rennes, France
1986 *Le Portrait à roulettes* (with George Apostu), Sales, France
1986 *Espace culturel*, Permanent Delegation of the Arab States to UNESCO, inaugural exhibition, Paris 1984 *Femina: In memory of Alicia Penalba*, UNESCO, Paris
1984 *Drawings for George Astalos*, Painters and Poets in Sologne, Aubigny-sur-Nère (Cher), France
1986 *Rajz/Drawing '86,* Pesci Galeria, Pesc, Hongrie
1985 *A thousand and one nights*, Centre culturel de Boulogne-Billancourt, Hauts-de-Seine, France
1984 *Lebanese artists*, Monaco Art Center, Monte Carlo
1984 *Painters and poets in Sologne: Drawings for Salah Stétié*, Alain Bosquet, Andree Chedid, Aubigny Sur-Nère (Cher), France
1980 Faris Gallery, Paris, France
1979 *Painters and poets in Sologne: Drawings for Alain Bosquet*, Aubigny-sur-Nère (Cher), France.
1972 *L'Estampe contemporaine*, Bibliothèque nationale, Paris
1971 *Contemporary Art from Lebanon*, Smithsonian Museum, Washington D. C.
1970 *Contemporary Lebanese Artists*, Museum of Modem Art, Tokyo
1970 *Grafica D'Oggi: 36th International Bienniale of Venice*, Venice, Italy
1970 *Sixteen Lebanese Painters*, Delta Gallery, Rome, Italy
1970 *Lebanese Artists: : Traveling exhibition in the US*, Smithsonian Institution, Washington D. C.
1970 *Atelier Caland*, Kaslik, Lebanon, with the painter Helen Khal
1969 Collective Exhibit of Lebanese Artists

Biennials and fairs

2025 (upcoming) 36th São Paulo Biennale
2024 Art Basel, Mennour Gallery
2024 Art Basel, Stephen Friedman Gallery
2024 *Foreigners Everywhere*, 60th Venice Biennale, Italy
2023 Taipei Biennale, Taïwan
2023 Art Basel, Stephen Friedman Gallery
2021 Frieze Masters, Kayne Griffin Gallery
2021 Armory Show, Kayne Griffin Gallery
2019 Sharjah Biennale 14: *Leaving the Echo Chamber*
2019 Frieze LA, Kayne Griffin Gallery
2017 *Viva Arte Viva*, 57th Venice Biennale, Italy
2016 Art Dubai Modern, Galerie Janine Rubeiz, Beirut
2015 Armory Show, Lombard Freid Gallery, New York and Galerie Janine Rubeiz, Beirut
2014 Frieze Masters London, Gallery Agial, Beirut
2014 Prospect 3 Biennial, New Orleans Museum of Art
2014 Art Dubai Modern, Galerie Janine Rubeiz, Beirut
2012 Art Dubai, Galerie Janine Rubeiz, Beirut
2011 Art Abu Dhabi, Galerie Janine Rubeiz, Beirut
2010 Art Dubai, Galerie Janine Rubeiz, Beirut
2009 Art Dubai, Galerie Janine Rubeiz, Beirut
2009 Amsterdam Art Fair
2009 Miami Art Basel
2009 Los Angeles Art Fair
2009 Chicago Fair
2009 New York Fair
1999 *Europ'Art*, Foire internationale d'art, Geneva, Galerie Janine Rubeiz
1996 *Europ'Art*, Foire internationale d'art, Geneva, Galerie Janine Rubeiz
1988 Grands et jeunes d'aujourd'hui, Paris
1984 XXIII Premi International of Dibuix Joan Miro, Joan Miro
1980 Arab Women Artists, Museum of Contemporary Art, Baghdad
1980 Salon de Mai, Paris
1980 Grands et jeunes d'aujourd'hui, Paris
1980 Union des femmes peintres et sculpteurs, Paris
1974 Festival international de la peinture de Cagnes-sur-Mer (Alpes-Maritimes), France
1974 Réalités nouvelles, Paris
1973 Salon de Mai, Paris
1973 Grands et jeunes d'aujourd'hui, Paris
1973 Comparaison, Paris
1973 American Cultural Center, Paris
1969 Salon de Printemps, Belgium
1968 Salon d'Automne, Beirut

Museums and private collections

MOMA, The Metropolitan Museum of Art, LACMA, Hammer Museum, Toledo Museum of Art, San Diego Museum of Art, Palm Springs Museum of Art, Museum of Fine Arts, Houston, TX, Frederick R. Weisman Art Foundation, British Museum, Centre Pompidou, Bibliothèque nationale de France, Paris Fondation nationale d'art contemporain, TATE Modern, Collection of Ministry of Culture – Saudi Arabia, Mathaf Museum Qatar, Sharjah Art Foundation, Barjeel Art Foundation-UAE, Kamel Lazaar Foundation – Tunis, etc.

Illustrations and publications

2024 *Dusk: Anthology Contemporary Lebanese Women Poets*, Kaph Books, Paris
2023 *Approaches to the Study of Pre-modern Arabic Anthologies*, Brill, Beirut (cover image)
2023 *The Story of Art Without Men*, by Katy Hessel, Random House, London
2022 *Sextarianism: Sovreignty, Secularism, and the State in Lebanon*, by Maya Mikdashi (cover image), Stanford University Press
2021 *Huguette Caland: Tête-à-tête*, The Drawing Center, New York
2021 *A Boundless Drop to a Boundless Ocean*, Orlando Museum of Art
2020 *Reflections: Contemporary Art of the Middle East and North Africa*, by Venetia Porter, The British Museum, London
2020 *Taking Shape: Abstraction from the Arab World*, 1950s-1980s, Grey Art Gallery, Munich, Hirmer Publishers
2019 *Vitamin T: Threads & Textiles in Contemporary Art*, Phaidon Press, London
2019 *Huguette Caland*, TATE Publishing, London
2017 *The Playful Provocations (and Erotic Kaftans) of the Lebanese Artist Huguette Caland*, by Dana Goodyear, The New Yorker
2017 *Huguette Caland, Everything Takes the Shape of a Person*, Aram Moshayedi (ed.), Skira, Lausanne
2016 *Made in L.A. 2016: a, the, though, only*, Hammer Museum, Los Angeles
2016 *The Anthologist's Art*, by Bilai Orfali, Brill, Beirut (cover image)
2013 *Huguette Caland, Works 1964-2012*, Solidere, Beirut
2012 *Le Corps découvert*, Institut du monde arabe, Paris (cover image)
1986 *Huguette Caland*, by Raoul Jean Moulin, Édition SMI, Paris
1982 Five illustrations for the magazine *Neighborhood*, New York (August)
1972 Ink drawing for the frontispiece of *Sade, système de l'agression*, by Noëlle Chatelet, Éditions Aubier-Montaigne, Paris

Symposium

1994 Asilah Summer Symposium in July-August, Asilah, Morocco

Design and fashion

1979 *Nour*, a haute couture line created for Pierre Cardin and for a fashion show at Espace Cardin, Paris
1970-1975 Creation of seven silk dresses, painted and embroidered

Film and Screenplay

1979 Wrote and starred in the short film Hubert Glotte, by Maryse Ebely
1978-79 Wrote *Sysphia*, a screenplay in collaboration with Maryse Ebely

Sculptures

2014 Created a series of 11 bronzes (edition of 3) based on terra cotta sculptures designed in 1984-1985
2009-2011 Produced 14 sculptures from a series *Rossinante* made of lime, wire, Japanese paper, and thread wool and papier-mâché
1984-1985 Produced more than 30 terra cotta sculptures, Paris

BIBLIOGRAPHY

Works

Alberoni, F., 1981, *Le Choc amoureux*, Éditions Ramsey, Paris.

Allendy, R., 1943, *Le Symbolisme des nombres*, Essai d'arithmosophie, Chacornarc, Paris.

Arrivé, M., 1986, *Linguistique et psychanalyse*, Méridiens Klincksieck, Paris.

Assoun, P. L., 1996, *Littérature et psychanalyse*, Ellipses, Paris.

Assoun, P. L., 2002, *Le Vocabulaire de Freud*, Ellipses, Paris.

Assoun, P. L., 2008, *Le Démon de midi*, L'Olivier, Paris.

Assoun, P. L., 2005, *Les Phobies*, Anthropos, Paris.

Bachelard, G., 2010, *La Poétique de l'espace*, PUF, Paris.

Barthes, R., 1973, *Le Plaisir du texte*, Le Seuil, Paris.

Bellemin, J. N., 2002, *Psychanalyse et littérature*, PUF, Paris.

Bensaid, C., Leloup, J.-Y., 2005, *Qui aime quand je t'aime ? De l'amour qui souffre à l'amour qui s'offre*, Albin Michel, Paris.

Berger, J., 1972, *Ways of Seeing*, BBC and Penguin Books, London.

Bodi D., 2001, *Petite grammaire de l'akkadien à l'usage des débutants*, Geuthner, Paris.

Butor, M., 2019, *Les Mots dans la peinture*, Flammarion, Paris.

Cheng, F., 1991, *Vide et plein, Le langage pictural chinois*, Le Seuil, Paris.

Christin, A.-M., 2011, *Histoire de l'écriture*, Flammarion, Paris.

Dufourmantelle, A., 2022, *Puissance de la douceur*, Rivages Poches, Paris.

El Khoury, B., 2007, *Réalités libanaises*, Éditions L'Orient-Le Jour, Beirut.

Foucault, M., 1976, *La Volonté de savoir*, Gallimard, Paris.

Freud, S., 1910, *Un souvenir d'enfance de Leonard de Vinci*, consulté en ligne.

Freud, S., 1914, *Le Moïse de Michel-Ange*, version numérique par Jean-Marie Tremblay, dans le cadre de la collection : "Les classiques des sciences sociales," traduit de l'allemand par M. Bonaparte.

Freud, S., 1986, *Les Délires et les Rêves dans la Gradiva*, Gallimard, Folio Essais, Paris.

Freud, S., 1988, *Le Mot d'esprit et sa relation à l'inconscient*, Gallimard, Paris.

Freud, S., 1997, *Psychopathologie de la vie quotidienne*, Gallimard, Paris.

Freud, S., 2004, *Cinq leçons sur la psychanalyse*, Payot, Paris.

Freud, S., 2006, *Dora*, PUF, Paris.

Freud, S., 2010, *Psychologie de la vie amoureuse*, Petite Bibliothèque Payot, Paris.

Freud, S., 2011, *Deuil et mélancolie*, Payot & Rivages, Paris.

Freud, S., 2012, *Pulsions et destins des pulsions*, Petite Bibliothèque Payot, Paris.

Groddeck, G., 1969, *La Maladie, l'Art et le Symbole*, Gallimard, Paris.

Klee, P., 1985, *Théorie de l'art moderne*, Denoël, Paris.

Klein, J.P., 1997, *L'Art-thérapie*, PUF, Paris.

Kristeva, J., 1969, *Recherches pour une sémanalyse*, Le Seuil, Paris.

Lacan, J., 2011, *Je parle aux murs*, Le Seuil, Paris.

La Marle, H., 2002, *L'Aventure de l'alphabet*, Geuthner, Paris.

Marin, C., 2019, *Ruptures, Comment les ruptures nous transforment*, Éditions de l'Observatoire, Paris.

Molesworth, H., 2015, *Leap Before you Look*, Black Mountain College, 1933-1957, ICA/Boston and Yale University Press, New Haven-London.

Pastoureau, M., 2008, *Noir, Histoire d'une couleur*, Le Seuil, Paris.

Pastoureau, M., 2005, *Le Petit Livre des couleurs*, Éditions du Panama, Paris.

Reuter, Y., 2009, *L'Analyse du récit*, Armand Colin, Paris.

Safouan, M., 1982, *L'Inconscient et son scribe*, Le Seuil, Paris.

Safouan, M., 2010, *La Parole ou la Mort. Essai sur la division du sujet*, Le Seuil, Paris.

Todorov, T., 1978, *Poétique de la prose*, Le Seuil, Paris.

Tomasella, S., 2012, *Les Amours impossibles, Accepter d'aimer et d'être aimé*, Eyrolles, collection "Les chemins de l'inconscient," Paris.

Tomb, M., 2016, *War Identities*, Human Rights Watch Organization, Beirut.

Winnicott, D., 2014, *Les Objets transitionnels*, Petite Bibliothèque Payot, Paris.

Articles

Christin, A.-M., 2001, "De l'image à l'écriture," in *Histoire de l'écriture*, Flammarion, Paris.

Deroche, F., 2001, "L'écriture arabe," in *L'histoire de l'écriture*, Flammarion, Paris.

Durand, J.M., 2001, "L'écriture cunéiforme," in *L'histoire de l'écriture*, Flammarion, Paris.

Eddé, D., 2013, "L'éléphant et le coquelicot," published in the exhibition catalog *Huguette Caland*, Solidere, Beirut.

Marinov, V., 2008, "L'oeuvre d'art est un crime parfait," in *L'Artiste et le Psychanalyste*, PUF, Paris.

Mopsik, Ch., 2001, "La Aleph des cabalistes," in *L'histoire de l'écriture*, Flammarion, Paris.

Moshayedi, A., Walker, H., 2016, "Sandy Lajer, Ed Moses and Robert Wilhite in conversation with Aram Moshayedi," in *Made in LA 2016*, catalog published by the Hammer Museum for the exhibition *Made in L.A, 2016*.

O'Connor, A. M., 2003, "Her magical world," *Los Angeles Times*, online, June 2003.

Schwendener, M., 2018, " Huguette Caland," *The New York Times*, February 15, 2018.

Seelye, K. Q., September 2019, "Huguette Caland, 88, Dies: Celebrated Freedom in Art and Life," *New York Times*, accessed 2023.

Tamraz, N., 2023, "Jouer, déjouer, transformer le corps: comme performance," catalog for the exhibition *Faces and Places*, Mathaf, 2020 (forthcoming).

Vigne, S., 2012, *Lipoedème: une entité mal connue*, www.sciencedirect.com, accessed March 2023.

Wilson-Goldie, K., *Huguette Caland, Body Works*, May 24, 2019, https://www.tate.org.uk/tate-etc/issue-46-summer-2019/huguette-caland-body-works-kaelen-wilson-goldie, accessed February 2023.

Wilson Goldie, K., 2021, in 4 Colunms.org, June 25, 2021, accessed February 2023.

Wilson-Goldie, K., 2023, "Liberated, Rebellious and Historically Consequential: Remembering Huguette Caland," *New Books Network*, accessed February 2023

Interviews

Ricardo Karam, *Warae elwoujouh*, with Huguette Caland, 2006, accessed February 2023.
Hanan el Cheikh with Huguette Caland, TéléLiban, October 1974.

Photographic credits

© Studio Huguette Caland, Los Angeles: Fig. 2, 3, 4, 5, 6, 7, 15, 16, 22, 24, 25, 26, 29, 30, 31, 32, 33, 34, 40, 41, 42, 43, 46, 49, 51, 52, 55, 56
© Brigitte Caland: Fig. 9, 10, 11, 15, 20, 21, 27, 28, 35, 38, 39, 44, 53, 54, 57
© H. La Marle (*L'Aventure de l'alphabet*, Geuthner, 2002, p. 26, 27, 150): Fig. 13
© F. Abillama : Fig. 17, 18, 47, 48
© M. Dib : Fig. 23, 50
© Unjoo Byers : Fig. 36
© Galerie Janine Rubeiz : Fig. 37, 45, 59
© D.R. : Fig. 59
Missing Credits: Fig. 1, 7, 19

Acknowledgments

I am deeply grateful to Nayla Tamraz for overseeing my research as part of my Master's in Art Criticism and Curatorial Studies at Université Saint-Joseph, Beirut, and for her generous editorial guidance.

I also thank José Belin, my first reader, for his insightful and enriching comments.

This research would not have been the same without the exceptional team at Studio Huguette Caland in Los Angeles —Salima Babakhyi, Ric Flaata, Malado Baldwin, Ron Griffin, and Karim Fazulzianov—whose support was invaluable. I am equally thankful to Galerie Janine Rubeiz in Beirut, especially Nadine Begdache and Shirine Nakhal, for their continued support. My warmest thanks to Nour Salamé as well as the Kaph Books and scope Ateliers teams for their enthusiasm, professionalism, and kindness. I also wish to thank Mansour Dib and the Huguette Caland Studio for providing the images, and Éditions Geuthner for granting permission to reproduce the images of *L'aventure de l'alphabet* by H. La Marle.

Finally, to my children, Guy Karim and L'Or Iman— your unwavering support means everything to me.

Untitled (From the Self Portrait series), 1992
Mixed media on paper, 61 × 45.7 cm

Private collection, Los Angeles, California

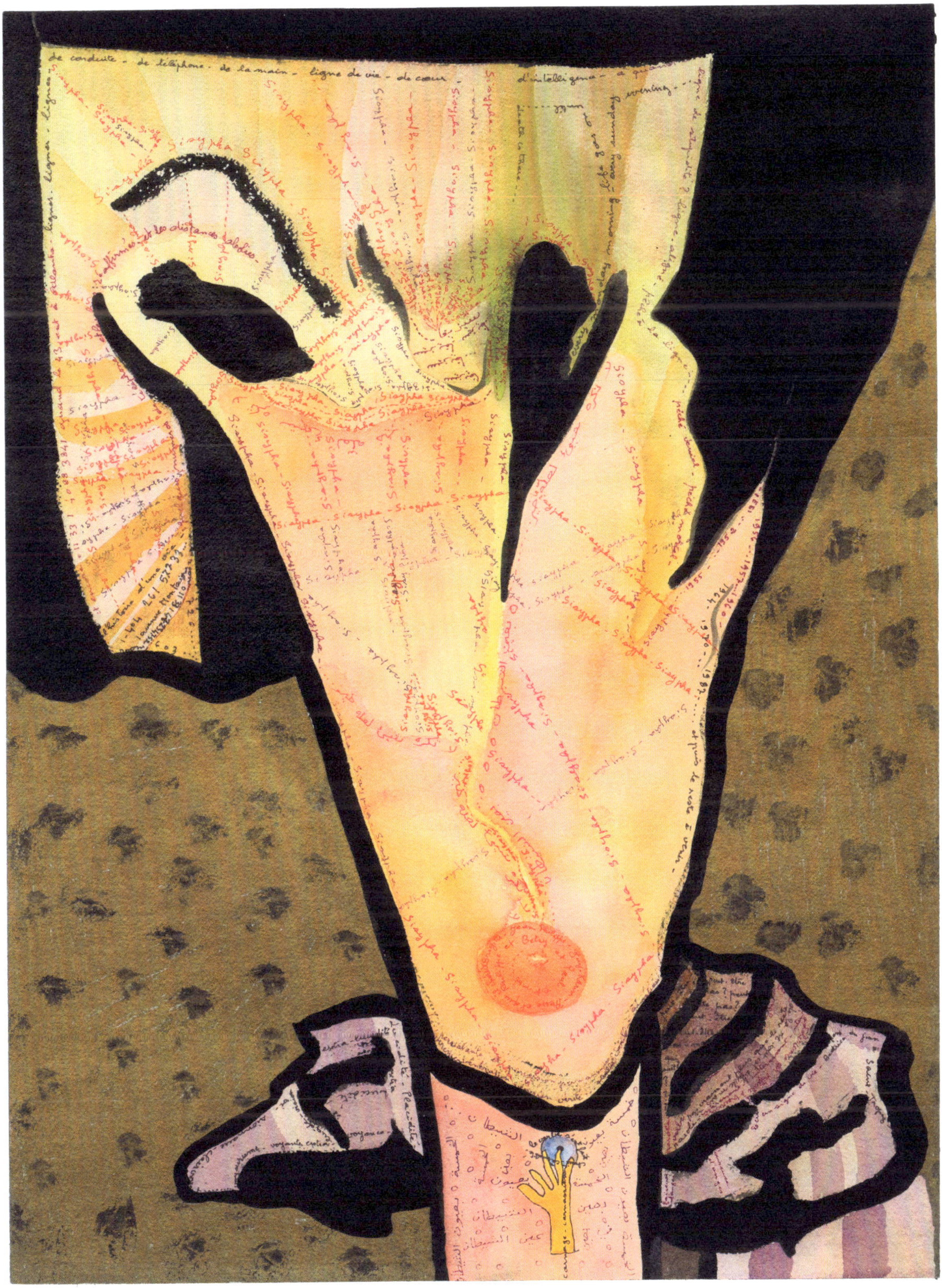

Text
Brigitte Caland

Editor
Nayla Tamraz

Proofreading
Zeina Assaf

Design
-scope Ateliers

Color Separation
Nadim Zablit, -scope Ateliers

Photo credits:
© Studio Huguette Caland, Los Angeles :
Fig. 2, 3, 4, 5, 6, 7, 15, 16, 22, 24, 25, 26, 29, 30, 31, 32, 33, 34, 40, 41, 42, 43, 46, 49, 51, 52, 55, 56

© Brigitte Caland: Fig. 9, 10, 11, 15, 20, 21, 27, 28, 35, 38, 39, 44, 53, 54, 57

© H. La Marle (*L'aventure de l'alphabet*, Geuthner, 2002, p. 26, 27, 150): Fig. 13

© F. Abillama: Fig. 17, 18, 47, 48

© M. Dib: Fig. 23, 50

© Unjoo Byers: Fig. 36

© Galerie Janine Rubeiz: Fig. 37, 45, 59

© D.R.: Fig. 59
Missing credits: Fig. 1, 7, 19

Printed by Editoriale Bortolazzi-Stei, Verona, Italy, July 2025

Legal deposit: August 2025

ISBN: 978-614-8035-80-7

Published by

KAPH
ART BOOKS FROM THE ARAB WORLD
كتب الفن من العالم العربي

Beirut / Dubai
www.kaphbooks.com

Distribution in Europe
Les Presses du Réel
35 rue Colson
21000 Dijon
France
www.lespressesdureel.com

Idea Books
Nieuwe Hemweg 6R
1013 BG Amsterdam
The Netherlands
www.ideabooks.nl

Distribution in the Arab world
CIEL Book Distribution
3rd Interchange, Al Quoz Industrial I
P.O.Box 282005
Dubai, UAE
www.ciel.me

MuseumShops Company / HAAL
Prince Turki Ibn Abdulaziz Al Awwal Rd,
Al Mohammadiyyah, Dooryard 1st floor
Riyadh, KSA

Distribution in the Americas, Asia and Australia
ARTBOOK | D.A.P.
75 Broad Street,
Suite 630
New York, NY 10004
www.artbook.com